Joseph Cornell

and Surrealism

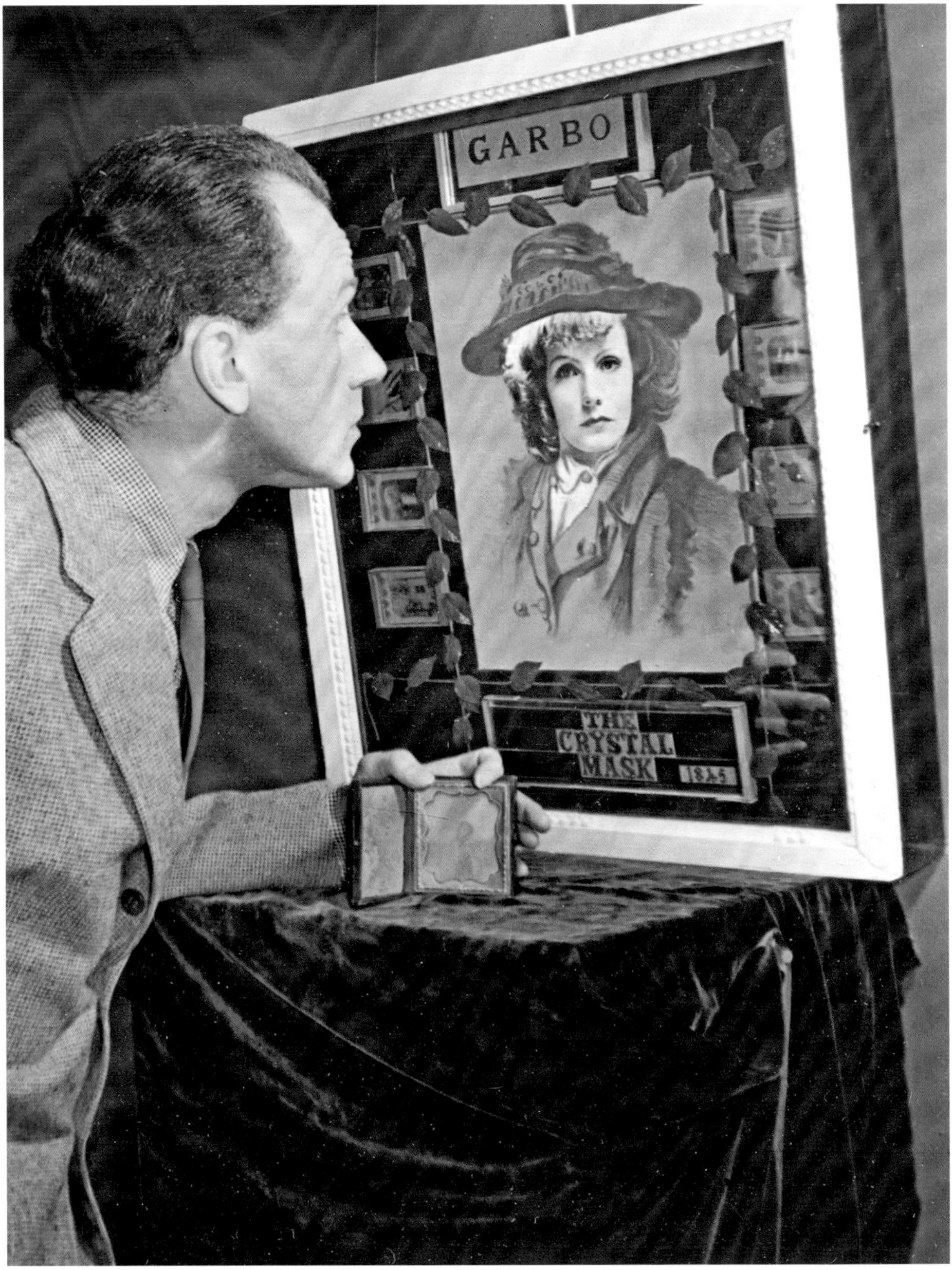
GARBO
THE CRYSTAL MASK

Joseph Cornell
and Surrealism

Edited by Matthew Affron and Sylvie Ramond

The Fralin Museum of Art at the University of Virginia

This publication is based on the exhibition catalogue *Joseph Cornell et les surréalistes à New York*. The exhibition was shown at The Fralin Museum of Art, University of Virginia, as *Joseph Cornell and Surrealism*, March–June 8, 2014

The Fralin Museum of Art's programming was made possible by the generous support of The Joseph and Robert Cornell Memorial Foundation.

The exhibition and associated programming was also made possible through the generous support of the Terra Foundation for American Art, the Annenberg Foundation/GRoW, the National Endowment for the Arts, The Fralin Museum of Art Volunteer Board, the Arts Enhancement Fund sponsored by the Vice Provost for the Arts, U.Va. Arts Council: Enriching the Arts on Grounds, the Office of the Provost & the Vice Provost for the Arts, the Suzanne Foley Endowment Fund, *albemarle* Magazine, and Ivy Publications LLC's Charlottesville Welcome Book. It was held under the auspices of FRAME (French Regional American Museum Exchange).

French essays translated by Ralph Tarica
Copy edited by Mary Christian
Permissions coordinated by William Auten
and Chloé Skye Delaney
Designed by Patrick Bell Design
Typeset in Bau and Stempel Garamond
Printing by Worth Higgins and Associates
Printed in the United States

Front cover (detail) and back cover: Joseph Cornell, *Surréalisme*, 1931–32, collage, Mark Kelman Collection

Frontispiece: Cornell with his *Construction Garbo (Greta Garbo in the Legendary Film* The Crystal Mask, c. 1845), 1939, detail of fig. 7.04

Page 6: Hans Namuth, Joseph Cornell with his record collection, detail of fig. 9.01

5 4 3 2 1

Library of Congress Cataloging-in-Publication Data

ISBN 978-0-9835059-7-6

The Fralin Museum of Art
University of Virginia
155 Rugby Road
PO Box 400119
Charlottesville, Virginia 22904-4119

THE FRALIN MUSEUM OF ART AT THE UNIVERSITY OF VIRGINIA · MUSÉE DES BEAUX-ARTS DE LYON · Furthermore: a program of the J. M. Kaplan Fund · TERRA FOUNDATION FOR AMERICAN ART · UNIVERSITY of VIRGINIA

ART WORKS. · National Endowment for the Arts arts.gov · FRAME French Regional American Museum Exchange · VILLE DE LYON · GROW ANNENBERG FOUNDATION

Contents

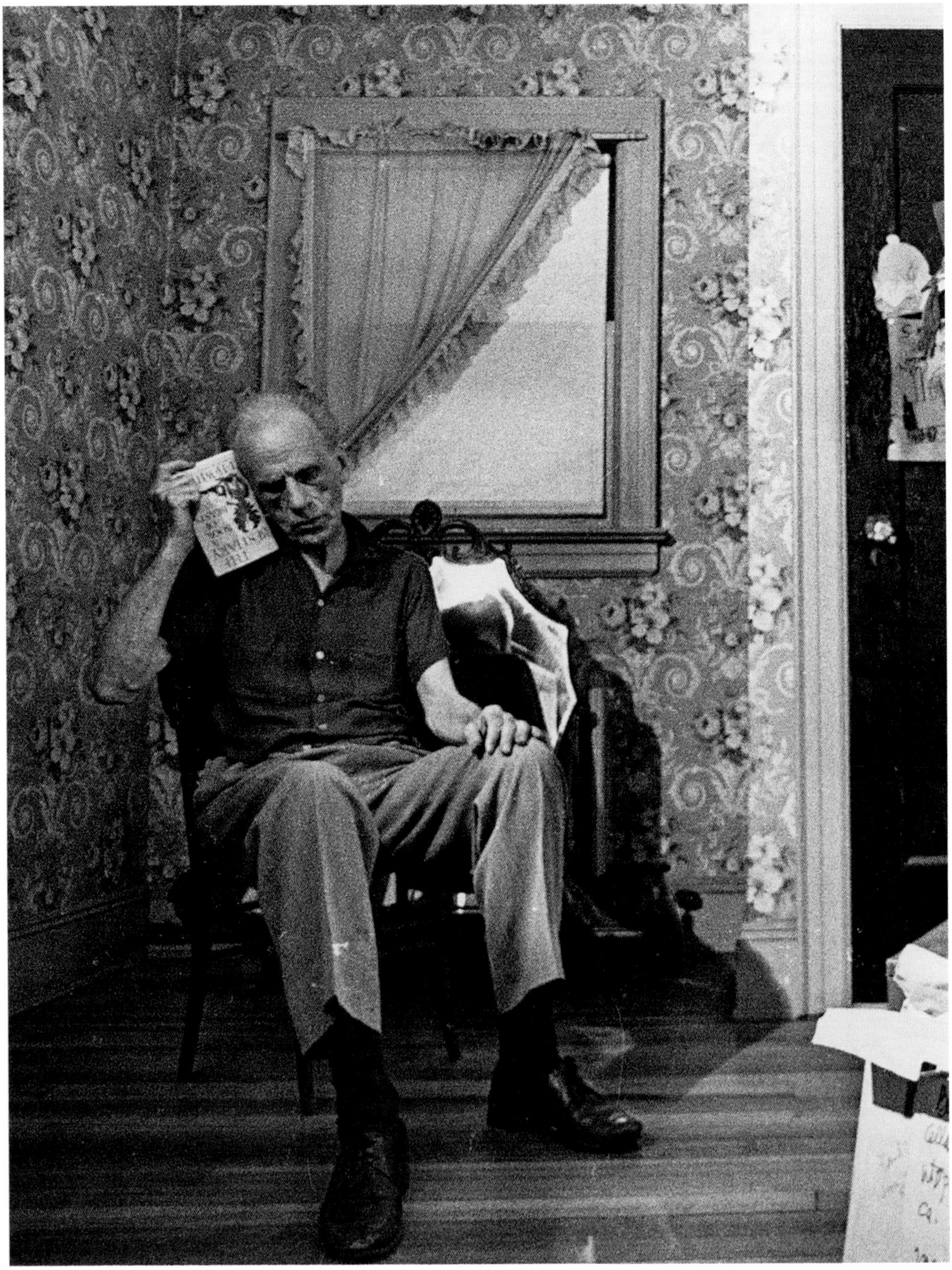

Foreword

Through his diverse and interrelated works in two and three dimensions, including collages and assemblages of found objects, Joseph Cornell coaxed poetry from the commonplace. Situated within the broader context of Surrealism, though, his creations are imparted with a wider global resonance—one that becomes powerfully evident in this book.

Positioning Cornell as an indisputably integral figure in the international Surrealist movement, the essays contained herein were initially developed for the exhibition *Joseph Cornell et les surréalistes à New York*, first seen at the Musée des Beaux-Arts de Lyon and later, with the title *Joseph Cornell and Surrealism*, at The Fralin Museum of Art at the University of Virginia. They were notable for delivering original perspectives on Cornell by authors from France, the United Kingdom, and the United States. However, until now this erudition existed only in French—this English edition makes important new scholarship accessible to Anglophone readers as well.

At the heart of the Terra Foundation's mission—to foster the exploration, understanding, and enjoyment of the visual arts of the United States for national and international audiences—resides a desire to stimulate robust cross-cultural dialogues. We accomplish this by collaborating with innovative partners and supporting original research, such as this publication. Implicit in these activities is the belief that art has the potential both to distinguish cultures and to unite them.

For more than thirty-five years, we've been connecting people worldwide with visual culture of the United States. On behalf of the Terra Foundation for American Art, we congratulate The Fralin Museum of Art at the University of Virginia and all of the contributing authors of this fine book for their dedication to inspiring new perspectives on American art and advancing international exchange through original scholarship.

Elizabeth Glassman

President
Terra Foundation for American Art

Director's Foreword

It is with great pleasure that I welcome the English edition of the catalogue *Joseph Cornell et les surréalistes à New York*. Having appeared first in France in the fall of 2013, the exhibition was shown at The Fralin Museum of Art for its only American version as *Joseph Cornell and Surrealism* between March and June of 2014. The project itself was an ambitious and complex undertaking that required years of preparation and collaboration with colleagues at the Musée des Beaux-Arts de Lyon and the numerous lenders to the exhibition. I am particularly grateful to Sylvie Ramond, director and chief curator, Musée des Beaux-Arts de Lyon, and Matthew Affron, formerly Associate Professor of Art History at the University of Virginia and now Muriel and Philip Berman Curator of Modern Art at the Philadelphia Museum of Art, for creating what was an illuminating experience. It is a testimonial to their stature and persuasiveness that so many important works by Joseph Cornell and his contemporaries were gathered together.

Differences in scale between the French and American versions of the exhibition rendered a simple translation of the exhibition catalogue implausible; consequently, we have decided to preserve the heart of the catalogue in this English version, namely the essays by a distinguished panel of experts. They shed new light on Cornell's relationship with Surrealism. While Cornell took pains to distinguish himself from the Surrealists, there is no doubt that there were strong reciprocal influences between him and his European contemporaries in terms of collage, assemblage, and cinema. The essays contained in this volume mark a tribute to the enduring appeal of Joseph Cornell and his "white magic."

This book and the exhibition associated with it have grown out of a long-standing relationship between The Fralin Museum of Art and The Joseph and Robert Cornell Memorial Foundation. Thanks to generous gifts from the Foundation, our Museum now enjoys a significant collection of collages and shadow boxes by Joseph Cornell, and the continuing support of the Cornell Foundation has had a transformative effect upon our educational programs. We hope that *Joseph Cornell and Surrealism* will serve as a tribute to the impact that the Foundation and its Trustees have had upon The Fralin.

Finally, I would like to acknowledge the generous support we have received from the following: the Terra Foundation, the National Endowment for the Arts, The Fralin Museum of Art Volunteer Board, the Arts Enhancement Fund sponsored by the Vice-Provost for the Arts at the University of Virginia, the Annenberg

Foundation, the University of Virginia Arts Council: Enriching the Arts on Grounds, the Suzanne Foley Endowment Fund, *albemarle* Magazine, and Ivy Publications LLC's *Charlottesville Welcome Book*. Publication of this volume was aided by a significant grant from Furthermore: A Program of the J.M. Kaplan Fund. This book owes a great deal to the collaborative efforts of Jérôme Gille and the staff of Hazan, a division of Hachette Illustré. The transformation of material from the original catalogue to the present volume was a complex project in itself. I would like to thank Mary Christian, our copy editor; Ralph Tarica, who translated the essays by Emmanuel Guigon, Ségolène Le Men, Camille Lévêque-Claudet, Patrick Mauriès, and Sylvie Ramond and François-René Martin; Anne Barriault, who created the index; William Auten and Chloé Skye Delaney, who coordinated image permissions; Patrick Bell, who adapted the book design and oversaw the production process; Katelyn Hobbs, formerly curatorial assistant at The Fralin; and my assistant, Laurie Hilsinger. Their combined efforts have been little short of heroic.

Bruce Boucher

Director
The Fralin Museum of Art, University of Virginia

Preface and Acknowledgments

Joseph Cornell (1903–1972), the American pioneer of collage, montage, and assemblage art, is sometimes regarded as a solitary star within the constellation of great Surrealists. This volume considers the essential connections between Cornell and the Surrealist group during the 1930s and 1940s, decades that saw both Cornell's development and maturation as an artist and the heyday of Surrealism in the United States. It presents essays that first appeared in French in the catalogue *Joseph Cornell et les surréalistes à New York*, published in 2013 to accompany the exhibition of the same name at the Musée des Beaux-Arts de Lyon. The Fralin Museum of Art, which had co-organized the exhibition, presented it as *Joseph Cornell and Surrealism* during the following year.

The conjunction announced in our title can still generate disagreement. Surrealism was an avant-garde movement in literature and the visual arts launched by the poet André Breton in Paris in 1924. Cornell lived his whole life in Queens, New York, and made his career within the New York art world starting in 1931. In looking at Cornell in the light of Surrealism, do we end up losing touch with the qualities of mind and the sensibility that make him an American original? Do we risk ignoring the distinctiveness of his key inventions, starting with the famous shadow boxes? We believe, to the contrary, that our view of Cornell's work across many mediums is enhanced by considering him as part of an international avant-garde community. His singular devotion to European culture, and to French culture above all, is another crucial part of the story of this American artist.

Cornell himself was never comfortable with the Surrealist label. He addressed this question in a letter to Alfred H. Barr, Jr., director of The Museum of Modern Art in New York, in November 1936, just as Barr was preparing to install his groundbreaking exhibition *Fantastic Art, Dada, Surrealism,* the exhibition that debuted Cornell's great first glass-paned shadow box, *Untitled* (*Soap Bubble Set*) (1936), now in the collection of the Wadsworth Atheneum Museum of Art in Hartford. "In the event that you are saying a word or two about my work in the catalogue I would appreciate your saying that I do not share in the sub-conscious and dream theories of the surrealists. While fervently admiring much of their work I have never been an official surrealist, and I believe that surrealism has healthier possibilities than have been developed."[1] Cornell rejected both Surrealism's Freudian theoretical apparatus and its penchant for the occult. For spiritual solace and renewal, he looked instead to a broader tradition in modern French literature, music, and art. His pantheon was populated by the poets Stéphane Mallarmé, Gérard de Nerval, Arthur Rimbaud, and Paul Verlaine; the composers Claude Debussy, Maurice Ravel, Emmanuel Chabrier, and Erik Satie; and the painters Odilon Redon, Paul Cézanne, Henri Rousseau, and Pablo Picasso.[2]

It was the Surrealist milieu, nonetheless, that fostered Cornell as an exhibiting artist. The network of artists, art galleries, and museums, as well as poets, critics, and magazines affiliated with Surrealism in New York was undoubtedly crucial for the development of his artistic identity during the first half of his career. Furthermore, it is difficult to understand Cornell's art without taking into account Surrealism's galvanizing impact. Cornell shared with the Surrealists his basic conception of the visual image as the product of poetic juxtaposition. And in his best-known works, the collages, small constructions containing found objects, and classic shadow boxes, he took key methods of Surrealist art in new directions. Moreover, Cornell's achievement cannot be understood without also considering his work in other formats, including both his ground-breaking work in collage film and the open-ended and nonlinear archives of printed materials that he called "explorations." The present volume addresses each of these topics. It also explores the ideas on art, literature, music, and dance that nourished his work.

The exhibition was realized in both Lyon and Charlottesville under the auspices of FRAME (French Regional American Museum Exchange). For their generous support, we acknowledge the Terra Foundation for American Art, the Annenberg Foundation/GRoW, the National Endowment for the Arts, and the Research and Academic Program at the Sterling and Francine Clark Art Institute. We extend warm thanks to our co-authors. We also acknowledge the colleagues who contributed to the realization of the French exhibition catalogue: at the Musée des Beaux-Arts de Lyon, Léna Widerkehr, Head of Publications; and Henrique Simoes, image services; and at Hazan in Paris, Jean-François Barrielle, director; Frédérique Cassegrain, editorial management; Julien Boitas, graphic design; Renaud Bezomes, copyediting; and Claire Hostalier, production. Additionally, we would like to make special mention of the many contributions made by Camille Lévêque-Claudet and Anne Théry throughout the preparation and realization of the exhibition in Lyon.

Matthew Affron and Sylvie Ramond

1 Joseph Cornell to Alfred H. Barr, Jr., November 13, 1936. Archives of the Museum of Modern Art, Registrar Exhibition Files, Exh. #55. The Museum of Modern Art Archives, New York.

2 Joseph Cornell to Hans Huth, July 20, 1953. Joseph Cornell papers, 1904–1986, bulk 1939–1972. Archives of American Art, Smithsonian Institution. Washington, DC.

Box constructions by Joseph Cornell in the collection of The Fralin Museum of Art at the University of Virginia

Six box constructions by Joseph Cornell are currently in the collection of The Fralin Museum of Art. Five of those works are shown on the following pages. The sixth work is awaiting conservation.

Not illustrated Joseph Cornell, *Untitled* (*Sand Box*), c. 1950–55, box construction, 7 5/8 x 12 5/8 x 1 3/4 in., The Fralin Museum of Art at the University of Virginia, Bequest of Buzz Miller. The Alan Groh–Buzz Miller Collection

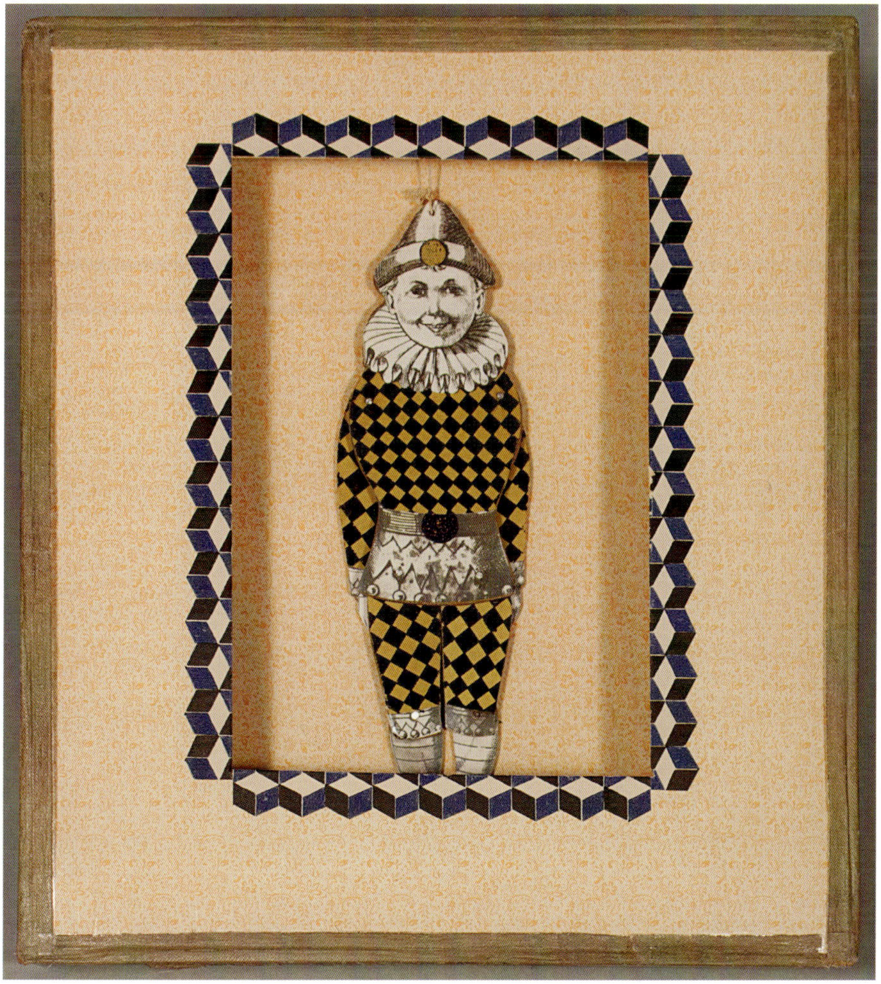

Joseph Cornell, *Untitled* (*Harlequin Jumping Jack*), c. 1935–38, box construction, 13 7/8 × 12 1/8 × 2 1/2 in., The Fralin Museum of Art at the University of Virginia, Gift of The Joseph and Robert Cornell Memorial Foundation

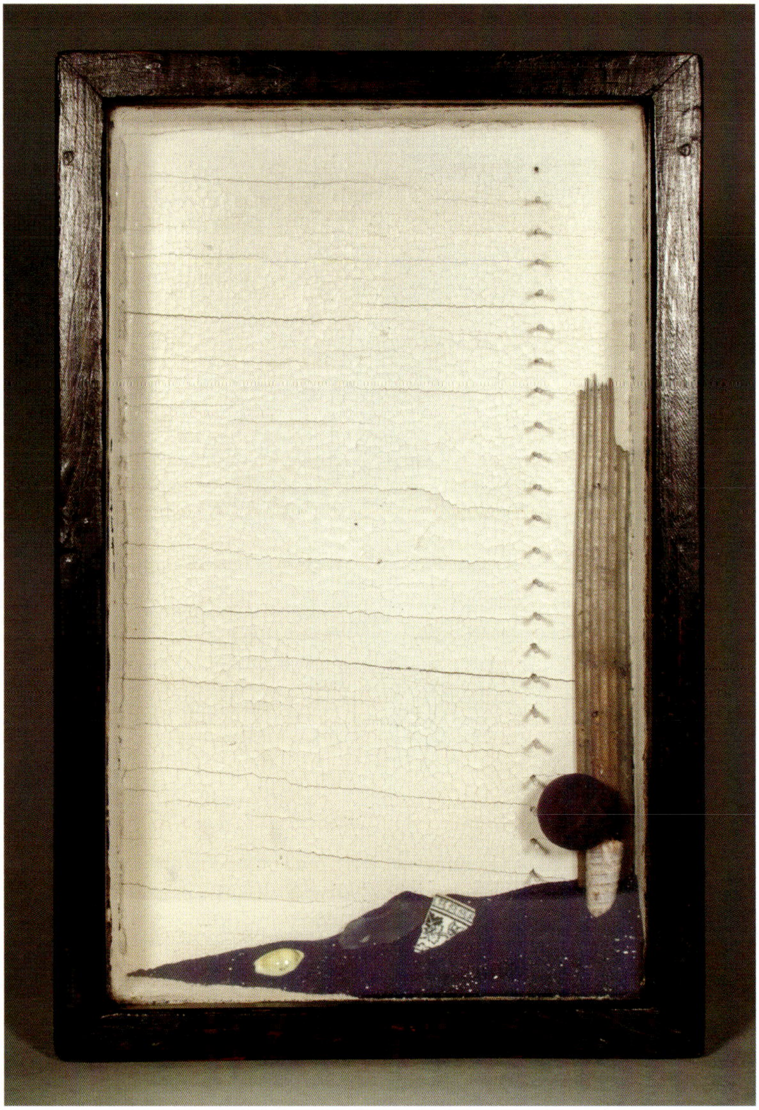

Joseph Cornell, *Untitled (Game)*, c. 1940, box construction, 14 7/8 × 7 7/8 × 5 in., The Fralin Museum of Art at the University of Virginia, Gift of The Joseph and Robert Cornell Memorial Foundation

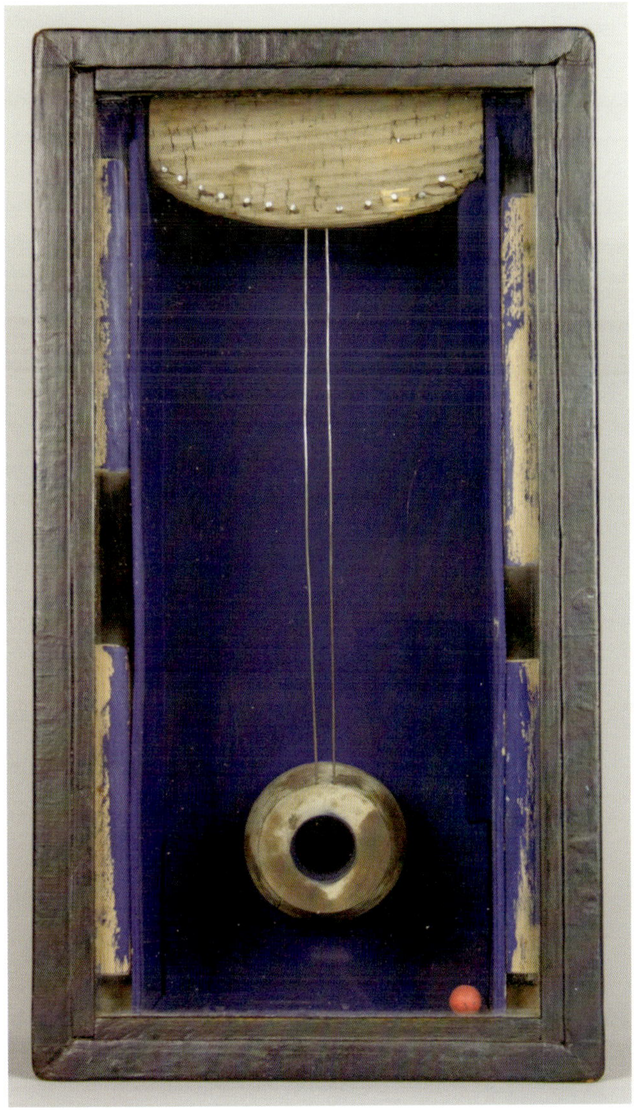

Joseph Cornell, *Untitled (Blue Sand Tray)*, c. 1954, box construction, 15 × 9 1/4 × 2 3/8 in., The Fralin Museum of Art at the University of Virginia, Bequest of Buzz Miller. The Alan Groh–Buzz Miller Collection

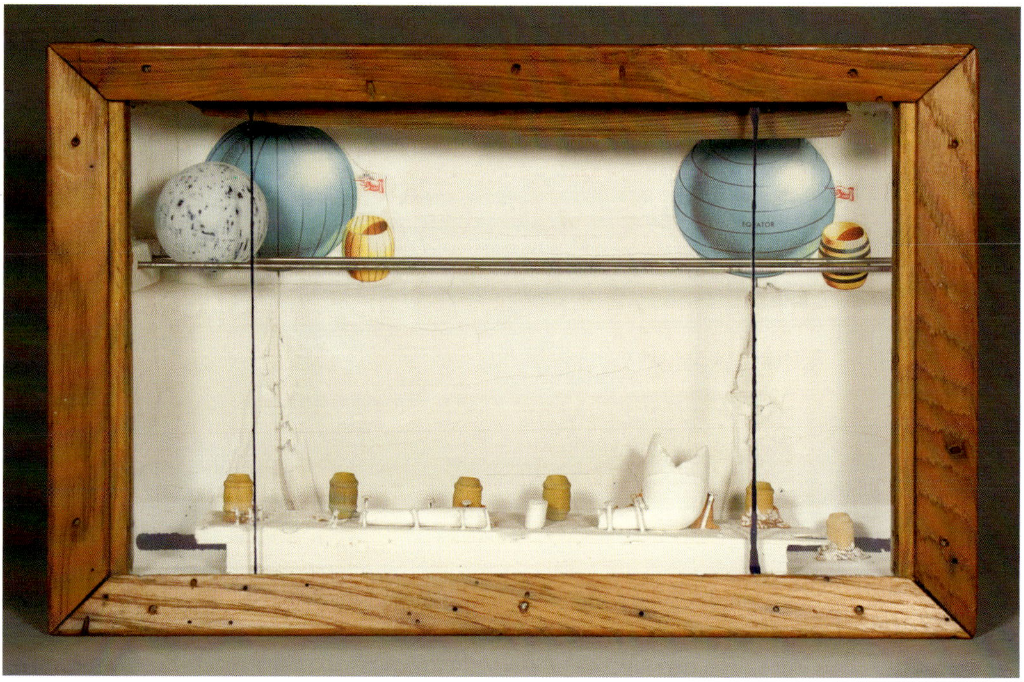

Joseph Cornell, *Untitled (Soap Bubble Set, Latitude and Longitude Box)*, c. 1960, box construction, 10 × 15 ½ × 4 ¼ in., The Fralin Museum of Art at the University of Virginia, Gift of The Joseph and Robert Cornell Memorial Foundation

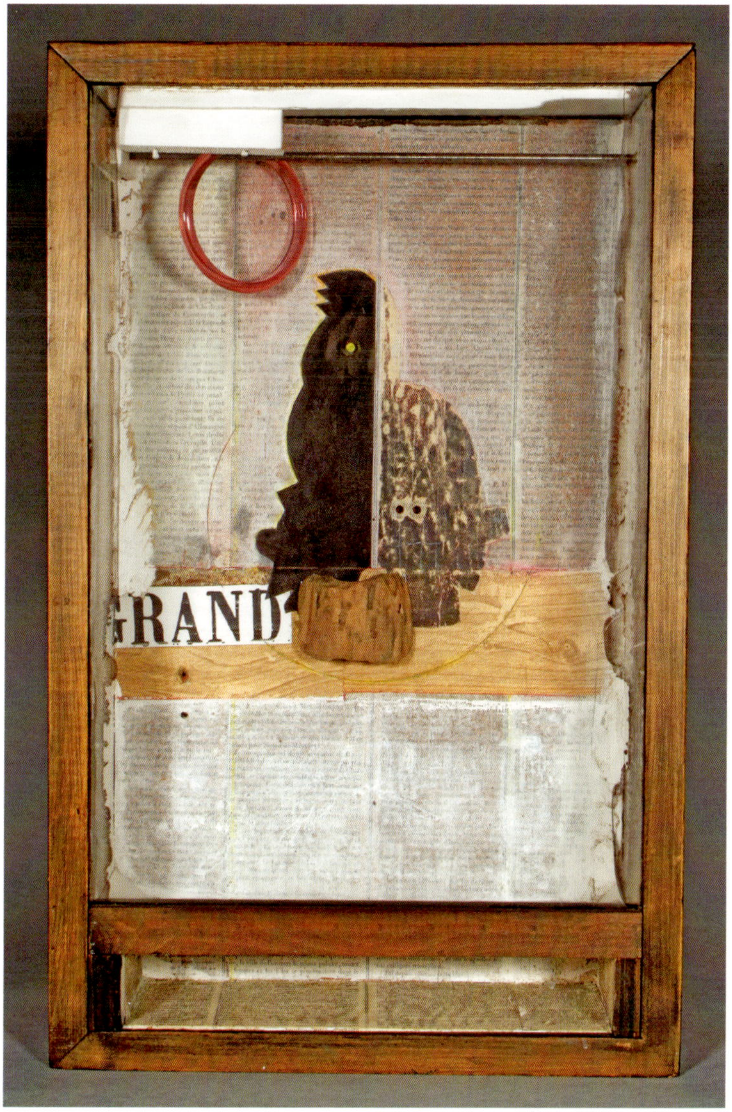

Joseph Cornell, *Untitled (Juan Gris Series, Black Cockatoo Silhouette)*, c. 1954–65, box construction, 19 5/8 × 12 × 4 3/8 in., The Fralin Museum of Art at the University of Virginia, Gift of The Joseph and Robert Cornell Memorial Foundation

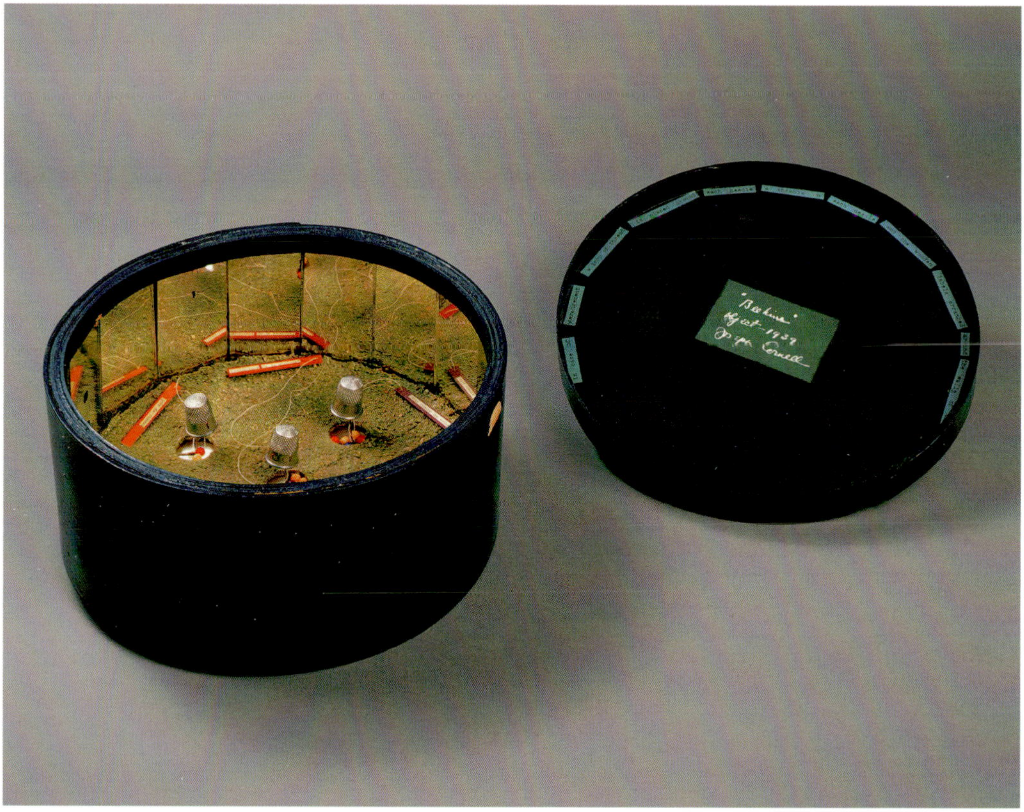

1.01 Joseph Cornell, *Beehive*, 1939, box construction, diam. 10 × h. 5 in., Private collection

Cornell and the Tradition of Curiosity

Stephen Bann

How can we categorize Cornell's work? Writing in 1942, Clement Greenberg had little doubt about the tradition to which it belonged. "Surrealism continues what Dada was the first to teach by actual examples. Dada stemmed, no matter how deviously, from art for art's sake, which asserted that works of art are self-sufficient and not required inevitably to be either mirrors of reality or decoration."[1] Continuing this problematic identification of Cornell's "objects" with "the abstract," Greenberg insisted: "The stuffed birds, thimbles, bells, cardboard cut-outs, and so forth which Cornell puts into boxes faced with glass please by their arrangement and the unspecified associations they call up, but mean or represent nothing not themselves."[2] But if Cornell's works are, for Greenberg, "abstract" in the sense that we should not bother to trace their extra-artistic "associations," they are unquestionably anchored in a recognizable modern genealogy. "They too derive from modern painting, from Chirico and Ernst—and Kurt Schwitters's 'trash' objects. (Cornell's only unsuccessful compositions, those relying on thimbles, have an emptiness resembling the duller canvases of Chirico)" (fig. 1.01).[3]

A few decades further on, this conviction that Cornell's work spoke only of its modernist antecedents had already begun to waver, spurred on by the increasing scrutiny directed at the historical roots of twentieth-century art. In the catalogue of her pioneering investigation of the "little magazines" of the first half of the century, Dawn Ades is much more discreet about aligning Cornell unequivocally with the modernist current. Commenting on *Box with a Perched Bird* (1948), she writes: "Cornell's boxes run a parallel course to the surrealist object; this one however uses a 'proscenium' setting, reminiscent of the toy theatres he played with as a child, and resembling a Victorian mantelpiece ornament."[4] On the one hand, we have there a reaffirmation of the relationship to Surrealism, however discreetly distanced; on the other, a frank admission that the artist's childhood memories have a major role to play in our appreciation of the work, not to mention the historical dimension that might lead us out of the twentieth century altogether. Ades adheres consistently to this double vision as far as Cornell is concerned. In relation to *Museum* (1945–47, The Menil Collection, Houston), for example, she notes his kinship with contemporary movements in sharing the "obsession with taxonomic arrangements that runs through Surrealism particularly at this time." But she also acknowledges, despite "a pointed lack of information about the exact contents of the box, [the] references to arcane knowledge and to alchemy."[5]

Between the date of Greenberg's review and that of Ades's exhibition essay, there had indeed been a quantum leap in the knowledge of Cornell's life and work, which would help to establish the complex singularity of his practice as an artist. Following on directly from his death in 1972, Dore Ashton's remarkable essay of 1974 had made it virtually impossible for any subsequent commentator to treat him directly as the dutiful follower of an avant-garde movement. Ashton forcefully emphasized Cornell's "certitude that his creations were not 'constructions' or 'sculptures' or 'collages' in the modern tradition."[6] She repeated his own forthright words that defined his practice primarily in terms of what it was *not*: "I can't draw, paint, sculpt, make lithographs."[7] One might add that Cornell even showed himself, on one occasion, to be so uneasy about being grouped with the Surrealists that he made a bid to be classed with their polar opposite, the Constructivists! When asked to exhibit work in an exhibition entitled *Fantastic Art, Dada, Surrealism*, he wrote to the organizer, Alfred Barr, to ask if he might be described instead as an "American Constructivist."[8] As is well acknowledged, Barr's position at the Museum of Modern Art in New York made him a virtual legislator in the matter of contemporary art movements, and this protestation must surely have fallen upon deaf ears. Moreover, Cornell's friend, Robert Motherwell, has attested that he was sometimes omitted from museum shows during his lifetime, precisely because the curators found it impossible to decide how to "place" him.[9]

How then should we categorize this artist who firmly refused to be categorized? Dore Ashton's solution—running directly counter to Greenberg's improbable view of the "abstract" foundation of the work—is to expatiate on the pre-twentieth-century world with which Cornell did without doubt cultivate multiple points of contact. On the first page of her eloquent essay, she describes Cornell quite simply as "the issue of nineteenth-century Romanticism."[10] The comment is surely justified by the many Romantic references that she uncovers in Cornell's artistic practice, and in his writings. Indeed, when we peruse the extracts from Berlioz, Stendhal, and Delacroix that Ashton incorporates as "Cornell's Recommended Readings" at the end of her study, there is a happy resonance between the subject matter of his boxes and the vanished world of these pioneers of the French Romantic movement. Ashton, nonetheless, concludes her essay with a slightly modified characterization of her view of Cornell as a Romantic, which locates his acquired historical consciousness not in the first flush of the nineteenth-century movement, but in a perspective that comprises both Gérard de Nerval and Stéphane Mallarmé: "Cornell saw himself in these terms, the terms of the nineteenth-century Symbolist."[11] There can be no doubt that this powerful reading has enriched our awareness of Cornell's art. At the very least, Ashton has made it impossible to accept as legitimate any "abstract," or purely "taxonomic," approach to its content.

There is, however a limitation in this or any such interpretation of the content of Cornell's thought world. This is quite simply that it pays too little attention to the material specificity of his practice, and to the significant historical antecedents that this unique practice brings to mind. I choose, almost at random, a telling sentence in which Ashton points out the similarity between poetic creation, which takes place within set forms like the sonnet, and Cornell's own artistic procedure: "Cornell always commenced by creating his frame, the box, and only then would drift into his procedure of association, putting in and taking out, much as a poet invests his poems with words that later may be changed or eliminated."[12] In this formulation, two things appear to be debatable. First (and most obviously), the addition and subtraction of words in a poem is simply not the same thing as the manipulation of objects. Mallarmé can invent the non-existent word *ptyx* to suit his rhyming scheme because language is a system of double articulation, consisting of phonemes as well having a semantic import. Objects may mean something to their owners, and another thing to the casual observer. But there is no level on which they could be said to mean nothing—or be the direct equivalent of *sound*—in the same way as a word is expressed as a concatenation of phonemes. This does not, of course, prevent objects from being reinterpreted in a second-order signifying system, by a process of metaphor, as when (in the case of Cornell's previously mentioned work of 1948), the little "thimbles" are grouped in to a "forest," in accord with the artist's chosen title.[13]

The second problem that emerges in relation to Ashton's comment is less obvious, but perhaps more telling. In referring to "his frame, the box," she passes lightly over a distinction that could prove to be of capital importance in coming to terms with Cornell's work. Frames and boxes are very different things, and specifically so in the sense that the very notion of a frame is integrally bound into the visual tradition of Western post-Renaissance art. Brunelleschi's *tavola* exposed on the steps of the Duomo at Florence has been taken as the almost mythical point of origin for the system of perspective applied from his time onward. Correspondingly, the conception of "framing" the image implicitly takes for granted a correspondence between the viewer's point of view and the construction of space within the picture. The frame is in this respect a guarantee of the correspondence between the viewpoint and what is depicted—and remained as such for the several centuries when perspective was the dominant system for the construction of pictorial space. What is more, the direction of modernist painting that comprehends Cubism, Surrealism, and Constructivism does not in fact abrogate this convention, so much as test it

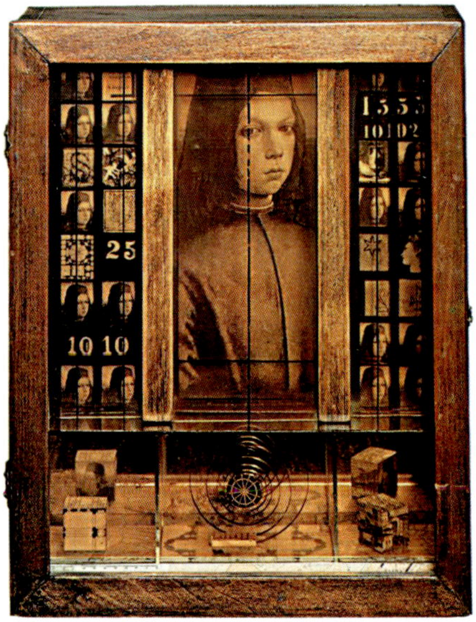

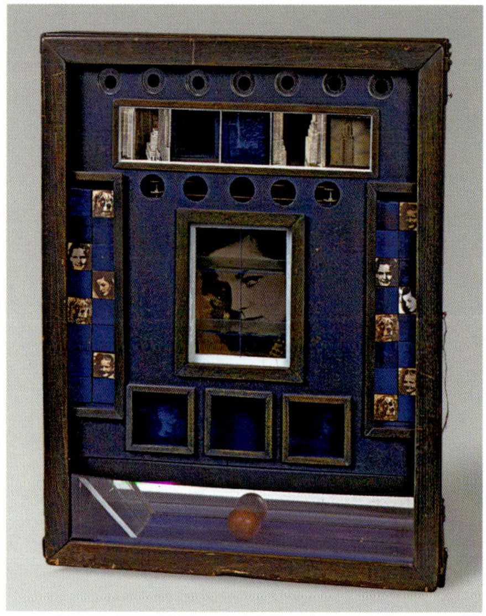

1.02 Joseph Cornell, *Medici Slot Machine*, 1943, box construction, 14 × 11 ¼ × 4 in., Private collection **1.03** Joseph Cornell, *Untitled* (*Penny Arcade Portrait of Lauren Bacall*), box construction, 20 ½ × 17 × 3 ½ in., Private collection

experimentally, while taking its constraints for granted. The shallow, fluctuating space of Cubism can only be perceived as such within the area demarcated by the frame, and the Cubist composition plays with the trained eye's disposition to move beyond the flat surface into space. Surrealism, moreover, brings back deep perspective in an accentuated form. In the paintings of Magritte and de Chirico the frame is constructed to contain a world all the more strange for being established by traditional pictorial norms.

Despite Cornell's undoubted admiration for both of these artists, it is surely clear that, on the material level, his work owes little or nothing to these post-Cubist manipulations of pictorial space. A more difficult judgment to make concerns the relation of Cornell's practice to that of Kurt Schwitters, whose "trash objects" (it will be recalled) appeared to Greenberg to be one of the chief contemporary sources from which Cornell's boxes derived. Here the connection might be said to reside, however, not so much in the framing of space as in the shared practice of collage, which without any doubt was a major factor in liberating Cornell from the constraints of conventional technique. Yet my recent viewing of a major exhibition of work by Schwitters confirms the impression that his is a practice radically distinct from that of Cornell, at least on the particular level that may be the most significant.[14] Whether or not Cornell was aware of the fact, Schwitters did certainly use collage in a way that anticipated its use in some of Cornell's works. Schwitters was by no means averse to using papers scraps that reproduced details of Renaissance paintings, just as Cornell did (fig. 1.02).[15] Schwitters, like Cornell, had a taste for movie stars (fig. 1.03). But the most significant thing about Schwitters's voluminous productions is that they remain, on the level of composition, absolutely orthodox Cubism. Whatever subtle connotations the paper scraps bring into the composition, their ordering on the surface is almost invariably in accord with the formal conventions of Synthetic Cubism, whose emergence coincided with the very point at which collage started to make its mark not as a minor craft and amateur pastime, but as the support for a novel revision of perspectival space. Even when Schwitters builds out from the surface by incorporating large and ungainly objects—as in *Untitled (Glass Flower)* 1940 (Museum Ludwig, Cologne)—he takes for granted the presence of the encompassing frame. The frame is not just a material support that secures the composition, and enables it to be hung upon the wall. It also serves, however vestigially, as a reminder that our viewing is still conditioned by the experience of looking into a delimited area that would allow a correct perspectival rendering of space.

If the concept of the frame is therefore rich in historical and cultural connotations, the box seems to have virtually none. It may be thought an advantage that Cornell's works are generally known by this fairly neutral term that seems to corroborate their individuality. But this advantage is perhaps outweighed by the distance that the term establishes from any form of historical genealogy that might appear appropriate to Cornell's way of working. As we have seen, Cornell has been happy to stress what his creations were *not*: neither "constructions," nor "sculptures," nor "collages," as Ashton underlines. But Ashton also quotes a fascinating comment that Cornell once made about his creative procedure in a catalogue of 1946: he writes of "impressions intriguingly diverse . . . that, in order to hold fast one might assemble, assort, and arrange into a cabinet . . . the contraption kind of the amusement resorts with endless ingenuity of effect, worked by coin and plunger, or brightly colored pin-balls."[16] The word *cabinet* is used here with exclusively contemporary connotations, in respect of the kind of interactive display that might be installed in a modern fairground or amusement arcade. But just a few pages earlier, Ashton herself employs the word *cabinet*, or an early modern variant of the word, in a passage that should indeed invite us to take a deeper historical view of Cornell's practice: "Closer to the *Wunderkammer* than to the chamber of horrors that so amused the Surrealists, Cornell's imagination harbored mementoes and anecdotes embellished by time."[17] It is indeed worth pursuing this new line of argument that associates Cornell's practice not with the practice of his contemporaries, but with a distinctive mode of practical interaction with the world of objects that had flourished several centuries before.

Cornell himself could hardly have predicted the much more widespread currency that the concept of the cabinet of curiosities has achieved over the past two decades. From being a somewhat esoteric object of study, familiar only to students of the Renaissance and the seventeenth century, the cabinet of curiosities has finally been widely acknowledged as, in many important respects, the chief ancestor of the museum as it exists today.[18] One landmark in this process was surely the installation, in 1998, of the Dutch collection of the National Gallery of Art, Washington DC, in a series of galleries henceforward known as the Dutch Cabinet Galleries. As the foreword to the accompanying catalogue of the collection noted, this installation was devised in order to "re-create the spirit underlying Dutch and Flemish encyclopedic collections."[19] No longer was the Dutch collection presented, like other national schools, as a mere sequence of framed paintings, identified by labels conveying details of authorship, title (if any) and provenance. Instead, the concept had been developed of recreating an imaginary collector's domain, which of course included the paintings, but placed them in the context of many different types of object in addition. "Art lovers, or *liefhebbers*," as the catalogue produced at the time explained, "brought together these fascinating collections in rooms, often referred to as *kunstkamers*, including artistic and natural wonders that ranged from paintings, sculpture, and decorative arts to books and musical instruments."[20] Although no particular art lover or collector was being designated, the aim was to remind the visitor that the world of art was at the time permeated by certain other classes of things. The blend of artificial objects and objects from the natural world that might be observed within the composition of a Dutch still life was made visible outside the frame, in the global context designated as a cabinet.

The Dutch Cabinet Galleries marked an interesting stage in the attempt to acquaint museum visitors with the collecting habits of the earlier period. But they did not focus the attention on perhaps the most striking feature of this past mode of connoisseurship, which was the fact that it went hand in hand with the development of a particular kind of furniture, that is, the cabinet, which was specifically intended to house, and so to protect, all the smaller items of the collection. At the present day, it has become fairly well known that the cult of the cabinet of curiosities in this sense of the term, arrived at its apogee in the second quarter of the seventeenth century with a number of outstanding specimens commissioned at Augsburg for the benefit of a small number of European monarchs and princes. A magnificent example, made for the Medici dukes of Florence, can still be seen in the Pitti Palace. But this

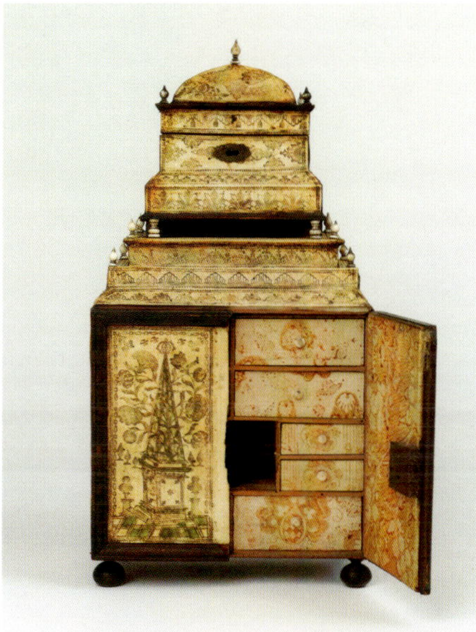

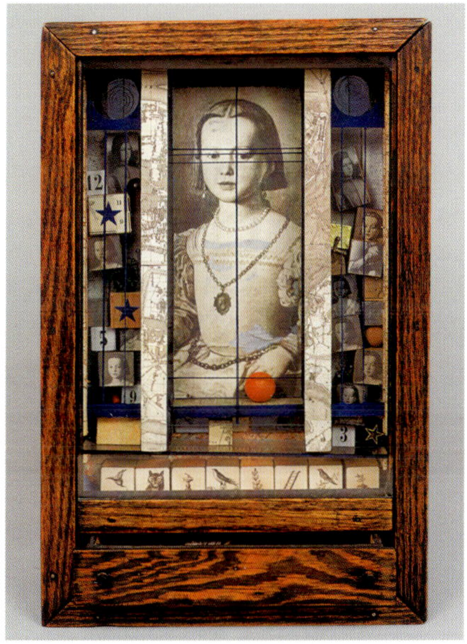

1.04 *Miniature Cabinet*, Germany (possibly Augsburg), c. 1700–1730, miniature cabinet of pine, covered with printed vellum, containing thirteen drawers of card, covered in red and white printed paper, 16½ × 8¼ × 5⅛ in., Victoria and Albert Museum, London **1.05** Joseph Cornell, *Untitled* (*Medici Princess*), 1948, box construction, 17⅝ × 11⅛ × 4⅜ in., Private collection

has lost all its contents. The sole example of such princely cabinets that survives in all its splendor, originally created for the Swedish King Gustavus Adolphus, is today displayed at the Museum Gustavianum at Uppsala, near Stockholm.

Yet examples so exceptional as these perhaps obscure the less dramatic development over several centuries of more modest but no less interesting cabinets. A recent exhibition at the Holburne Museum, Bath, made up for this omission by carefully tracing the evolution of such cabinets over the seventeenth century.[21] Notable in all cases was the exceptional beauty and virtuosity of the exterior claddings, whether they consisted of elaborate marquetry depicting flowers and architectural details or sported miniature oil-painted panels with a complex narrative iconography. The essential feature of all of them, however, was a central compartment that preserved the owner's secrets. Sometimes locked with a key, and quite often arranged as a miniature theatrical proscenium, this was the very heart of the cabinet. It symbolized the intersection between the public face of the cabinet and the concealed treasure that it might be required to hide.

What is the possible advantage of looking at Cornell's work in this light of this new-found interest in the history of the cabinet of curiosities? And how does it help us to focus on this term, the *cabinet*, rather than on the more neutral notion of the box? Certainly the connection with the regal and princely cabinets already mentioned here would be an inappropriate one. These were the contemporary equivalent of Hollywood productions, put together with the use of materials obtained at enormous expense, crafted by delegated artisans and designed above all to enhance the patron's reputation. Only a small number of cabinets survive, which, by contrast, relate more approximately to the size of Cornell's works. One might be the miniature cabinet, designed probably at Augsburg around 1700, which is "covered with vellum printed, tooled and painted with . . . allegorical figures and a woodland hunting scene" (fig. 1.04).[22] This was, to repeat the words of the catalogue, "probably intended for a private closet or study to house some of the owner's most personal possessions" and it incorporated "two secret drawers hidden beneath the molding above the doors."[23] However, the point of any such a comparison is surely not just to establish a physical relationship between the two objects. The point in common is rather the link that can be imagined between the psychology of the collector and this distinctive means of enhancing and reflecting value that draws our attention to a secret space (fig. 1.05).

Clearly there is a dialectic between revelation and concealment that is implied in the case of the cabinet of curiosities and in the work of Cornell. The Age of Curiosity featured not only locked cabinets, but also still-life paintings that emblematized the accessibility of precious objects through an open display. The well-known work of Georg Hainz, *Cabinet of Curiosities* (Hamburger Kunsthalle), is a good example, which invites an immediate comparison with the stocked and open shelves of Cornell's *Untitled* (mid-1950s) box construction (figs. 1.06, 1.07).[24] But the role of the box in Cornell is generally not to emblematize accessibility in this way: it is to remind us from the start that what is stored within the box has been placed there in such a way that it functions as an emissary from a private world.

Is there anything more concrete that can be said about the seemingly far-fetched comparison between the seventeenth-century collector of curiosities and Cornell, a contemporary of Marcel Duchamp? I believe so. Having myself written a study of one such collector, I am perhaps more prone than most to see points in common between the conventions of that period, and certain features of the "expanded field" (to borrow Rosalind Krauss's term) of twentieth-century art. I certainly believe that the concept of curiosity has surfaced again with a vengeance in relation to work that is most commonly described as an offshoot of Surrealism, but appears to me to have a much more complicated historical genealogy.[25] At a time when the traditional

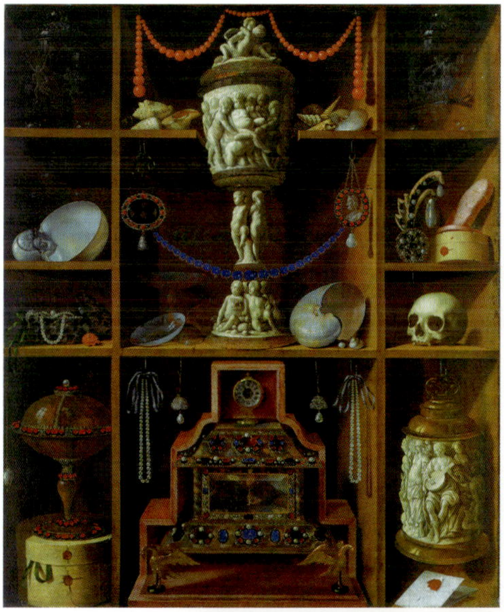

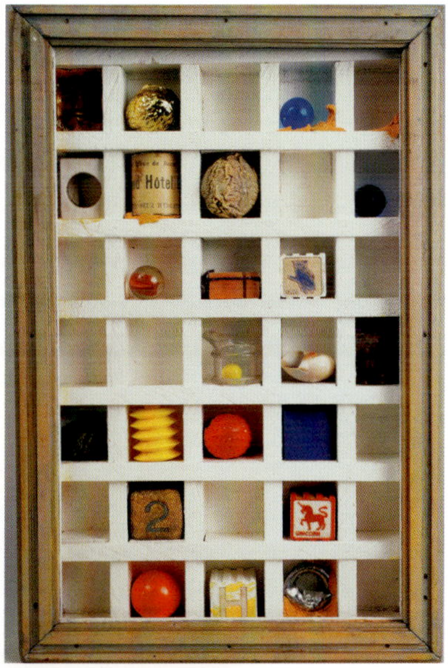

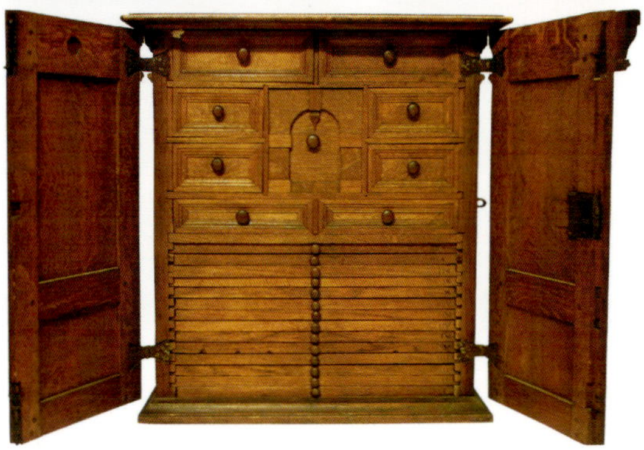

1.06 Georg Hainz, *Cabinet of Curiosities*, 1666, oil on canvas, 45 ¼ × 36 ⅝ in., Hamburger Kunsthalle **1.07** Joseph Cornell, *Untitled*, 1950s, box construction, 18 × 11 ½ × 2 ¾ in., Private collection **1.08** Cabinet made for Dr. Meric Casaubon in Canterbury during the 1630s and bequeathed to Dr. John Bargrave 18 × 11 ½ × 11 in., Canterbury Cathedral archive, Canterbury

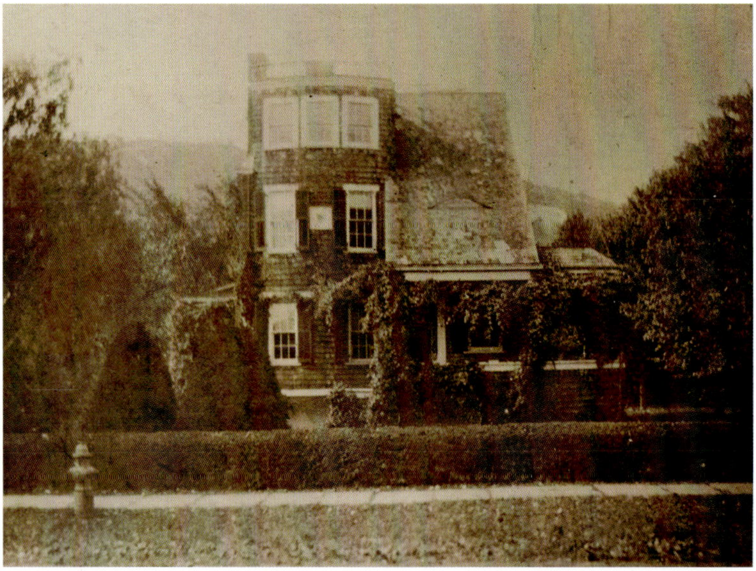

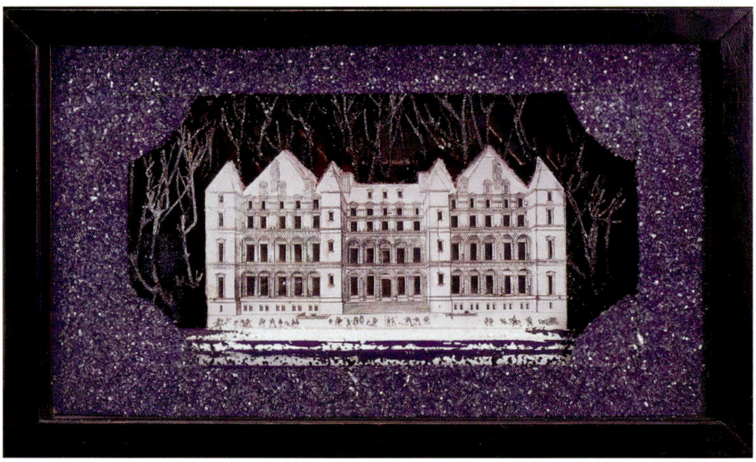

1.09 House where Joseph Cornell was born, Nyack, NY, photograph dated between 1890 and 1950, Joseph Cornell papers, Archives of American Art, Smithsonian Institution **1.10** Joseph Cornell, *Untitled (Pink Palace)*, c. 1946–48, box construction, 10 × 16½ × 3¾ in., The Robert Lehrman Art Trust, courtesy of Aimee and Robert Lehrman

aesthetic category of the beautiful appears increasingly inappropriate, the productions of artists as different as Hubert Duprat and Damien Hirst can be understood as having reactivated a type of spectator involvement that is indeed comparable to the early modern engagement with the natural world.[26] The differences are, of course, also obvious. But in tracing the career of the seventeenth-century churchman, traveler, and collector John Bargrave, I discern something of the same signifying process at work in his collecting enterprise as in the creations of Cornell: first of all, there is the passion for collecting over many years a motley assortment of objects, all of which are vividly imprinted with his memories; and secondly, there is the need to focus that amalgam of objects and memories through the physical form of the cabinet (fig. 1.08 and Cornell, *Untitled* [*Pocket Matchbox Treasury*], 1947, collection Mark Kelman). For Bargrave, the small wooden pieces of furniture—with their sliding trays, drawers, and secret chambers—became the embodiment of a mental universe not completely closed to the spectator but still possessing a hermetic character that could never entirely be dispelled.

Another point of comparison that can be made between Cornell and Bargrave touches perhaps more precisely upon the nostalgic mood that the boxes persistently evoke. Robert Motherwell was clearly fascinated by the anachronistic aspect of Cornell's practice. As he expressed it, "we all felt that nostalgia was the enemy of Modernism, and [Cornell's] work is saturated with it."[27] But this "nostalgia" may be understood as having taken a very particular form in Cornell's adult life, namely a yearning for the sense of security that he had experienced as a child, before the death of his father compelled the family to move out of the large house where they had been comfortably installed (fig. 1.09). Lindsay Blair remarks on this point: "His whole preoccupation . . . with Malba House, Willet Mansion, Lawrence Farm—large homesteads with outbuildings set in the landscape—brought back a sense of the past, his own past, and nostalgia for a bygone era of imagined gentility" (fig. 1.10).[28] This "preoccupation" chimes in very much with the story of Bargrave, who lived as a child in the great country house Bifrons, which his father had built, and continued to sport in his portraits the coat of arms that his father had been granted in the time of his prosperity. Bargrave's father's virtual bankruptcy while he was still an adolescent, and the subsequent devastation wrought upon the family by the English Civil War, gave him an enduring sense of loss, for which his collection built up over the difficult years of exile provided seemingly some sort of panacea.[29] Cornell did not have to travel widely to acquire his objects and artifacts. He could rely on the prodigality of mass merchandising and modern communications to bring them all within his reach. But the overwhelming influence of this remembered past upon his creative persona can hardly be doubted.

One of the most interesting recent essays on Cornell happens to strike a similar note. Tony Fabijancic takes the general knowledge of Cornell's boxes for granted, and turns to exploring their ramifications in contemporary American literature. William Gibson's "cyberpunk novel *Count Zero*" of 1987 introduces the notion that boxes of unknown provenance are appearing on the art market, and these can be traced back to a deliberate forgery of a Cornell box that was once sold in an art gallery and subsequently caused a scandal. The point of these references, according to Fabijancic, is precisely that Cornell's boxes embody fantasies of the past that the false and recently manufactured boxes cannot achieve. The author uses the example of Cornell to point to the loss of authenticity that is the disease of contemporary society. "Gibson's description of objects in his boxes suggests longing for waning humanism and for the potential value of emotionally invested objects in a commodity-ridden world."[30] Taking this point of view into account, it is worth stressing that the authenticity of Cornell's work makes it even more of a legitimate protest against dehumanization than it could be when he was putting together his boxes. To a certain degree, he eludes contemporary artistic terms of classification only to emerge as having an effective solidarity with the great writers of the past who were his constant study. Words written by Julia Kristeva on the significance of Proust for our time seem to capture something of Cornell's special resonance: "If you will only be so good as to open up your memories of felt time, *there* will rise the new cathedral."[31]

Notes

1 Clement Greenberg, "Review of a Joint Exhibition of Joseph Cornell and Laurence Vail," *The Nation*, Dec. 26, 1942, republished in Clement Greenberg, *The Collected Essays and Criticism*, ed. John O'Brian (Chicago: University of Chicago Press, 1986), 1: 131–32.

2 Ibid., 131.

3 Ibid., 132. The "thimble" boxes stigmatized by Greenberg may have included *Beehive* (1939), illustrated in Blair 1998, 30. Cornell was evidently not discouraged by Greenberg's comment in pursuing this theme, since *Beehive* reappears in a modified form as *Thimble Forest*, 1948 (illustrated in Ashton 1974, 179).

4 London 1978, 389.

5 Ibid.

6 Ashton 1974, 4.

7 Ibid.

8 Blair 1998, 32. His letter included the comment: "I do not share in the dream theories of the Surrealists. While fervently admiring much of their work I have never been an official Surrealist" (letter to Alfred H. Barr, Jr., of Nov. 13, 1936, first published in Ades 1980, 19).

9 Blair 1998, 33.

10 Ashton 1974, 1.

11 Ibid., 111.

12 Ibid., 58.

13 See Stephen Bann, "'The Mythical Conception is the Name': Titles and Names in Modern and Post-modern Painting," *Word & Image* 1, no. 2 (1985): 176–90, for a discussion of the role of titles in Western art.

14 *Schwitters in Britain*, Tate Britain, London, Jan. 30–May 12, 2013.

15 Compare for example, *Holy Night by Correggio Worked through by Kurt Schwitters* (1947) with Cornell's *Medici Slot Machine* (*Bernardo Pinturicchio*) (1943, fig. 1.02). I imply no significant influence here, in either direction, since the life experience of Schwitters could scarcely be more different than that of Cornell.

16 Ashton 1974, 77–78.

17 Ibid., 74.

18 See Stephen Bann, "The Return to Curiosity: Shifting Paradigms in Contemporary Museum Display," in *Art and its Publics: Museum Studies at the Millennium*, ed. Andrew McLellan (Oxford: Blackwell, 2003), 17–30; and Stephen Bann, "Un retour à la curiosité: Sur certains aspects de la situation actuelle," in *Histoire de l'art et musées*, ed. Dominique de Viéville (Paris: Ecole du Louvre, 2005), 21–28.

19 Arthur Wheelock, *A Collector's Cabinet* (Washington, DC: National Gallery of Art, 1998), 7.

20 Ibid., 7.

21 *Secret Splendour: The Hidden World of Baroque Cabinets*, exh. cat. (Bath: Holburne Museum, 2012).

22 Ibid., item 11. Its dimensions are 42 x 21 x 13 cm.

23 Ibid.

24 See Blair 1998, 127.

25 See Stephen Bann, *Ways around Modernism* (New York and London: Routledge, 2007), 103–72, for a broad sketch of the development of the concept of curiosity since the early modern period.

26 Hal Foster has reminded me, in this connection, that Sol LeWitt required of his work that it should simply be "interesting."

27 Quoted in Blair 1998, 67.

28 Ibid., 63.

29 See Stephen, Bann, *John Bargrave, Collector, Traveler, and Witness* (Ann Arbor: University of Michigan Press, 1994), especially 25–61, "Rise and Fall of the House of Bargrave."

30 Tony Fabijancic, "The Sadness Is in Your Memory in the Boxes of Joseph Cornell, William Gibson, and E.L. Doctorow," *Word & Image* 28, no. 3 (2012): 233.

31 Julia Kristeva, *Proust and the Sense of Time*, trans. Stephen Bann (New York: Columbia University Press, 1993), 7.

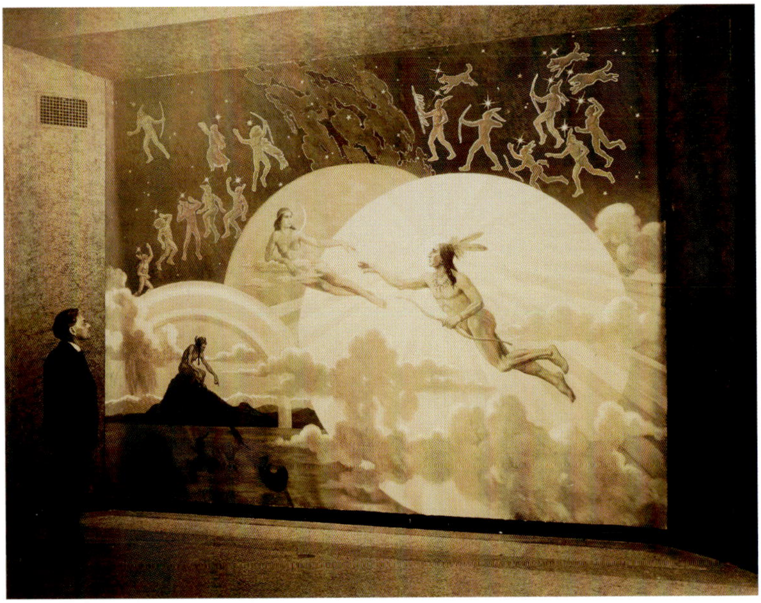

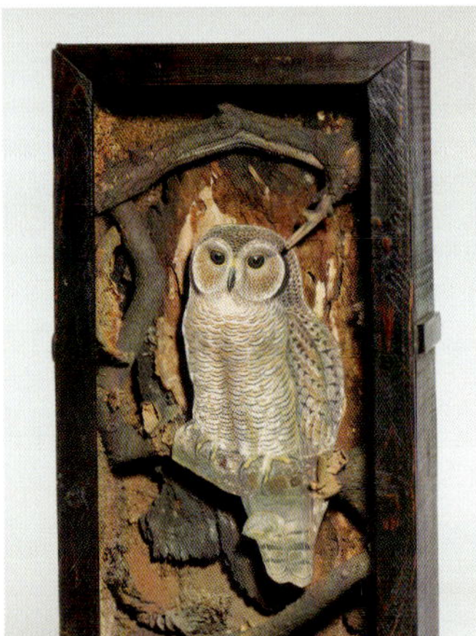

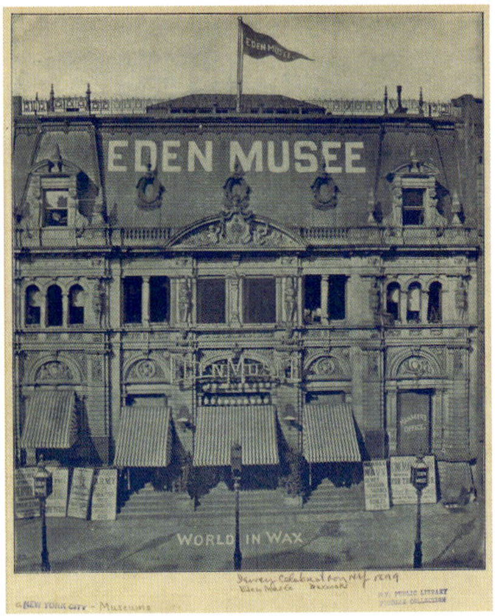

2.01 Wurts Bros., 200 Central Park West. American Museum of Natural History. View of C. R. Knight, artist, with his mural painting, 1935, gelatin silver print, 10 × 8 in., The Museum of the City of New York **2.02** Joseph Cornell, *Owl Box*, c. 1945–46, box construction, 25 × 14 ⅛ × 6 ¼ in., Musée National d'Art Moderne, Centre Georges Pompidou/Centre de création industrielle, Paris **2.03** *Eden Musée—"World in Wax,"* n.d., The New York Public Library, Astor, Lenox, and Tilden Foundation

Museums, Muses

Notes on Joseph Cornell

Sylvie Ramond and François-René Martin

Joseph Cornell was passionate about visiting movie houses, theaters, libraries, used book stores, department stores, and museums. His imaginary world and his artwork cannot be dissociated from the shows and merchandise offered by a city as excessive as New York in the twentieth century. To return to that source, to the profusion of images and objects of all kinds that accompany those places, allows us to perceive a particular topography and economy. In this respect, one could even conceive of Cornell's work as an attempt to fight against the proliferation of images and objects—an uninterrupted immersion in which fantasies are endlessly manipulated in a chain of transformation leading to the artist's files, then to his boxes. But at the same time, guiding Cornell's resistance, before all the steps he needed for selection, concentration, and association, we find a love of images, a fascination with odds and ends and, above all, a constant experiencing of all the places where the creatures who haunt his work live—actresses, dancers, birds.

It is at the beginning of the 1940s, in Cornell's journal, that we find the first traces of what he calls his "expeditions" to museums. In the summer of 1941, the artist writes from memory how one of these excursions took place:

> (another day) Trip to the Metropolitan Museum of Art in connection with VIEW article, "The Enchanted Wanderer," the Quattrocento Montage portrait of Hedy Lamarr. Fine sunny day—went into town in morning experiencing an unexpected exaltation that stayed until five o'clock. Lunch in 86th St. Automat. Evocation from material above of presence. Never have visited museum with such an unhurried sense of pleasure. The panoramic landscape of Patinir stands out now as an unusual experience, made vividly authentic by the mood, etc. Bought some postcards, among them Predis' Madonna of the Cherries. Hypnagogic musings of same on subway express. Very warm in Times Square. Saw Dietrich in "Destry Rides Again." Disappointing after the above mood. The midtown section was filled with an odour of heavy smoke from a fire across the river in Jersey. Came home on subway.[1]

A visit to the museum, in this case with the specific intention of finding some work that would help him prepare the page of *Enchanted Wanderer* for the magazine *View*, is never anything other than the conclusion to a true wandering about in the center of New York, where the cinema is the extension of the museum, Marlene Dietrich connects to some Italian Madonna seen in the rooms of the Metropolitan Museum of Art, the New Jersey shores to the landscapes of Patinir. As to the intense, unexpected pleasure offered by the visit, it does not exclude other pleasures, such as lunch at the 86th Street automat, or other sensations. Thus, visiting museums—but such an observation would also probably apply to shows and movies—is associated with a physical journey to some very specific places in Manhattan or Brooklyn, where the artist comes to glean visions, relics, and sacred images. It is the journey of a pilgrim, or even more so that of a hunter: he actually does define himself precisely in the text proposal given to *View* as a "hunter of images."[2] These images collected by Cornell in reality have many faces: the face of actresses like Hedy Lamar, the faces of women painted several centuries ago, like the *Young Girl with Cherries* by Giovanni Ambrogio de Predis, a painter of the school of Leonardo active in Milan between 1472 and 1508, but also probably everything coming from his "hypnagogic meditations" in the express train taking him back to his neighborhood in Flushing, Queens.

In 1921, when he started to work as a traveling salesman for the William Whitman textile company, Cornell had been looking forward to crisscrossing Manhattan and stopping in at its many museums: the Met; the Morgan Library; the American Geographical Society; the Whitney Studio, ancestor of the Whitney Museum of American Art; the Brooklyn Museum and its collection of Asian art discovered in 1929; and so on. For many years, the artist would assiduously visit these places favorable to all kinds of daydreaming, places where so many apparitions congregated, which necessitated making visits to the picture collection at the public library, or to the Bettmann Archives to make photostats of his favorite works. But here again, we must wait until the summer of 1941 to find in his journal the description of those days, such as the entry for July 15, when he found the doors of the Museum of the American Indian closed, choosing in compensation the Geographic Society, guarded over by a totem pole made by Alaska Indians. The Museum of Natural History is another one of those places Cornell frequented assiduously. It was a whole collection of museums unto itself, where one could, from one room to the next, from one floor to the next, apprehend by sight and mind every realm of creation: Indian ornaments (fig. 2.01), planets, animals (fig. 2.02), extinct creatures—all sorts of *naturalia* which, along with effigies of actresses and some works from the past, would create what can be called the *paraphernalia* of Joseph Cornell's artistic creation; the term appears in his journal, simply in connection with astronomy:

> Down to the Museum of Natural History to trace Indian designs. Copied in the library with its oil paintings of early pioneer days and an Indian princess. Had never been in this department before which is so peaceful and probably has not changed in at least seventy years. It seems even longer. Decided to stay and take in for the first time the Hayden Planetarium. Wandered around downstairs and noticed (also for the first time) the breath-taking collection of birds' nests in their original condition complete and replete with eggs. From the hummingbird's half-inch miniatures to eagles'. Many of the nests could be inserted intact into the fabulous fairyland of Tchelitchew, of whom I could not help thinking. The sweetness and the ingenuity of some of the smaller ones! Into the bookshop. Couldn't resist a mottled blue and green coiled shell, also a shiny white and pink one, for an ONDINE box for Fanny Cerrito.[3]

New York could thus appear as the gathering place of what in the past used to be scattered all over in different places, at the outside peiphery, now brought together, concentrated in a few places, museums or otherwise, which then took on the position of "prompting points," where an almost immeasurable number of images and objects, coming from a multitude of distinct universes, were available for all kinds of uses, for all kinds of rearrangements.[4]

Museums

Claude Lévi-Strauss best expressed the particular status of New York just before the middle of the century, during the war years. He lived in Manhattan from 1941 to 1944 and he, too, frequented some of Cornell's favorite places. In 1943 the anthropologist wrote: "There is in New York a magic place where the dreams of childhood hold a rendezvous, where century-old tree trunks sing and speak, where indefinable objects watch out for the visitor, with the anxious stare of human faces, where animals of superhuman gentleness join their little paws like hands in prayer for the privilege of building the palace of the beaver for the chosen one, of guiding him to the realm of the seals, or of teaching him, with a mystic kiss, the language of the frog or the king-fisher."[5] The vast hall on the ground floor set up by Franz Boas, where the works of Indians of the North Coast of the Pacific, from Alaska to British Columbia, were displayed, was where the French anthropologist could strengthen his conviction that there, at that very moment, a great upheaval of aesthetic categories was about to take place imminently: "Surely it will not be long before we see the collections from this part of the world moved from ethnographic to fine arts museums to take their just place amidst the antiquities of Egypt or Persia and the works of medieval Europe."[6]

But New York does not simply stand for this extension of the domain of art museums, with due justice finally given to this art of greater diversity than European art. New York stands for something larger and more composite, which Lévi-Strauss had understood. America had started late, compared to Old Europe, but it had known how to seize what the latter had neglected: the rejected old stones used to build the Cloisters, arms collections, and ancient clothing—areas neglected by the great European museums—Egypt and its items for daily use, and, even more so, the natural sciences. "America . . . had assiduously created galleries of mineralogy, paleontology, ornithology, as well as aquariums. All these sumptuous palaces dazzled the European visitor not only because of their treasures from an unspoiled and therefore prodigal continent, but also as they compared with our own rundown galleries of natural history. In Europe, our interest in these collections has reawakened after an eclipse of two centuries—a revival that may well have been sparked, at least in part, by a certain familiarity that Europeans acquired after the Second World War with American museums."[7]

Lévi-Strauss was possibly referring to the taste that the Surrealists showed for assembled objects, and perhaps to André Breton himself, with whom he would go about foraging in the antique shops on Third Avenue and Sixth Avenue or on Madison. But his remark implies at the same time something deeper, which does not refer so much to the diversity of the objects and works exhibited as to their quantity, their heterogeneity, and the museum form itself. The logic of the availability of an infinite number of treasures is the logic of rejected objects. Each generation, believed Lévi-Strauss, when leaving the stage, leaves behind a page of humanity's past, with its remnants; each wave of immigrants had arrived, for over a century, with its fetishes, "each new group . . . bearing rich or meager treasures, which necessity forced it to disperse very quickly. The immense resources which the local plutocracy had to satisfy its whims, made it seem as if examples of the whole of humanity's artistic legacy were present in New York. Shuffled and reshuffled, like flotsam and jetsam, to the capricious rhythms of social ups and downs, some of these examples still decorated drawing rooms or had made their way into museums, while others piled up in unexpected nooks."[8]

It is, in fact, the coexistence of those "rich or meager treasures" that made Manhattan this extraordinary place described by Lévi-Strauss; and, even more so, it was the coexistence of museums of the poor or the rich which made it into a gigantic *Kunstkammer.* Side by side with institutions created on the model of European museums, such as the Met or even The Museum of Modern Art, which had recently opened, there were places related to the museum industry, dime museums, where crowds of visitors mingled to see great quantities of unrelated objects or shows, dioramas, exotic animals, automatons, wax statues, midgets, Siamese twins, mummies, specimens from indigenous peoples, and more. The P. T. Barnum American Museum, which opened in 1842 at the corner of Broadway and Ann Street, had been the pioneer by presenting "an encyclopedic synopsis of everything worth seeing in this curious world"[9] and was receiving up to twenty-five thousand visitors per day, eager to see these popular *mirabilia.* Dime museums, typically American institutions, although present throughout the whole country, were mainly concentrated in Boston, Philadelphia, and New York. They offered in a single location various types of popular entertainment and reached their peak in the years 1880–90 before disappearing after the First World War. Another of these temples of entertainment was the Eden Musée (fig. 2.03), open between 1883 and 1915, located on 23rd Street between Fifth and Sixth Avenues, and especially renowned for its waxworks. All sorts of entertainment were offered, from a Hungarian orchestra to Japanese acrobats, from Spanish dancers to magicians. In 1887, a show devoted to an orchid, a newly discovered flower, met with great success. A horror chamber showing instruments of torture was also one of the crowd's favorites. The museum exhibited a spectacular collection of paintings in its art gallery and was one of the first among dime museums to show movies, as early as 1897, in its winter garden, with the Lumière Brothers' projector, including a film version of the Oberammergau passion play.[10]

Vaudeville and the cinema brought on the demise of these museums, which could not compete with places that offered, on the one hand, the ordinary spectacle of human passions, and on the other the marvels of technical achievements and the miracles of human presence. And yet, dime museums had succeeded in filling in the great gaps left by other museums and they had in some ways defined themselves as the mirror to specialized museums: the spectacular won over contemplation, the single event over the long term, profusion over rarity, artifice over authenticity, automation over art, the presence or the immediate appearance of real beings rather than their representation. The fascination Cornell felt for these shows and their installations is what, finally, places him outside the Surrealist universe, where the found object never totally leaves the world of rare things. In his youth, Joseph Cornell had frequented the Eden Musée, where his grandmother would take him.[11] Another collection of treasures that would, years later, impress him was the World's Fair set up at the former Corona Dumps in 1939–40, near

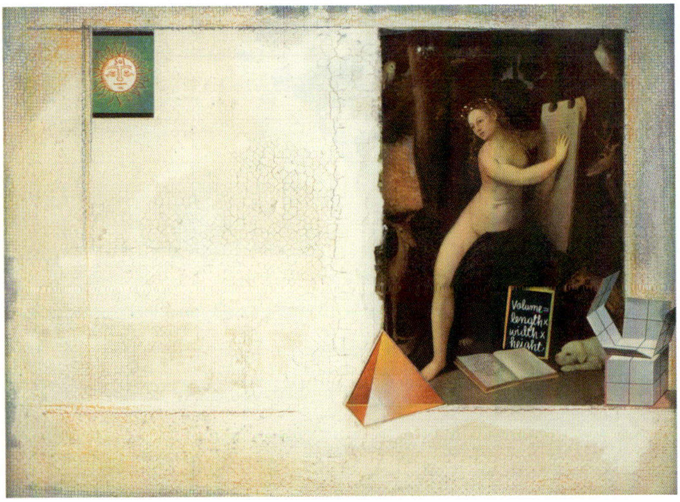

2.04 Joseph Cornell, *Circe—Surface and Volume in Nature*, c. 1965, collage, 8 7/16 × 11 7/16 in., National Gallery of Art, Washington, DC. Andrew W. Mellon Fund

Flushing Meadows, not far from Utopia Parkway. What seemed to have a special impact on Cornell was not so much the *Dream of Venus* pavilion by Salvador Dalí (a project spearheaded by Julien Levy), but the three pavilions devoted to the presentation of masterpieces of European art from the thirteenth to the nineteenth centuries. Here he discovered works that would later wind up populating his boxes: *Portrait of a Young Man* by Bronzino, *Circe and Her Lovers in a Landscape* (c. 1525) by Dosso Dossi (fig. 2.04), *Maria Theresa, Infanta of Spain* (1651–54) by Velázquez, *Manuel Osorio Manrique de* Zuñiga (possibly 1790s) by Goya, and *Soap Bubbles* (probably 1733–34) by Chardin.[12]

Images and fetishes are connected to all these places. Cornell collected reproductions of works of art that he discovered and admired during his wanderings, or better, souvenir objects such as the shells he found in the shop of the Museum of Natural History. And this first gleaning was further supplemented with the help of used-book dealers on Fourth Avenue and their vast depositories of texts and illustrations—Doubleday, Gotham Book Mart, Hacker Art Books, the Sanctuary, Vanity Fair Bookshop—which the artist frequented assiduously. But one source stands out far above the others in Cornell's work: the museum, at the same time the source and the horizon for the creation of many of the artist's boxes, like so many reliquaries for the saints he venerated in movie houses and magazines, but also like condensed museums, or even portable chambers of marvels.

Muses

Untitled (*Soap Bubble Set*) (1936, The Wadsworth Atheneum Museum of Art, Hartford, Connecticut) and *Cabinet of Natural History* (*Object*) (1934, 1936–40), presented within an installation of objects entitled *The Elements of Natural Philosophy* at the exhibit *Fantastic Art, Dada, Surrealism* at the Museum of Modern Art in 1936, are among the first works by Cornell to take on the appearance of an armoire or of one of those displays seen in seventeenth-century vanities, such as the one by Sébastien Stosskopf—a display cleverly playing with precarious and almost ethereal elements, bubbles, droplets, shadows, reminiscent of the orbits of the stars, the movement of the tides, but also the universe of childhood.[13] In 1948 Cornell writes of these compositions: "Shadow boxes become poetic theatres or settings wherein are metamorphosed the elements of a childhood pastime."[14] Can we find here the origins of this love of Cornell's for shows and museums, which is the underlying principle of his work? An event in his youth immediately comes to mind, both obvious and yet undecipherable: four months after his father's death, of leukemia, in 1917, Cornell decided to distract his family by organizing a show at the rear of their garden.[15] On the admission ticket was written:

GROUP TICKET GIVING ACCESS TO:
The Professional Burglar
Relic Museum
Candy
Shadow Play[16]

Another event also deserves some attention: Cornell's theft of a doll from his cousin Ethel, which will become Bébé Marie, the idol that the artist would wind up encasing in a box, placed among some branches. This kidnapping, recounted by one of Joseph's sisters, takes on the look of one of those *translationes* of relics of saints in the Middle Ages, the doll carrying with itself the aura of the enchanted places where it had come from: a magnificent house—an Old Hudson River–type of house—which, as Elizabeth Cornell Benton recalls, was a true "museum of antiques."[17]

These installations or objects, small theaters of memory bearing souvenirs of childhood or relic-dolls, all had in common the recourse to the museum as their setting. The same applies to a box as important as the one Cornell devotes to Cléo de Mérode (fig. 2.05), the dancer made famous by her chaste beauty, the great commotion over her alleged love life and especially the great number of photographs showing her as a Javanese dancer, as Phryné, as a Gypsy or simply as Cléo de Mérode.

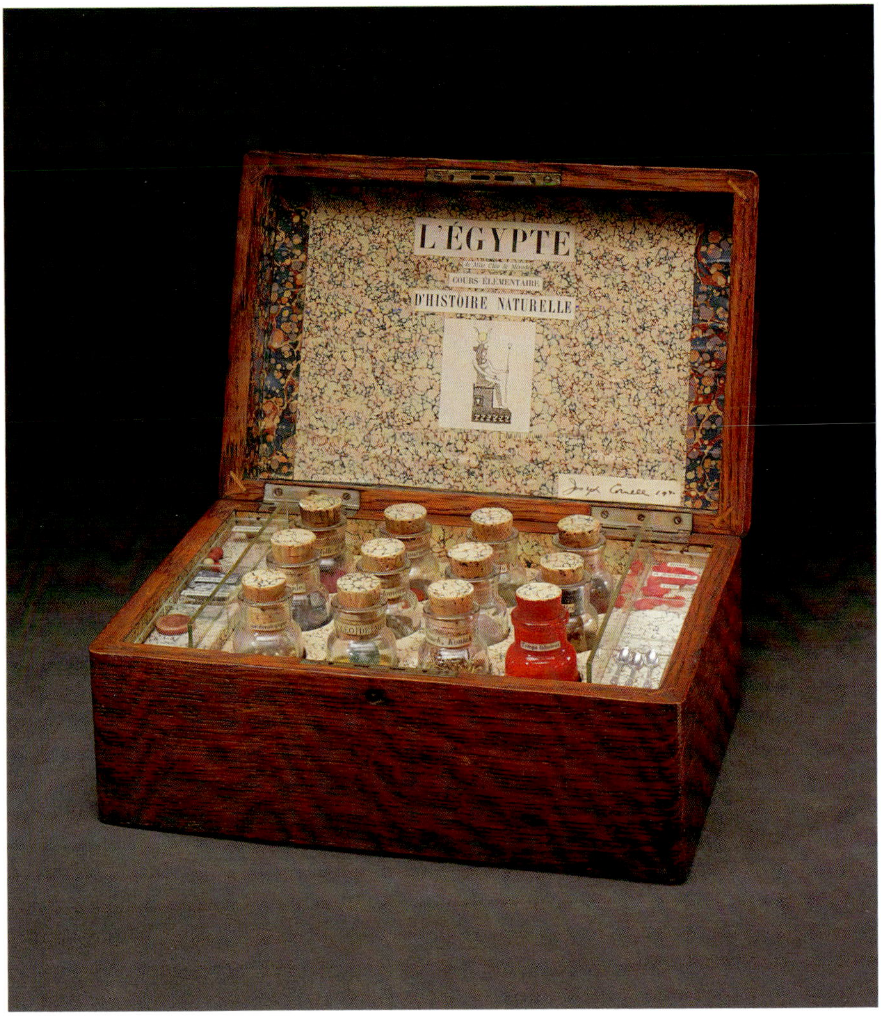

2.05 Joseph Cornell, *L'Egypte de Mlle Cléo de Mérode: cours élémentaire d'histoire naturelle*, 1940, box construction, 4 ⁵⁄₈ × 10 ⁵⁄₈ × 7 ¼ in., The Robert Lehrman Art Trust, Collection of Aimee and Robert Lehrman

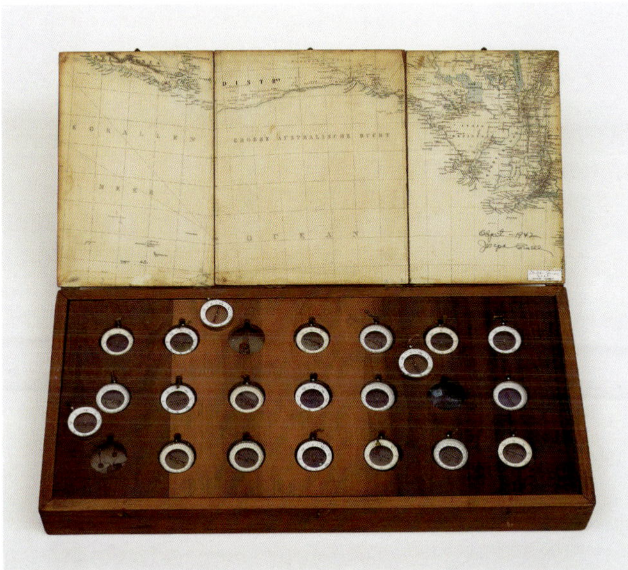

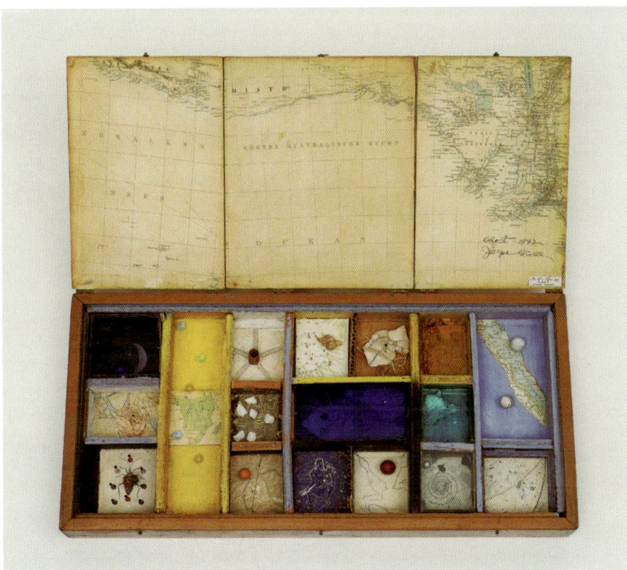

2.06a, b Joseph Cornell, *Object* (*Roses des vents*), 1942–53, box construction, 2 5/8 × 21 1/4 × 10 3/8 in., The Museum of Modern Art, New York. Mr. and Mrs. Gerald Murphy Fund

Playing on her first name, Cléo-Cléopatre Diane de Mérode, Cornell associates this heroine with ancient Egypt, and particularly with the goddess Hathor, wife of the falcon-god, associated with festivities and with love. He no doubt was aware that she had fascinated the old king of Belgium, Leopold II, during a production of Verdi's Egyptian opera *Aida* at the Paris Opera. Thus, the *Cours élémentaire d'histoire naturelle* (Elementary course in natural history) on *L'Egypte de Mlle Cléo de Mérode* takes on the form of a relic case, with its vials holding small flasks containing plastic rose petals labeled "Dew with rose leaves" or the famous photograph by Nadar, but also a few fragments referring to Egypt such as grasshoppers or a Nilometer, an instrument that measured the level of the Nile, in particular at times of flooding. Other boxes such as *Object* (*Roses des vents*) (fig. 2.06) already held a whole gamut of maritime articles, with samples, maps, and measuring or orientation instruments. The *L'Egypte de Mlle Cléo de Mérode* construction mixes the world of nymphs and actresses with the world of stars, rivers, and seas, according to some geodesy of the muses.

Another venerated character was Hedy Lamarr, to whom Cornell devotes "a journey album" in his contribution to the magazine *View*.[18] It is still the world of museums, of its galleries and of the screens created by certain paintings, that is expressed in the long daydream at the end. Scenes from the movie *Come Live with Me* (1941), the musical images of *Thus Spoke Zarathustra* by Richard Strauss, chiaroscuro scenes by Caravaggio or Georges de La Tour, a man in armor by Carpaccio, a young woman by Giorgione—all are piled together as though in superimposed impressions. This capacity to make faces painted by masters of the past communicate with those of actresses of the present is not solely Cornell's; Henri Gervex had enjoyed representing Cléo de Mérode as *Belle Ferronière*.[19] But in Cornell's case, these associations give to these fugitive visions of movie stars both an unexpected extension and an origin to faces set down a few centuries ago (see figs. 7.05, 1.03). Through this montage, the actress is transformed into a fifteenth-century androgynous-looking character, and even as an artist doing a self-portrait, "she slipped herself without difficulty into the role of painter . . . the hunter of images."[20] But this kind of associative process, as soon as it promotes communication between looks coming from different sources and different stages, comes into contradiction with the reserve earlier expressed by Breton in "Surrealism and Painting": "I have stalked furiously through the slippery-floored halls of museums: and I am not the only one. In spite of a few marvelous glances thrown in my direction by women looking exactly like those of today, I have never been taken in for a moment by the purportedly unknown which those subterranean, immovable walls had to offer me. I have abandoned some adorable supplicants without compunction. There were too many theatre stages available on which I did not have the heart to act."[21]

Ephemera

For his part, Cornell was ready to play on these various stages—movie houses as well as museums, or even the street—as he shows in his journal when he relates, under the seal of innocence and beauty, the follow-up to a dream in 1944—the arrival of a young girl, barely eight years old, traveling by herself on a bus and holding a book (*Little Women*) under her arm. The artist describes in detail her dark hair and her almost imperceptible expression of sadness.[22] All these encounters, these faces, formed a mental gallery joining together a multitude of relics methodically collected, piously filed away in folders or exhibited like treasures in precious boxes. Thus, the "Romantic Museum" conceived by Cornell in December 1946 takes on the values of a manifesto. Alexandre Iolas, the director of the Hugo Gallery in Manhattan, had offered him the use of the smaller of the two rooms of his gallery. Cornell, re-baptizing the gallery by the name "Romantic Museum" and thereby inaugurating his own museum with a show called *Romantic Museum: Portraits of Women: Constructions and Arrangements*, had intended to celebrate the women who occupied the highest place in his personal pantheon: divas (Giuditta Pasta, Conchita Supervia), ballerinas (Marie Taglioni, Fanny Cerrito), actresses (Eleonora Duse, Greta Garbo, Lauren Bacall) to whom was added a fictional character, the young Berenice. We only have a very imprecise idea of what that show was like. In it Cornell had installed flowers and cages from which birdsong flowed. In the four-page brochure accompanying the show, one can read—following the sections on "The Crystal Cage," the "Penny Arcade Portrait of Lauren Bacall" and the "Portrait of Ondine"—this announcement:

METAPHYSICS OF EPHEMERA
The unknown past and present
Fugitive impression[s]
Faces seen once—Faces seen in the crowd
Tabloid Portraits

The Pathetic of the Ordinary
Young girl[s] with braids—New York City
Summer 1946[23]

A man in New York in the year 1946 decided to become the curator of minute objects, of faces seen once, of faces seen in a crowd, of fugitive impressions, of smiles of women, likewise inaccessible. In his own way, he was interested in expressions that were both immemorial and instantaneous. The "young girls with braids" who held his attention, as part of "the pathetic of the ordinary," were in fact the cousins of other nymphs, pursued by other inventors of atlases who were stalking other manifestations of the sentimental. The term *ephemera* deserves some attention. It is in contrast to the terms *mirabilia, naturalia,* or even *memorabilia* (which, however, appear in the brochure *Romantic Museum*), thus indicating the wide field covered by these arrangements and constructions—the transitory and fugitive nature of certain women, after original sin, modern-day courtesans that the painter of modern life would try to represent. But perhaps more than Baudelaire, Gérard de Nerval was the poet Cornell venerated and to whom we should turn for consideration here. In *Aurelia,* the narrator experiences enormous inner torments, believing he has committed a sin and having lost through his conduct the love of the woman now buried, searches in vain for her tomb and remembers that he had kept its precise location in a chest that used to belong to her, a sort of relic case in which, along with her last letter, were piously placed: "a rose picked in the gardens of Schoubrah, a strip of cloth brought back from Egypt, laurel leaves picked in the Beirut river, two little golden crystals from the mosaics of Hagia Sophia, a bead from a rosary, and I know not what else? . . . finally the paper given to me the day the grave was dug, so that I could find her again."[24]

Finally, we might even regard the word *ephemera* itself as a direct reference to a famous letter, a *bagatelle* addressed by Benjamin Franklin to one of his French admirers, a talented harpsichordist, Anne Louise Brillon de Jouy, which ends with the following statement: "To me, after all my eager pursuits, no solid pleasures now remain, but the reflection of a long life spent in meaning well, the sensible conversation of a few good lady ephemerae, and now and then a kind smile, and a tune from the ever amiable Brillante."[25] In this letter, often designated under the title *The Story of Ephemera,* Franklin was describing a day in the summer of 1778 spent in the company of the lady musician at the Moulin-Joly near Passy, where after observing an infinite number of cadavers of small flies called "ephemeras," which live and die in one day, he imagines and writes down the conversations of these creatures discussing the progress of nations or of universal destruction without being concerned with the briefness of their life. It would not have been very difficult to get hold of this letter, which can be found in anthologies of American literature.[26] Undoubtedly Cornell, after reading it, would have understood the elegiac meaning of the address to these "good Ladies" and of collecting all possible traces of ephemera: flies, smiles, musical chords.

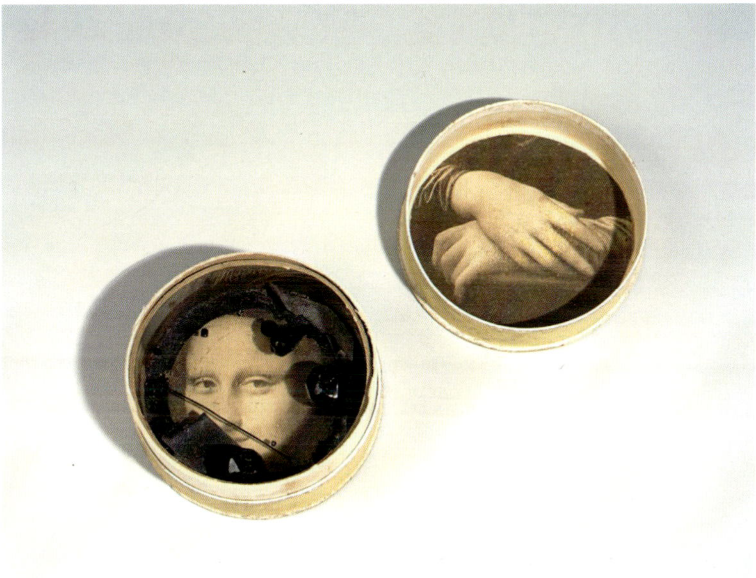

2.07 Joseph Cornell, *Untitled* (*Mona Lisa*), c. 1942, box construction, diam. 3 × h. 1 3/8 in., The Robert and Marguerite Hoffman Collection

Ephemera could mean a great number of forms and substances: a smile, a gesture like the ones of Hollywood stars or of the *Mona Lisa* (fig. 2.07), or else the most minuscule residues of time, represented by relics from brooms, or watchmakers or chimneysweeps ("Watchmaker's Sweepings," "Chimney Sweepers Relics"), the motions of a juggler ("Juggling Act")—these being phrases on a box entitled *Museum* (c. 1944–48, The Menil Collection, Houston) that holds in its bottles all sorts of minuscule traces, revealed by the titles of the containers or by the little pieces of paper that are housed in them. "Mouse Material" is the title of one of these twenty little bottles—but also of a box in the artist's garage workshop—designating the dust balls found under beds or in corners, alluding to Duchamp or Marx. Travelers' suitcases, pharmacies—the museum can finally take the shape of an archive, as in files growing ever larger, such as the one Cornell created beginning in 1944, when he started working in a garden center (*GC 44*, that is, Garden Center 44), collecting works of art, postcards, quotations, descriptions of movie scenes, reproductions of leaves and flowers, illustrations coming from tales in children's books, all having to do with a garden center. At the time of Cornell's death in 1972, no fewer than 162 files were found in the Utopia Parkway house, mainly in the garage that he used as a workshop.

Just as in his boxes, Joseph Cornell's *Wunderkammer* could be found in this accumulation of pictures and texts organized in the most complex way in that garage. The labels on the boxes and files reveal an idea for the project that was buried in them, which went far beyond the infinite wealth of Manhattan to draw near associations created by André Malraux in his books *Metaphysics of Ephemera*, *Museum without Walls*, and finally *Center of a Labyrinth*.

Notes

Research for this study would not have been possible without a grant from the Terra Foundation, thanks to which I was able to work at the Center for Advanced Study in Visual Arts (CASVA) and at the Joseph Cornell Study Center, the Smithsonian Institution in Washington, D.C., in April and July 2013. My thanks go to Elizabeth Glassman, as well as to Matthew Affron, Corinne Bayle, Charlotte Eyerman, Uriko Jackall, Camille Lévêque-Claudet, Anne Théry, Léna Widerkehr (S.R.).

1 As cited in Caws 1993, 95.

2 See the essay by Lynda Hartigan in this volume.

3 As cited in Caws 1993, 96.

4 This is according to the sense that Patricia Faiguières gives to this term in *Les Chambres des merveilles* (Paris: Bayard, 2003), 16.

5 Claude Lévi-Strauss, "The Art of the Northwest Coast at the American Museum of Natural History" (1943), quoted in "Enigma of a Mask," in Claude Lévi-Strauss, *The Way of the Masks*, trans. Sylvia Modelski (Seattle: University of Washington Press, 1982), 3.

6 Ibid.

7 Claude Lévi-Strauss, "New York in 1941," in Claude Lévi-Strauss, *The View from Afar*, trans. Joachim Neugroschel and Phoebe Hoss (New York: Basic Books, 1985), 265.

8 Ibid., 262. See Jeffrey Mehlman, *Emigré New York: French Intellectuals in Wartime Manhattan, 1940–1944* (Baltimore, Johns Hopkins University Press, 2000).

9 P. T. Barnum, quoted in Andrea Stulman Dennette, *Weird and Wonderful: The Dime Museum in America* (New York: New York University Press, 1997), 27.

10 See Dennette, *Weird and Wonderful*, particularly 44–56.

11 Howard Hussey writes: "I consider it miraculous that he had the chance to discover what a lantern slide is and what a photograph is, all on his terms, never losing the shock value of that experience when as a child, being taken by his grandmother on excursions and outings to N.Y.C., a favorite haunt, the Eden Musée (c. 1911) became indelibly engraved in memory. Or should he have said photoengraved on his memory?" Howard Hussey, "Collaging the Moment," in New York 1978, 17.

12 Waldman 2002, 25.

13 New York 1936, 155. On the evolution of his work see Dawn Ades, "The Transcendental Surrealism of Joseph Cornell," in New York 1980, reprint 1990, 15–41, 19–20.

14 Joseph Cornell, in *Joseph Cornell: Objects*, exh. cat. (Beverly Hills: Copley Galleries, 1948), cited in Waldman 2002, 28.

15 Solomon 1997, 18.

16 Ibid., 18.

17 Elizabeth Cornell Benton, interview with Lindsay Blair, cited in Blair, *Joseph Cornell's Vision of Spiritual Order* (London: Reaktion, 1998), 109–10.

18 Joseph Cornell, "'Enchanted Wanderer': Excerpt from a Journey Album for Hedy Lamarr," *View*, Series 1, nos. 9–10 (Dec. 1941–Jan. 1942), 3. See also Catrina Neiman and Paul Nathan, eds., *View Parade of the Avant-Garde: An Anthology of View Magazine* (1940–47) (New York: Thunder's Mouth Press, 1991), 24–26.

19 Christian Corvisier, *Cléo de Mérode et la photographie: La première icône moderne* (Paris: Patrimoine, 2007), 58–59.

20 On the subject of these reversals see Tashjian 1992, 41–61, and Dickran Tashjian, *A Boatload of Madmen: Surrealism and the American Avant-Garde, 1920–1950* (New York: Thames and Hudson, 1995), reprint 2001, 235–60; Hauptman 1999, 1–10.

21 André Breton 1945, 351. Breton, "Surrealism and Painting" (1928), in Breton, *Surrealism and Painting*, trans. Simon Watson Taylor (Boston: MFA Publications, 2002 (1978), 3.

22 Caws 1993, 143.

23 *Romantic Museum*, brochure, New York, Hugo Gallery, December 1946. See the reproductions and very enlightening analysis in Hauptman 1999, 11–54.

24 Gérard de Nerval, *Aurelia ou le rêve et la vie*, in Albert Béguin and Jean Richer, eds., *Oeuvres* (Paris: Gallimard, Bibliothèque de la Pléiade, 1966), 1: 357–414, 389–90. Mary Ann Caws and Jodi Hauptman indicate this possible source from Nerval, but without developing their case (Caws 1993, 136; Hauptman 1999, 35–36). Our thanks to Corinne Bayle who pointed out this important passage.

25 Benjamin Franklin, "Letter to Madame B., Passy" (Print shop of B. Franklin, 1778).

26 For example, Brander Matthews, ed., *The Oxford Book of American Essays* (New York: Oxford University Press, 1914), 1–3. The letter can likewise be found in Walter Isaacson, *A Benjamin Franklin Reader* (New York: Simon & Schuster, 2003), 279–80.

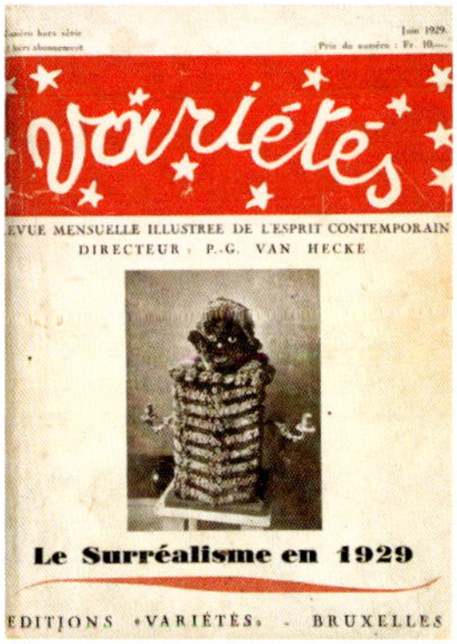

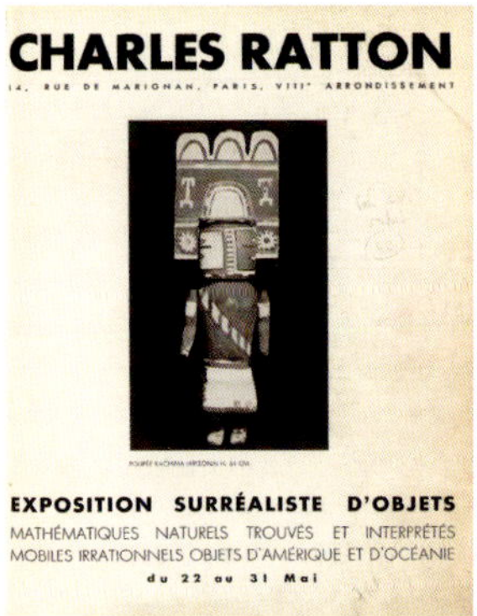

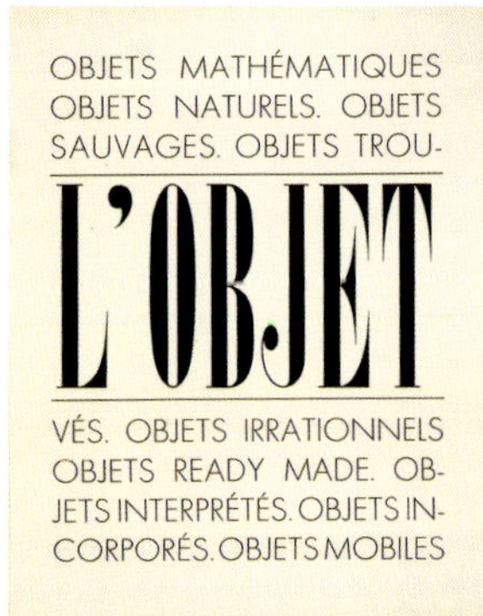

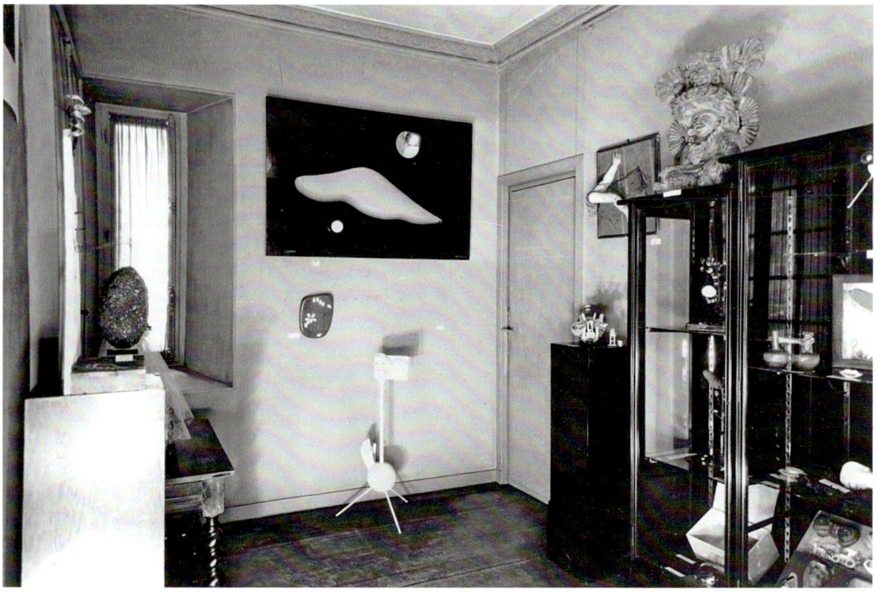

3.01 Cover of "Le surréalisme en 1929," special issue of the Belgian periodical *Variétés* (June 1929) **3.02, 3.03** Announcements for the *Exposition surréaliste d'objects* at the Galerie Charles Ratton, Paris, published in *Cahiers d'art* 11, nos. 1–2 (1936) **3.04** Man Ray, View of the *Exposition surréaliste d'objects*, Galerie Charles Ratton, Paris, May 22–31, 1936, with Man Ray's *L'Orateur* (1935) on the far wall

With Hidden Noise

Emmanuel Guigon

Hourglass:
"The hourglass of a dress falling and of a nude body rising up" (P.E. [Paul Éluard])
"A thread of milk endlessly flowing from a breast of glass" (A.B. [André Breton])

—*Dictionnaire abrégé du surréalisme* (Abridged Dictionary of Surrealism), 1938[1]

Surrealism. Signed by Jacques-André Boiffard, Paul Éluard, and Roger Vitrac, the preface to the first issue of *La Révolution surréaliste* of December 1924 affirms the appropriateness of the Surrealist act to its object: "Since every discovery changes nature, the destination of an object or a phenomenon constitutes a Surrealist fact."[2] Into this programmatic declaration is further inserted the photograph of Man Ray's object, *L'Enigme d'Isidore Ducasse* (The enigma of Isidore Ducasse, 1920). Published two months before by André Breton, the *Manifesto of Surrealism* pays particular attention, as early as its second sentence, to the objects of daily life. "Man, that inveterate dreamer, daily more discontent with his destiny, has trouble assessing the objects he has been led to use, objects that his nonchalance has brought his way, or that he has earned through his own efforts." Surreality, the equivalent of a kind of "absolute reality," might be able to widen our experience of objects, in order to liberate their latent life. Breton also speaks about words whose meaning he has forgotten and of "the *poetic consciousness* of objects" that he could "acquire only after a spiritual contact with them repeated a thousand times over."[3] In 1929, "Objects that upset" is the first of the twelve definitions of Surrealism on the announcement flyer for a special issue of the Belgian magazine *Variétés* (fig. 3.01). The *Dictionnaire abrégé du surréalisme* of 1938, composed of quotations collected by André Breton and Paul Éluard, reproduces no less than about forty objects and defines Surrealism as "old pewter tableware before the invention of the fork."[4] The apparent care they took in popularizing their material can barely hide the irrational and confusing intentions of the work. Surrealism, the highest form of subjectivity, quickly came to grips with the object. And out of that object, it made another object, perpetual and ever changing.

The Surrealist object would not have happened without the shocks produced by a certain number of artistic inventions that would have a definitive influence on the way to future Surrealists envisaged creation. In the eyes of André Breton, what distinguishes these inventions is the audacity with which artists disregard traditional representation in favor of a "revolution in appearances." In 1918, the article that Breton devotes to Guillaume Apollinaire sanctions the introduction onto the scene of problematical ideas. He quotes a long passage from a short story of 1917 by Paul Morand, "Clarisse ou l'amitié" (Clarisse). Clarisse collects objects, all kinds of objects, from the rarest to nails and doorknobs: "Small, unimaginable, ageless objects, never even dreamed of: the museum of a wild child, curiosities from insane asylums, the collection of some consul made anemic by the tropics." She keeps around her a thousand objects to use in ways not ordinarily intended for them, books that open into boxes, pen-holders that are telescopes, chairs that become tables, tables that transform themselves into screens. Breton likes these false objects that are masked or disguised—"this latent mockery of the false object"—that surround Paul Morand's beautiful and mysterious heroine.[5] They remind him of the "idiotic paintings" of Rimbaud's *Une saison en enfer* (A Season in Hell).[6] Clarisse for him is the image of the modern woman with incongruous and unexplainable tastes. In his *Introduction au discours sur le peu de réalité* (Introduction to the discourse on the paucity of reality), whose publication precedes that of the *Manifesto of Surrealism* by a few months, André Breton for the first time proposes to make and circulate oneiric objects, without any use or aesthetic value, such as a rather curious book whose back was formed by a wooden gnome with a white beard, cut in the Assyrian style, that comes all the way down to his feet. He hastened to acquire it and regretted not finding it upon awakening. Breton adds: "It would be relatively easy to reconstruct. I'd like to put a few such objects into circulation; their fate seems to me eminently problematic and disturbing."[7] In "Crisis of the Object," written in 1936 on the occasion of the *Exposition surréaliste d'objets* (Surrealist exhibition of objects) at the Charles Ratton gallery in Paris (figs. 3.02–.04), Breton comments on the effect of this undertaking as follows: "I certainly hoped that the multiplication of such objects would entail the depreciation of objects of often dubiously accepted *usefulness* which clutter up the so-called real world; such a depreciation seemed to me a prerequisite for the unleashing of the *powers of invention* which, within the limits of our present understanding of the dream process, must surely be vitalized by contact with dream-engendered objects representing pure desire in concrete form. But the aim I was pursuing went far beyond the mere creation of such objects; it entailed nothing less than the objectification of the very act of dreaming, its transformation into reality." Breton continues that, more generally, it is the "reconciliation of two

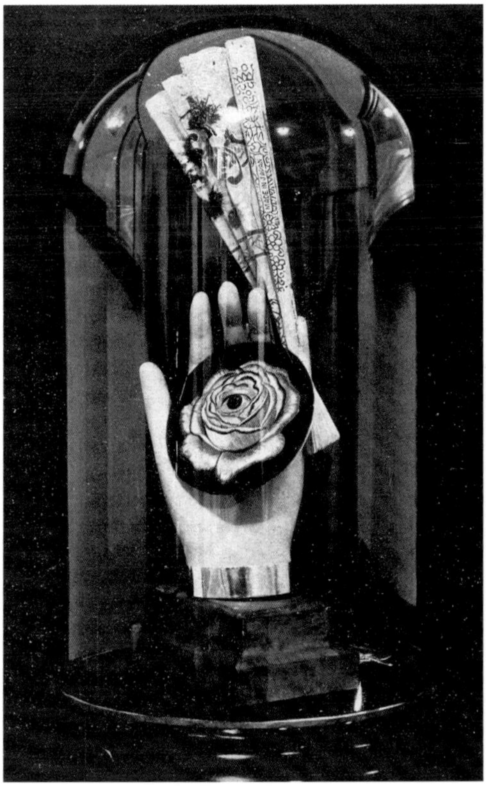

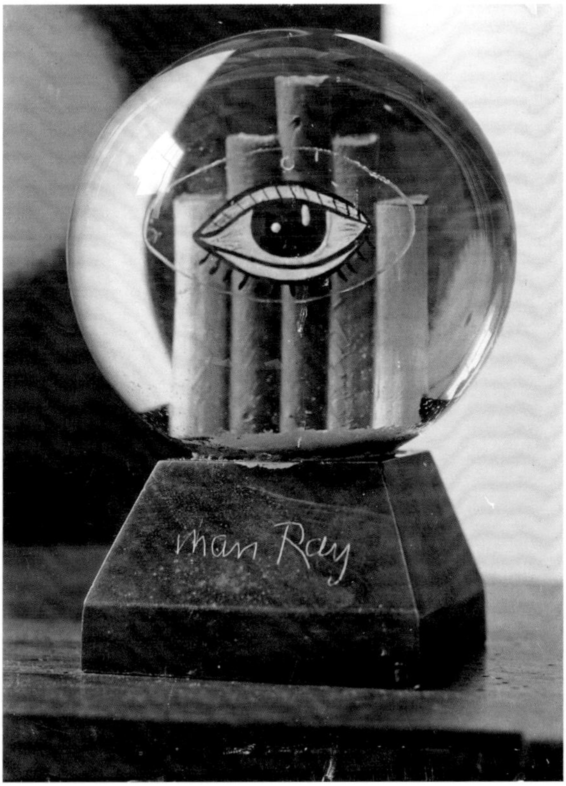

3.05 Joseph Cornell, *Untitled* (*Glass Bell*), c. 1932, as published in *Minotaure* 3, no. 10 (Winter 1937) **3.06** Man Ray, *Snowball*, c. 1935, positive scan from a negative, 4 1/2 × 3 3/8 in., Centre Pompidou, Musée National d'Art Moderne/Centre de création industrielle, Paris

different images" which allows poets, artists, scientists, to "transcend the generally limiting factor of the object's manifest existence" whose "conventional value then becomes entirely subordinate, in the eye of the observer, to its dramatic value, leading him to see it more in terms of its picturesque aspect and its evocative power." There exists in fact no object of human activity that cannot be recycled, whether it be mutilated by time, found on the street or in an attic, or by the edge of a body of water. "Every piece of flotsam and jetsam within our grasp should be considered a precipitate of our desire," adds Breton—as fine a definition of the Surrealist object as we can have.[8]

The appeal he made in 1924 did not, however, result in any concrete response. We could of course pick out this announcement in *La Révolution surréaliste* of December 1, 1926: "Coming soon: EXHIBIT OF SURREALIST OBJECTS. Keep the catalogue which, starting now, will formally define the Surrealist object and will reproduce the types of objects exhibited." But there was no reply to the announcement, no doubt because sufficient material was lacking. In October 1930, the Surrealist group was again interested in the problem of the object and of the need for an exhibit, but still in an unclear manner. It was only in the spring of 1931, with the creation of "Surrealist objects functioning symbolically," that the great wave of Surrealist objects appears.

Working in Flushing, Queens, in the 1930s, in self-imposed isolation, Joseph Cornell would also develop the foundations for his art of the object. In January 1932, he participated in the legendary first Surrealist exhibit, organized in New York by Julien Levy, and designed the cover for the catalogue. Here can be seen a young boy blowing into a pastry bag with the letters of the word *Surrealism* undulating upward, as though playing in the wind. To go up, to rise toward the sky, always means to become light, to free oneself from weight and gain a new status by reaching a new space. Here we already have a "soap bubble machine," where the bubbles are letters. One might also think of the first definition of reality in the *Dictionnaire abrégé du surréalisme*, given by André Breton: "Reality is at the fingers of that woman blowing on the first page of dictionaries."[9] That woman is the one we see blowing the famous dandelion flower printed on the cover of the *Petit Larousse Illustré*. It is perhaps our fragile world blowing away. For this first exhibit, Cornell presents a glass bell under which a model's hand is holding up an open fan covered with roses, and which is entitled very simply *Glass Bell* (c. 1932). It would be reproduced later in *Minotaure*, issue no. 10 (fig. 3.05). The object is mentioned in the catalogue under the category "Pot-pourri" along with Man Ray's sensational *Snowball*, with an enlargement inside of an eye by Lee Miller (fig. 3.06). *Pot-pourri*: a mixture of spices, plants, and dried flowers chosen for their perfumes and aromas;

by extension, a more or less well-matched assemblage, collage. This might be one of the possible readings: patchwork, bric-a-brac, kaleidoscope, thrown together pell-mell; disturbances introduced by great thrusts of the knife into reality; seeds of narratives or little ambiguous myths are forged, where ridiculous materials are conjoined, something akin to a childhood emotion felt, for example, upon looking at the pictures in a dictionary, on a world globe, or in illustrated books.

Joseph Cornell occupies a particular status relative to Surrealism. He was certainly not a "militant"; he always proclaimed his independence, but he was inspired by it from his earliest work on. Shortly after discovering Max Ernst's novel-collage, *La Femme 100 têtes* (Hundred headless woman) (1929) in November 1931, Cornell showed Julien Levy his first attempts at collage. From collages he moved on very quickly to his singular collections: to "pots-pourris," flasks, and pots of all sorts, filled with powders and various substances, then to the constructions under glass and inside boxes that constitute the main part of his work. He made a great many, of which many are not dated, just as he completed numerous versions of the same box and numerous boxes on the same theme. In the fall of 1932 Julien Levy organized his first personal exhibit: *Objects by Joseph Cornell: Minutiae, Glass Bells, Shadow Boxes, Coups d'Oeil, Jouets Surréalistes.*

A discreet man, indifferent to fashion, having no concern for fame, Joseph Cornell lived in his modest frame house on Utopia Parkway from 1929 to his death in 1972. He was a sedentary sort. And yet, throughout his work, he never ceased recounting the Thousand-and-One-Night hotels of Europe (*Grand Hôtel de la Boule d'Or*, early 1950s, Dallas Museum of Art). At Ostende the Grand Hôtel Fontaine has a hydraulic elevator. Two twin kings are staying at the *Hôtel de l'Étoile* (1950, private collection). At the Hôtel du Cygne, "a house with an old reputation," a chariot-driver is spending the night. Parrots and cockatoos live alternately at the Hôtel Beau-Sejour, at the Grand Hôtel Semiramis, at the Hôtel Voyageurs, at the Grand Hôtel de la Pomme d'Or, at the Hôtel Neptune. They are Cornell's collaborators. The Grand Hôtel Bon Port shelters the reproduction of the *Antea* or *Portrait of a Young Woman* by Parmigianino and at the Hôtel du Nord one can glimpse an engraving of Sagittarius (*Untitled* [*Hôtel du Nord*], c. 1954, private collection). The Hôtel de la Mer is also called Hôtel des Trois Rois or Hotel Blue Star; it houses "Apollinaris." This constant dual referencing to travels and to art history and literature is one of the touchstones of his art. Cornell is always enthusiastic about grand voyages in time and space.

In 1936, Cornell participated in an important exhibit, *Fantastic Art, Dada, Surrealism*, organized by the Museum of Modern Art. Here he presented his first box under the title *Untitled* (*Soap Bubble Set*) (1936, The Wadsworth Atheneum

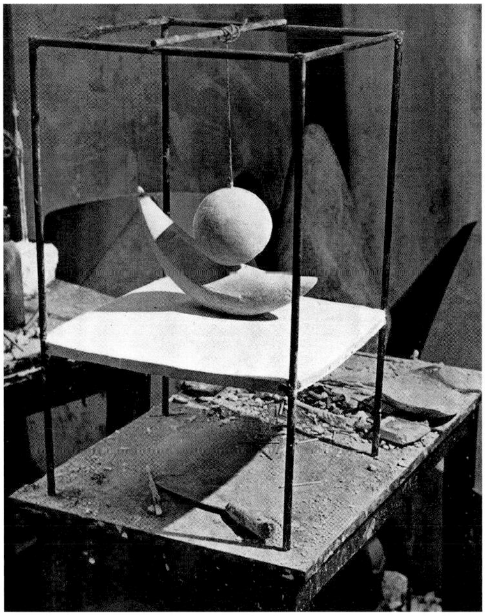

3.07 Brassaï, *Suspended Ball* (1930–31) in Alberto Giacometti's studio, 1947, gelatin silver print, 11 3/8 × 8 5/8 in., Collection Fondation Giacometti, Paris

Museum of Art, Hartford, Connecticut) described in the catalogue as a "composition of objects 38.8 × 35.3 photographed with additional effects by George Platt Lynes." Here for the first time appear earthen pipes, glasses, engravings, maps ("geographical map of the moon"), and mirrors, which would become his main elements of reference. From this point on, all his work would present itself almost exclusively in the form of boxes, generally with glass, divided into sections and drawers that are empty or filled with tiny knickknacks that notably play up our mania for classification and enumeration. Like the Surrealists, Cornell is an archivist. He haunted flea markets. He accumulated document "files," which he used as the material for the creation of his boxes. He liked this way of isolating and enlarging the details of the world. Using the least prestigious materials, Cornell manages to create a striking impression of melancholy, like Paul Morand in *Clarisse*, at times evoking legendary treasures hidden in some land or other of our childhood, at other times mysterious medicines shelved in little jars like those of apothecaries. Objects for him are just so many "pieces of booty," which become the scene of actions, the accuracy of which is beyond any verification. We find ourselves, in the best of cases, like puzzled spectators looking at a setting that offers partial objects and terse information. "Shadow boxes become poetic theaters or settings wherein are metamorphosed the elements of a childhood pastime. The fragile, shimmering globules become the shimmering but more enduring planets," he wrote in 1948 in a catalogue published on the occasion of an exhibit that took place in California, "a connotation of moon and tides . . . the association of water less subtle, as when driftwood pieces make up a proscenium to set off the dazzling white of sea foam and billowy cloud crystallized in a pipe of fancy."[10] An unending chain of visual associations sets off the successive identification of a ball of cork hanging on an upper beam with a soap bubble, then with a curtain ring and with the circumference of the moon. The circles here that circumscribe so many orbits keep growing larger; a tennis ball slides over two metal rails before bouncing onto a girl's bracelet and conjures up the movements of the cosmos. To these spherical and light forms are sometimes added characters as diverse as a Medici princess, a Harlequin, ballerinas, and navigators, or a blue swan. Theater, operetta, and ballet make him dream. Cornell always looks at the world through his soap bubbles.

The movements are not always just imaginary. Certain elements are mobile or already in motion, like the first Surrealist objects functioning symbolically (fig. 3.07). They can be moved about freely, as in Giacometti's game boards—which he admired. Like him, he addresses himself to the spectator. They are, for example, objects to be manipulated such as the white wooden cubes of *Multiple Cubes* (1947) that move about in their boxes at the slightest tilting of the box. Little wooden balls roll on parallel metal wires, along which hanging rings can also slide (*Untitled* [*Soap Bubble Set, Latitude and Longitude Box*], c. 1960 and *Untitled* [*Juan Gris Series, Black Cockatoo Silhouette*], c. 1954–65, The Fralin Museum of Art at the University of Virginia, Charlottesville, see pages 16, 17). Likewise, his "Sand boxes" are composed of several layers of sand of different colors, separated by sheets of glass, in which bits of broken glass, ball-bearing balls and other tiny items move about and mix together, coming and going according to the movements applied to the box (*Untitled* [*Blue Sand Tray*], c. 1954, The Fralin Museum of Art at the University of Virginia, Charlottesville, see page 15). Collages of words and poetic verse are often set randomly on these objects, producing effects that are comparable to those of the poem-objects of Breton (who during his exile years in America wrote the only essay devoted to these and completed his best-known poem-objects during that time). In the *Mémoires inédits de Madame la Comtesse de G.*[*enlis*] (c. 1939, private collection), Cornell enclosed into a little round box a series of verses cut out from French poetry, which he slipped into stiff plastic holders in such a way as to allow one to remove and assemble them into a practically unlimited series

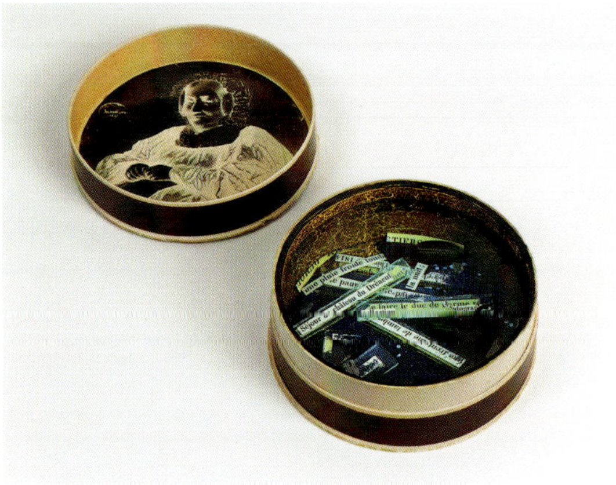

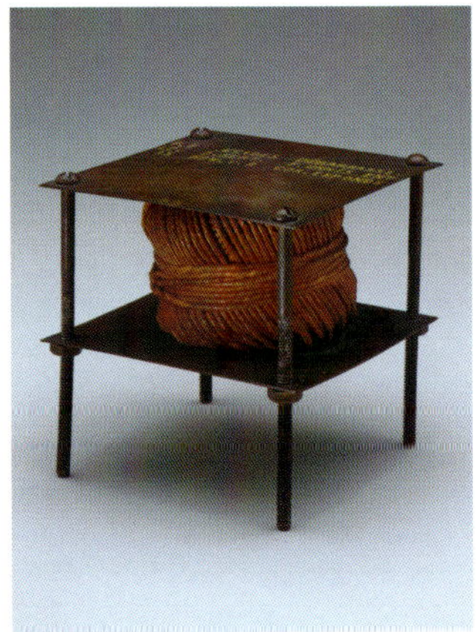

3.08 Joseph Cornell, *Mémoires inédites de Madame la Marquise de la Rochejaquelein*, 1943, box construction, diam. 4 1/4 × h. 1 15/16 in., San Francisco Museum of Modern Art. Gift of Leo Castelli, Richard Feigen, and James Corcoran **3.09** Marcel Duchamp, *With Hidden Noise*, 1916, assisted readymade, 5 × 5 × 5 1/8 in., Philadelphia Museum of Art, the Louise and Walter Arensberg Collection

of accidental poems—a principle that he carried over a few years later to another box dedicated to a woman of letters of the *ancien régime*, Madame la Marquise de la Rochejaquelein, 1943 (fig. 3.08). Another box, *Taglioni's Jewel Casket* (see fig. 10.06), 1940, conserved at the Museum of Modern Art in New York, presents, behind a necklace of paste jewelry and embedded in the brown velvet that lines the cover, this inscription by Cornell: "On a moonlight night in the winter of 1835, the carriage of Marie TAGLIONI was halted by a Russian highwayman, and that enchanting creature commanded to dance for this audience of one upon a panther's skin spread over the snow beneath the stars. From this actuality arose the legend that, to keep alive the memory of this adventure so precious to her, TAGLIONI formed the habit of placing a piece of artificial ice in her jewel casket or dressing table where, melting among the sparkling stones, there was evoked a hint of the atmosphere of the starlit heavens over the ice-covered landscape."[11]

"His work makes you use the word 'beautiful.' What more do you want?" wrote Robert Motherwell, who saw him often.[12] Cornell is one of the most original and most important artists whose work is devoted entirely to the object. It is an extremely mysterious work and absolutely without comparison in its very simplicity, forcing itself to use so few elements, and where nothing appears gratuitous—it is the "gathering of a dream," as Mallarmé wrote.[13] Truth to tell, these boxes do not look like anything—anything, at least, to which one could give an exact name. They are objects *with a hidden noise*, in which the hidden part is also a part preserved from changes in time (fig. 3.09). Stopping time neutralizes time. We can understand how Breton was particularly sensitive to this message, which he was one of the first to salute in the following terms, in "Genesis and Perspective of Surrealism" in 1941: "at the extreme limits of a point of view which may be characterized as stereotypical and anaglyphic, or of the stereotyped vision of things, Cornell has devised an experiment which completely overturns the conventional use of the object."[14]

Notes

1 "Sablier," in *Dictionnaire abrégé du surréalisme* (Paris: Galerie des Beaux-Arts, 1938), 24.

2 Jacques-André Boiffard, Paul Éluard, and Roger Vitrac, "Introduction to *La Révolution surréaliste*" (Dec. 1924), in *Surrealism against the Current*, ed. and trans. Michael Richardson and Krzysztof Fualkowski (London: Pluto Press, 2001), 23.

3 André Breton, "Manifesto of Surrealism" (1924), in *Manifestoes of Surrealism*, trans. Richard Seaver and Helen R. Lane (Ann Arbor: University of Michigan Press, 1972), 3, 14, 34.

4 *Dictionnaire abrégé du surréalisme* (supplément), 76.

5 André Breton, "Guillaume Apollinaire" (1918), in *The Lost Steps*, trans. Mark Polizzotti (Lincoln: University of Nebraska Press, 1996), 17.

6 Arthur Rimbaud, "Delerium III: Alchemy of the Verb," in *A Season in Hell and Illuminations*, trans. Bertrand Mathieu (Brockport, NY: BOA Editions, 1991), 33.

7 André Breton, "Introduction to the Discourse on the Paucity of Reality" (1925), in *Break of Day*, trans. Mark Polizzotti and Mary Ann Caws (Lincoln: University of Nebraska Press, 1999), 16.

8 André Breton, "Crisis of the Object" (1936), in *Surrealism and Painting*, trans. Simon Watson Taylor (New York: Icon Editions, 1972), 277, 279, 283.

9 André Breton, "Réalité," in *Dictionnaire abrégé du surréalisme*, 23.

10 Cornell, in *Objects by Joseph Cornell*, exhibition announcement (Beverly Hills, California: Copley Galleries, 1948), n.p.; quoted in Dore Ashton, *A Joseph Cornell Album* (New York: Viking, 1974), 64–65.

11 Ibid., 26.

12 Robert Motherwell, "Preface to a Joseph Cornell Exhibition" (1953), in New York 1976, n.p.

13 Stéphane Mallarmé, "Apparition," in *Poems*, trans. Roger Fry (New York: Oxford University Press, 1937), 39.

14 Breton 1941, 26. See essay by Matthew Affron, "Joseph Cornell's Optical Toys," in this volume.

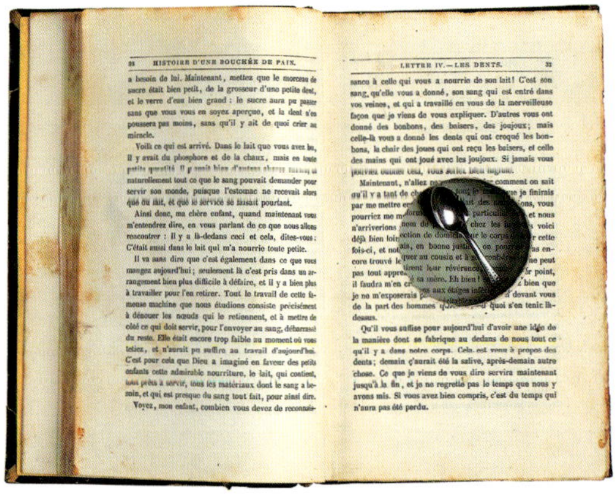

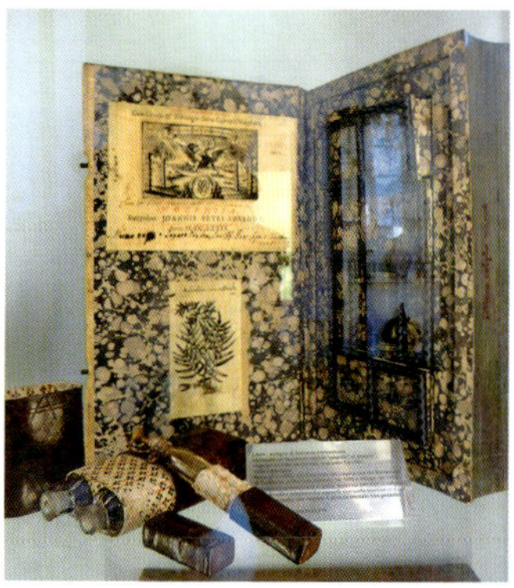

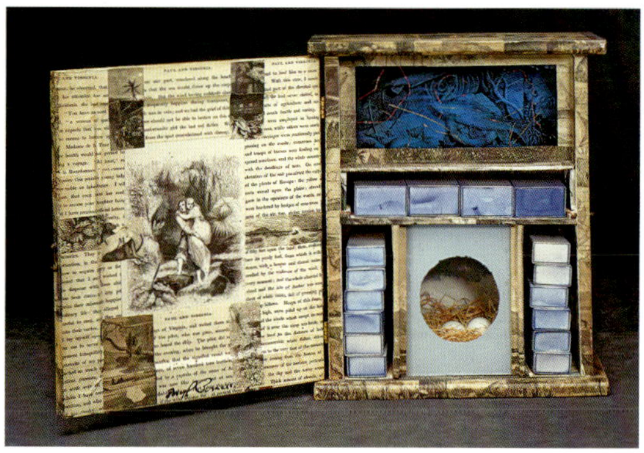

Left to right, top to bottom: **4.01** Joseph Cornell, *Untitled* (*Paul and Virginia*), c. 1946–48, box construction, $12\frac{1}{2} \times 9\frac{15}{16} \times 4\frac{3}{8}$ in., The Robert Lehrman Art Trust, courtesy of Aimee and Robert Lehrman **4.02** Joseph Cornell, *Object* (*Histoire d'une bouchée de pain*), c. 1939, book object, 7 × 4 × 11 in., Allan Stone Gallery, New York **4.03** Apothecary book object with secrets of botanical pharmacopoeia, 16th-century binding, marbled paper, in-quarto, from the library of the Capucin convent of Türkheim, Bavaria, Aboca Museum, Sansepolcro **4.04** Joseph Cornell, *Untitled* (*Paul and Virginia*), c. 1946–48 (compare fig. 4.01): box open

The Box-Books of Joseph Cornell

A Romantic Art?

Ségolène Le Men

"But whoever the author, I adored the works in the Hetzel collection, little theaters with gold-tasseled red covers for curtains: the powdery gilding on their edges was the footlights. I owe my first experiences of beauty to these magic boxes."

—Jean-Paul Sartre, *Words,* 1964.[1]

The constructions that Joseph Cornell devoted to books and reading turn the metaphor of the book box around, the metaphor itself announcing others, like that of the theater depicted at the beginning of Sartre's sentence evoking the red and gold binding covers of his childhood books. He made them in his home on Utopia Parkway in New York around 1946–48 and covered these constructions with cutouts of pictures and pages from nineteenth-century publications. This aspect of Cornell's work encompasses cultural practices, the aesthetic, and types of illustrated edition that had been disseminated on either side of the Atlantic since the time of the Romantics, to the point of becoming a kind of standard art of nostalgia. Yet even as he appropriates these familiar practices, Cornell adapts them in his own manner.

An Art of Revival

With these book boxes, Cornell places himself in a tradition of private books that lasted as an amateur art form into the twentieth century.

Various forms of private book-like creations were widespread in the social circles of the Romantic age. Albums, scrapbooks, and keepsakes, associated with the culture of children and young people, used the codex format of the book and transformed it by applying to all sorts of practices of collage, cutout, and montage into a "magic box." It was from these experiments that a new form of book was invented—the illustrated Romantic book—that used the techniques of illustrated publishing that were available within the context of the Franco-British publishing world and were very quickly adopted throughout Europe and the United States. In a counterpoint of text and image, vignettes engraved on wood or steel could attract the eye of the reader who became the viewer of an "armchair spectacle," according to

Alfred de Musset's formula, and stimulate the imagination using familiar materials. Lithographs decorate albums; steel engravings are brought together in keepsakes;[2] given as gifts; embellished by literary pages, poems, or souvenirs of travel and feminine beauties—for example, *Le Livre de Beauté* in 1834 and *Les Beautés de l'Opéra* in 1845.[3] Cornell echoes the idea of keepsake with titles such as *Untitled (A Keepsake for John Donne)*, around 1935–39, *Untitled (Sylphide Souvenir Case)*, around 1940–42, and *Perles de l'Opéra*, around 1948.[4] Further, he introduces steel engravings from the *Beautés de l'Opéra* into certain of his collages such as *The Uncertainty Principle*, 1966,[5] and constructions such as *A Swan Lake for Tamara Toumanova*, 1946.[6] Finally, when in 1940 Cornell began his first file inspired by Romantic ballerinas, *Portrait of Ondine*[7] (1940, Smithsonian American Art Museum, Washington, DC), which he continued working on in the 1950s, he transposed Marcel Duchamp's *Box in a Valise* (1936–41) in his own manner by making reference to the universe of these engravings as well as to the ways of composing these illustrated anthologized collections. For example, he slips in a Romantic brochure entitled *Pâquerette* and a few keepsake engravings alongside the reproduction of a painting by de Chirico.

The notion of album[8] brings to mind a white background for writing purposes, as the Latin etymology for this substantivized adjective reminds us. One interpersonal form was the *album amicorum* that gained currency in the eighteenth century before being adopted during the Romantic era when the "craze for albums"[9] became widespread; Henry Monnier evoked this vogue and traced its Germanic origins. This "book from the heart" enjoyed wide success among sophisticated ladies and romantic girls. In 1859 the Danish storyteller Hans Christian Andersen, whose work had an impact on Cornell's childhood, composed *Christine's Picture Book*, along with a friend, for the third birthday celebration of that friend's granddaughter, using color illustrations cut out from magazines or Épinal pictures captioned in French. He also fashioned numerous cutouts and long strings of silhouettes in which the motifs, relating to the universe of his tales, were clowns, swans, and ballerinas.[10] Picture albums would come to have a widespread vogue in Victorian England, which made scrapbooks popular. These homemade collections of cutouts were found across Europe and the United States; they were often done using vignettes made for cutting out, following the French tradition of *macédoines* (hodgepodges) of traditional popular imagery, which was carried over to the lithography in the Romantic period. Color prints with various subjects were sold in sheets to be cut out, or else offered as advertising images, the main providers being Liebig and the Menier chocolate company.[11] Scrapbooks also included friends' autographs, short texts, watercolors, and dried flowers. Use of photography during the Victorian period allowed for photocollages,[12] while the album also offered its pages to collections of family photographs and, around 1900, to postcards.

Max Ernst's collages, like those of Jacques Prévert, appear to turn away from but also to extend this bourgeois family culture issuing from Romanticism and linked to childhood, with its startling Surrealist effects. Postcards of the *belle époque*, with their sentimental photomontages, represent another incarnation. Walter Benjamin identified the nostalgic implications of these elementary and familiar forms of collectorship. While clearing out his library he found "two albums with stick-in pictures which my mother pasted in as a child and which I inherited."[13] Regarding these albums of *Oblaten* ("stick-in pictures"), he states that "There is no living library that does not harbor a number of booklike creations from fringe areas," and pursues his search among the books spread out about him, evocative of his travels, bearers of traces of the moment of their acquisition. This nostalgic pleasure, with its Romantic tone of the intimate, bourgeois, Biedermeier style, is based on the association between the object-souvenir and the evocation of the person who put together the album of these holy objects or of the place where the books were bought and, finally, of the boyhood room: "O bliss of the collector, bliss of the man of leisure. Of no one has less been expected, and no one has had a greater sense of well-being than the man who has been able to carry on his disreputable existence in the mask of Spitzweg's 'Bookworm.'" And the article concludes with an analogy between books and the stones of a palace of reminiscences: "So I have erected one of his dwellings, with books as the building stones."[14]

Cornell's vignette boxes are related to Walter Benjamin's "book-like creatures" that go back to the sentimental tradition of the amateur arts, as well as to the memories of childhood or adolescent books and to the nostalgia for a return to the past, as his biography indicates, and as witnessed by certain elements of his archives. Cornell was born in 1903, on December 24, a Christmas Eve when presents and books with pictures are distributed to the children. His father, a fabric designer, and his mother, a housewife, both cultivated amateur arts. A taste for books and pictures is associated with his childhood, as well as with the early education from his mother that had exposed him to the tales of Grimm and Andersen. Even beyond that, he had gorged himself on illustrated encyclopedias and children's magazines that offered manual activities and paper games.[15] In 1931 he gave Julien Levy, who was to become his art dealer, some cardboard collages done with steel engravings taken from keepsakes (*Untitled*, 1930s, The Museum of Modern Art, New York), which Levy immediately compared to those by Max Ernst.[16] In the 1930s he made numerous collages taken from cutout illustrations. Some resemble those of the amusing physics experiments of Tom Tit,[17] already Surrealist before their time, reproduced in *View* in April 1942, a series expressly paid homage to Max Ernst, the creator of *La Femme 100 têtes* (The hundred headless woman) (1929).[18] Many of them recalled the fantasy world of natural elements in the novels of Jules Verne, published by Hetzel with illustrations by Riou and Neuville, from the aerial flights of *Five Weeks in a Balloon* to the deep-sea world of *Twenty Thousand Leagues under the Sea*.

The Joseph Cornell Study Center Collection, conserved at the Smithsonian Institution, Washington, DC, allows a glimpse into the originating elements for his boxes. The Joseph Cornell papers at the Archives of American Art permit us to approach his practice as a diarist and letter writer, two activities that developed, beginning in the Romantic period, with the association of text and image. Cornell exchanged postcards with his friends, carefully choosing the stamps, those Readymades that were fully in circulation, betraying their common passion for pictures and vignettes. The postage stamp, a minuscule rectangular vignette whose invention in Britain goes back to 1840, is one of the symbols of this passion. His correspondence with Dorothea Tanning is particularly revelatory of this shared game that many artists and writers of the period indulged in, from Salvador Dalí to Paul Éluard. A postcard sent by Tanning in August 1943 announces that she is on her way to France via Cuba, while the reverse side has a reproduction of a Romantic painting by the Dresden painter Adrian Ludwig Richter representing a boat loaded with passengers on the Rhine; one of them meditates, another plays the harp, a third contemplates a castle, while a pair of lovers are placed nearby in front of the rower. The transatlantic voyage is thus in tune with this Romantic sailing.[19] In the correspondence exchanged with Anne Reigel in 1969 one finds a social game practiced in scrapbooks until the twentieth century: collecting friends' autographs (notably in Germany) which, upon being folded, become Rorschach ink blots; the pages are signed vertically on sheets folded in two while the ink is still wet. Cornell wrote the first name "Anne" in this manner; she then had to return—unwillingly but to comply with the artist's request—three of her "little souvenirs" composing a fantastic bestiary of "delightful Rorschachs"—some "Anne-lobster fantasies."[20]

A Taste for Books: *Object* (*Story of a Mouthful of Bread*)

Cornell's papers, his postcards, and the Rorschach autographs inspired by social games for scrapbooks show what he inherited from the private formats of books derived from Romantic and Victorian albums. Not unrelated to these activities in the boxes he composed, he availed himself of a variety of techniques in the manipulation and elaboration of pictures, collected objects, optical games, and reappropriation through recycling. He gave new life to old, often familiar things, which he went about gleaning at random in bookstores and second-hand shops, while reconfiguring them and bringing them together in the tight and constraining framework of boxes that he constantly reinvented. By delving into these elements of material culture that he assembled and associated according to the principle of the Surrealist image—i.e., to extol the disparate and the incongruous—he created a world of memory and imagination that was personal to him while remaining open to the appropriations of spectators, who were in their turn prompted to manipulate these concrete artifacts derived from a poetic *bricolage*. His work, focused on the construction of these boxes, extends along major thematic categories that often cross over—notably those of maps, books (with or without pictures), and what in his titles he called "hôtels." I shall be interested here in the second, books, which can be further divided into two groups.

The first will deal with the object-book, with typographical space, and with popularized scientific and technical writing, as well as with books on practical instructions or ordinary readings, in hopes of opening a few windows on the subject.[21] In *Object* (1940), Cornell cuts up a copy of volume 12 of the *Bibliothèque du médecin-praticien: maladies respiratoire et circulatoire* (Baillière, 1850).[22] He does the same for *Object* (*Histoire d'une bouchée de pain*) (Object [Story of a mouthful of bread]) in 1939 (see fig. 4.02),[23] which presents a copy opened onto a double page, where one can recognize the typographical norms for "scripturation" perfected in the nineteenth century:[24] The title at the top of the page on the left side repeats the title of the book, which Cornell's title cites in parentheses and as a subtitle, and specifies on the right page the textual unit of which the double page is a part: *Lettre IV: Les dents* (Letter IV: teeth). The text is printed in two typographical columns—rectangular, justified, and framed inside white margins. The right page has a neatly traced circle cut out and an open hole obliterates the entire second paragraph, in the center of the page, going all the way down through the thickness of the book. At the bottom is set an intruded object, as unexpected as the Surrealist pipe in Magritte's painting, which, because it is a picture, is not an object but a representation. What this presence of an object-spoon expresses in the object-book is that this *is* a spoon, shining before the spectator's eyes. If, as the title tells us, Cornell transforms the book into an object, the text into texture, and shows the conditions for reading an ordinary book by exhibiting its three-dimensional reality as a *codex*, he nonetheless has not forgotten the act of reading; the reader's glance can move quickly across the page, all the more easily because the circle cut out of the right page obliges the eye to skip the middle paragraph. He can also read back and forth from left to right and from one line to the next, following a pendulum-like rhythm that is to some extent suggested by the diagonal orientation of the spoon. By means of metonymy, the spoon also introduces the semantic field of food, as indicated by the title and treated in the body of the text, thus reflecting the idea of a double nourishment for human beings, physical and mental, that has been expressed in the verb "to nourish" since medieval times. The reader is open to the associations suggested to him by the coexistence of the spoon and the text printed on the page of this object that reveals a taste for the book, savored since childhood. The theme is developed by the passage that can be read on the double page, devoted to the first food absorbed by the child's stomach, which is his mother's milk; the content of the book, addressed by the narrator to his "dear little girl," extends the physiological lesson into a moral lesson. And the making of this object-book, signed by Cornell, becomes the allegory of his art, a story of nourishment and digestion, of assimilation and appropriation that goes back to memories of a mother nursing her child.

By making reference, without naming its author, to the *Histoire d'une bouchée de pain. Lettres à une petite fille sur la vie de l'homme et des animaux* (Story of a mouthful of bread: Letters to a little girl on the life of man and animals) by Jean Macé (1861), Cornell takes account not only of the most widely known title by a certain boarding-school master who became the literary director of the *Magasin d'éducation et de récréation*, the publisher and artistic editor of which was Jules Hetzel, but also a whole vast domain of printed culture of the bourgeoisie in the nineteenth century, with its children's books and popular science. He inscribes his object into the sphere and tradition of natural-history lessons and in pedagogy by means of consideration of physical aspect, while also introducing the distance of a context far removed from the American public and in a language other than English, all of which strengthens the dominance of the little spoon as a real object, in the hollow of a book that serves as its box.

The "Vignette" Look

The second group of box-books includes those in which Romantic vignettes cover over the main part of the box in conjunction with typography or with a literary text stated in the title or subtitle. They share an identical setting that can be shown open or closed, evoking not only the book but other personal items. Vignettes proliferate on the exterior sides and the outer frame of the main side, whereas the interior has a more enigmatic character and is organized differently in each of the boxes. In *Comédies et Proverbes (le petit de crac)* (Comedies and proverbs [The little lord of Crac], c. 1948, private collection), which takes us back to children's theater, the closely traced silhouettes of the characters have been cut and pasted, not unlike children's scissors activities. In *Les Trois Mousquetaires* (*The Three Musketeers*, c. 1948, private collection), illustrated rectangular pieces are arranged end to end, and the typographic elements appear only on the lower part of the box, on what constitutes the base or footing. On the outside parts, the cutouts have been dyed in pale rose. A glass window lets us look into the interior compartments, where other closed boxes are guarding their secrets. The metaphor of a miniature mirrored armoire comes to mind. It is entirely bedecked with a profusion of characters; wide-brimmed hats, capes, and moustaches take us back to the universe of Dumas's historical novels suggested by the title. In the fragments of text on the footings, no continuous text can be read but one can recognize the names of heroes: "ma foi, mon cher Aramis, dit d'Artagnan" (yes indeed, my dear Aramis, said d'Artagnan). Finally, in *Untitled (Paul and Virginia)* (see figs. 4.01, 4.04), rectangular cutouts juxtapose textual elements and vignettes in a structured set of hidden compartments and mirrors on the inside, transforming the book into a cabinet, not without evoking the tradition in convents of apothecary box-books that preserve secrets of botanical pharmacopeia (see fig. 4.03).

The notion of Romantic vignette, used in all three boxes, is a complex composition where the sense of the original meaning of the word is linked to the vocabulary of illuminated pictures. Its extension, very widespread in the terminology of the period (where the word *illustration*, taken in the sense still in usage in our time, came into use only progressively), ultimately the idea of a new form of symbolic image, as analyzed thusly by Henri Zerner and Charles Rosen:

> If this new type of book illustration was so apt and definitive an expression of Romanticism, it was not only because the close association of text and image satisfied the desire to unite different forms of art. The vignette, by its general appearance, presents itself both as a global metaphor for the world and as a fragment. Dense at its center, tenuous on the periphery, it seems to disappear into the page: this makes it a naïve but powerful metaphor of the infinite, a symbol of the universe; at the same time, the vignette is fragmentary, sometimes even minute in scale, incomplete, mostly dependent upon the text for its meaning, with irregular and ill-defined edges, not unlike Schlegel's hedgehog. It is the perfect Romantic formula.[25]

The absence of a frame is the corollary of the fact that the vignette spreads out from its center, but that is also the stake the Romantic vignette claims in its conflict with the classical concept of representation, that of painting-as-window: "The image . . . emerges from the paper as an apparition or a fantasy. The uncertainty of contour often makes it impossible to distinguish the edge of the vignette from the paper: the whiteness of the paper, which represents the play of light within the image, changes imperceptibly into the paper of the book, and realizes, in small, the Romantic blurring of art and reality."[26] In Cornell's boxes with applied vignettes, the framing of the book page and the metaphor of the secret closet or cabinet, with their system of imbricated rectangles, are in tension with the floating effect of the vignettes that cover the surface.

Yet on the other hand, these surfaces, with their repetitiveness and characteristic graphic treatment, also become subjects, according to the vocabulary of the decorative arts of the period, where vignettes, like decals, can travel from one support to another, migrating from the book to wallpaper or to fabric designs and illustrated plates, taking along with them more or less precise memories of texts and literary genres. This vignette look comes into play in the box inspired by Bernardin de Saint-Pierre's novel *Paul et Virginie* (first published in 1788), a literary theme abundantly revived from the end of the eighteenth century to the nineteenth in its various registers, and also adapted for the opera and ballet. The textile print of the Petitpierre factory in Nantes (c. 1795, see fig. 4.08),[27] for example, takes as its inspiration a very free rewriting of the novel by the librettist Favières, for Kreutzer's opera created in Paris in 1791, then transposed into a ballet choreographed by Gardel and presented from 1806 to 1828 at the Paris Opera. The spectator's eye is prompted either to call to mind the story, if he knows it, or to imagine a new one, or else again to dream nostalgically of a mythic state of nature from which society has distanced itself through industrialization, on the basis of scenes that stand out against a tropical vegetation.

Untitled (Paul and Virginia)

Paul et Virginie, despite the wide distribution it achieved earlier in the United States, once again became a tabula rasa theme for the contemporary American reader who would hardly have been familiar with this novel. Cornell's title, combining "Untitled" with the exact title of a book, can nevertheless be understood by itself, since the union of two first names becomes associated with the evocation of two lovers by means of vignettes in an exotic and luxuriant setting, suited to the utopia of the idyll narrated by the text. Virginia, which is also the name of one of the states of the South, can be understood as a suggestive first name that betokens the virginity of the girl and lets her personify a land untouched by any culture, an idea that might have interested Cornell as a disciple of Thoreau. This expressivity of the myth associated with a virginal first name had already occurred to Baudelaire when he wanted "confront with [the diabolically comic] an absolutely primitive soul, as given by the hands of Nature, so to speak. Let us take as our example the noble and typical character of Virginie, who is a perfect symbol of absolute purity and simplicity."[28]

Despite the relative obscurity into which it had fallen, this novel—which had inspired Balzac in *Le Vicaire des Ardennes* (*The Vicar's Passion*, 1822), *Le Vicaire de*

Village (*The Village Rector*, 1839–41) and *Les Amours de deux bêtes* (*The Love of Two Beasts*, 1840), Lamartine in *Graziella* (1849), and Flaubert in *Madame Bovary* (1856) and *Un coeur simple* (*A Simple Heart*, 1877)—had an enormous critical and artistic success.[29] One ardent collector, having the same first name as the hero, Paul Toinet, applied himself as of 1939 to gathering an iconography of the book.[30] He claimed he was "preserving the elements of a history of the illustrated book over more than a century and a half." His repertory does not broach the fine arts, even though the theme gave rise to numerous works, whether in painting—among others, those by Landon, Broc, Géricault, and Courbet (see fig. 4.09)—or sculpture, with the sketch by Carpeaux[31] as an example. But it includes series of prints, popular imagery, and all the illustrated props of Neoclassical and Romantic art forms, from panoramic wallpaper to fans, screens, and chintzes, and including pill boxes[32] and plates,[33] with a central scene in vegetal border from Gien or Choisy that can be found in the Deglos collection, now at the Museum of the Quai Branly and formerly at the National Museum of Arts of Africa and Oceania (Historical Collection). This variety of derived objects could not help but attract the attention of Cornell to the theme.

The 1788 novel was illustrated the following year, the year of the French Revolution, by Moreau le Jeune and Joseph Vernet, in small format, and the first separate sequel, by Schall, appeared in 1791, the same year as William Blake's collection of poems, *Songs of Innocence*. In 1806 Didot Publishers released a major illustrated Neoclassical edition with seven inset plates for which the author, who had ordered it, had himself prepared and dramatized the argument, following the example of Rousseau for the subjects of *La Nouvelle Héloïse* (*Julie: Or the New Heloise*). Participating in this were the painter-illustrators Gérard, Girodet, and Prud'hon, for the famous engraving on the death of Virginie. The Curmer edition, published in thirty installments from October 1836 to July 1837, then in book form in 1838 (450 vignettes, twenty-nine wood engravings, and seven portraits in steel engravings) and supplemented by *La Chaumière indienne* (*The Indian Cottage*), is the one Cornell would draw on for the elements of his own version, using the English edition that appeared in 1839 at Orr publishers.[34] Unlike the Neoclassical book that contained only a few plates, inspired by the *tableau-fenêtre* (painting window), the illustrated Romantic book with vignettes throughout became a "museum of pictures" in this edition, considered by the bibliophile Jules Brivois to be "the pearl of illustrated books in the nineteenth century."[35] Léon Curmer had called upon Tony Johannot for "the dramatic part and the 'touching scenes' in the novel"[36] (see figs. 4.05–.07), as well as on Paul Huet (see fig. 4.10), Eugène Isabey, and Charles Marville—for the landscapes and seascapes, remarkably condensed into small engravings that are often panoramic—and finally Louis Français and Ernest

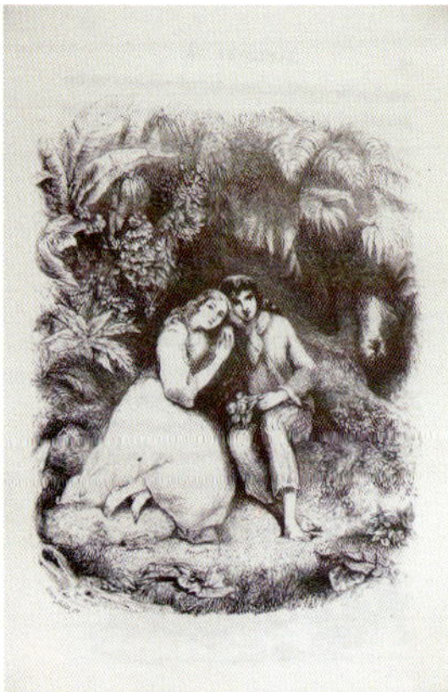

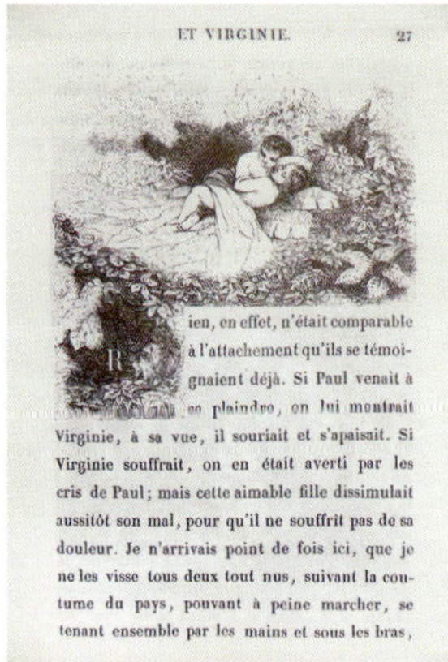

ET VIRGINIE. 27

Rien, en effet, n'était comparable à l'attachement qu'ils se témoignaient déjà. Si Paul venait à se plaindre, on lui montrait Virginie, à sa vue, il souriait et s'apaisait. Si Virginie souffrait, on en était averti par les cris de Paul; mais cette aimable fille dissimulait aussitôt son mal, pour qu'il ne souffrît pas de sa douleur. Je n'arrivais point de fois ici, que je ne les visse tous deux tout nus, suivant la coutume du pays, pouvant à peine marcher, se tenant ensemble par les mains et sous les bras,

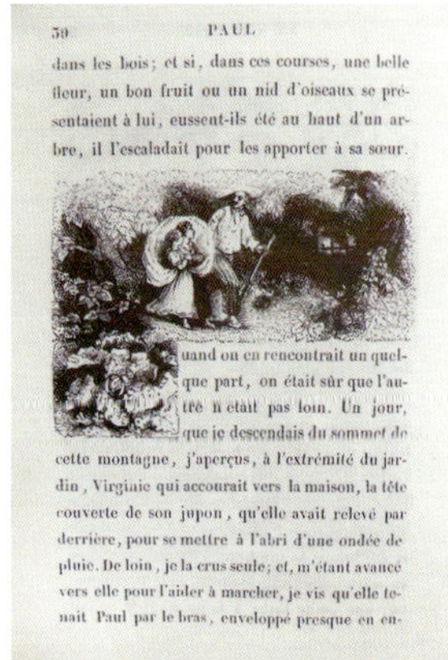

30 PAUL

dans les bois; et si, dans ces courses, une belle fleur, un bon fruit ou un nid d'oiseaux se présentaient à lui, eussent-ils été au haut d'un arbre, il l'escaladait pour les apporter à sa sœur. Quand on en rencontrait un quelque part, on était sûr que l'autre n'était pas loin. Un jour, que je descendais du sommet de cette montagne, j'aperçus, à l'extrémité du jardin, Virginie qui accourait vers la maison, la tête couverte de son jupon, qu'elle avait relevé par derrière, pour se mettre à l'abri d'une ondée de pluie. De loin, je la crus seule; et, m'étant avancé vers elle pour l'aider à marcher, je vis qu'elle tenait Paul par le bras, enveloppé presque en en-

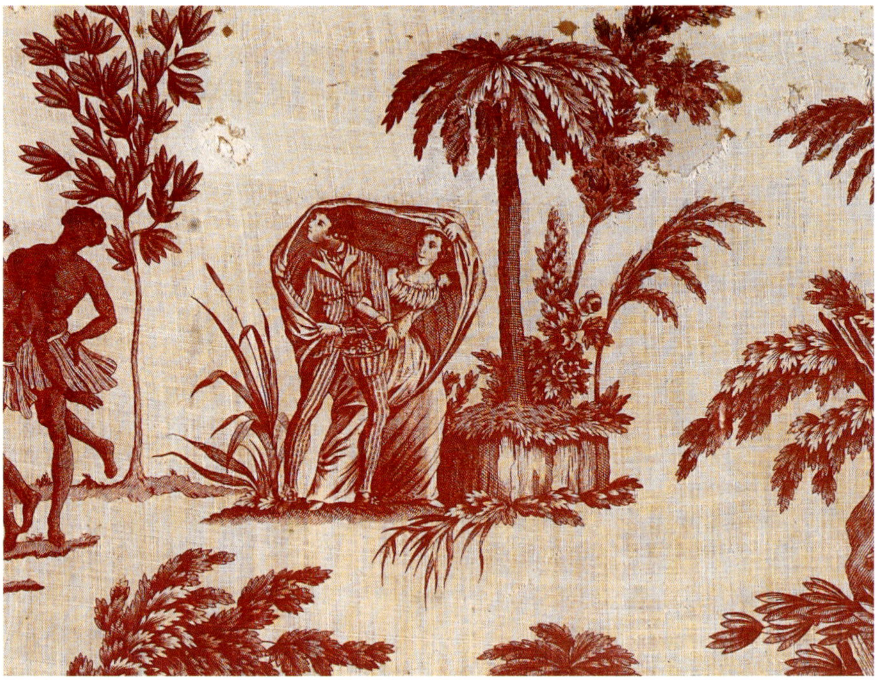

4.05–4.07 Wood engravings after Tony Johannot and Louis Français, from Bernardin de Saint-Pierre, *Paul et Virginie* (Paris: L. Curmer, 1838), applied by Cornell to the exterior of *Untitled* (*Paul and Virginia*) (see fig. 4.01) **4.05** *Adolescence of Paul and Virginia*, large plate by Orrin Smith (facing p. 34) **4.06** *Children with Cradle*, engraving by C. Gray (p. 27) **4.07** *The Old Man and the Children*, engraving by Samuel Williams (p. 30) **4.08** Printed textile (detail) inspired by *Paul et Virginie*, c. 1795 (compare fig. 4.07) Linen, Favre, Petitpierre et Cie., Nantes, Museum of Printed Textiles, Mulhouse

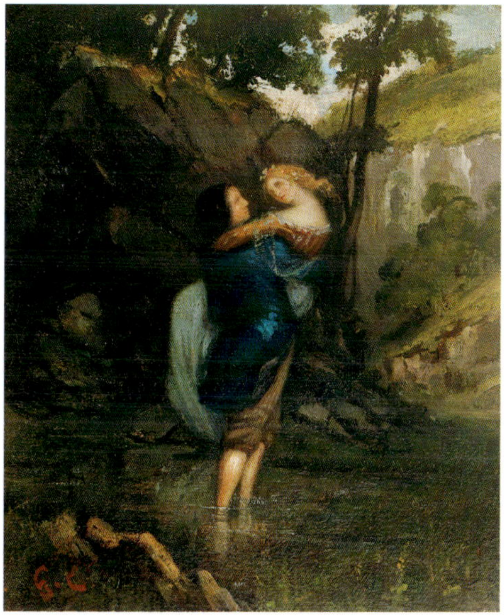

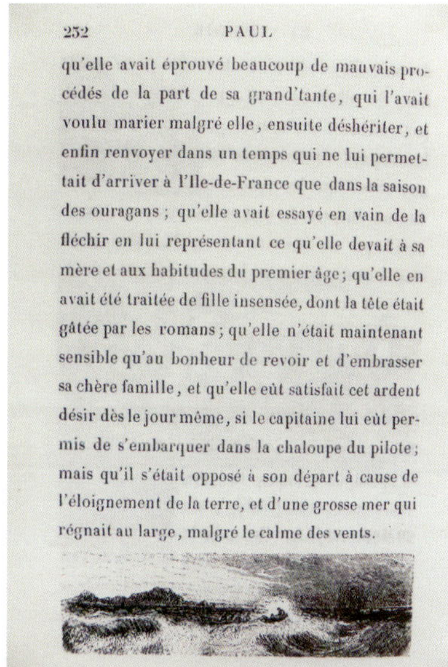

252 PAUL

qu'elle avait éprouvé beaucoup de mauvais procédés de la part de sa grand'tante, qui l'avait voulu marier malgré elle, ensuite déshériter, et enfin renvoyer dans un temps qui ne lui permettait d'arriver à l'Ile-de-France que dans la saison des ouragans ; qu'elle avait essayé en vain de la fléchir en lui représentant ce qu'elle devait à sa mère et aux habitudes du premier âge ; qu'elle en avait été traitée de fille insensée, dont la tête était gâtée par les romans ; qu'elle n'était maintenant sensible qu'au bonheur de revoir et d'embrasser sa chère famille, et qu'elle eût satisfait cet ardent désir dès le jour même, si le capitaine lui eût permis de s'embarquer dans la chaloupe du pilote ; mais qu'il s'était opposé à son départ à cause de l'éloignement de la terre, et d'une grosse mer qui régnait au large, malgré le calme des vents.

4.09 Gustave Courbet, *Flooded Passage*, 1841, oil on paper mounted on canvas, 10 3/8 × 8 5/8 in., Institute Gustave Courbet, Ornans **4.10** Paul Huet, *High Sea*, cul-de-lampe wood engraving by Powis for *Paul et Virginie*, 1838, applied by Cornell on the interior left surface, to the right of the central plate, in *Untitled* (*Paul and Virginia*) (see fig. 4.02)

Meissonier for the ornamental first letters, frequently protracted into square shapes and devoted to botany and natural history. The epistolary sections offered reproductions of illustrated letters (p. 153, at the end of Virginie's letter). Inscriptions on rocks ("the discovery of friendship," p. 71), and maxims set squarely in the midst of nature on tree trunks (pp. 74–75, see fig. 4.05), infinitely repeated by means of the vignette, introduced the poetry of picturesque gardens into this evocation of tropical paradise.

The choice of plates, vignettes, and fragments cut out by Cornell a century later, and pasted in their turn on his box, is in many regards closely related to the job of editor. All this is done as if he had chosen engravings to be reused for a new edition, *Untitled* (*Paul and Virginia*).[37] In closed position (see fig. 4.01), the box shows on its main outside surface a rectangular mirror surrounded by a framework decorated with vignettes of yellow paper. One might recall here Madame Bovary's identification with the story and characters in the novel, as she becomes moved by the keepsake engravings: "She had read *Paul et Virginie*, and she had fantasized about the little bamboo house, the Negro Domingo, the dog Fidèle, but even more the sweet friendship of some good little brother."[38] The vignettes chosen by Cornell are drawn from the first part of the novel, the Robinson Crusoe–type adventure of a small, Eden-like community living in full nature. The theme of love between the foster brother and sister, from the cradle (see fig. 4.06) to adolescence (see fig. 4.05), is reiterated through the repetition of the motif of the fraternal pair who then fall in love presented in eight of the nine scenes depicted (see figs. 4.05–.07). The colonial episodes and plot developments are left aside through this focus on Paul and Virginie, which tends to overly sweeten the contents of the book. To the mirror phase corresponds that of the album of pictures, without text, like a comic strip for children.

Once opened (see fig. 4.04), the box offers, to the left, a flat surface covered with a set of other vignettes and text fragments framing a large central engraving, framed again, *Le passage du torrent* (Crossing the Torrent), a striking scene that had been used, among others, by Courbet (see fig. 4.09) and symbolizing the rite of passage to a new age of life, with the awakening of feelings of love and sexuality. If one looks a bit closer, the story moves forward as dramatic elements are announced, by antiphrasis, through typographical fragments of the cut pages that reference the end of the novel, from Virginie's letter announcing her return (see fig. 4.07) to her shipwreck, and where the running title, *Paul and Virginia*, appears recurrently. The disconnected nature of the reading makes it almost subliminal. The artist has placed his signature on this inside panel, at the place where the publisher's name would appear on the title page of a book, while the running head, *Paul and Virginia*, is repeated several times, including in the center, where it is turned into the legend for the central plate. This second surface is no longer a place simply for reading pictures, like that on the outside, but for the reader-spectator is similar to the kind of reading that is a relationship between text and picture, with its movement from an anchored spot to back-and-forth movements or contradictions between picture and text. Cornell is no longer merely the editor but assumes the role of author of the literary box construction, which recycles the Curmer edition of *Paul et Virginie* by adding a network of imaginary associations to this new passing through the mirror—a passing whose embodiment can be found in Lewis Carroll's *Through the Looking Glass* and in the films of Jean Cocteau (from *Blood of a Poet* to *Orpheus*), who himself composed a theatrical transposition of *Paul et Virginie* with Léon Radiguet.

To the right, the box is metamorphosed into a kind of cabinet-museum with many compartments, several of which are filled with empty match boxes (see fig. 4.04). The uprights and separation walls are covered with pasted engravings and typographic bits, in small sections, juxtaposed in a patchwork pattern and assembled in such a way as to paper over the surface, making it impossible to recognize the constituent elements. Only a graphic texture remains, lending its particular vibrations to this "magic box." The principle of collage here reminds one of fabric prints or boxes decorated with little cut-out assortments. The compartments of this little case, when turned around, commemorate—through various techniques of exposition, from diorama to an aquarium, associated with the museography of natural history—the sadly touching destinies of the heroes. The arrangement in three superposed registers functions as a simultaneous evocation of the three cycles of the novel. Childhood is symbolized in the lower diorama by the twin eggs lying on bits of straw on a nest. This naturalistic metaphor appears at the beginning of Saint-Pierre's text (p. 27). It comes up again in the ornamental capital letters of the Curmer edition (p. 28), echoes the astrological allusion to the constellation of Gemini (p. 28), and then extends its mythological reference when the children in the same crib, on the island, are compared to those of Leda in the same shell (p. 30), and winds up constituting one of the main leitmotifs of the novel. The cycle of adventures in the ages of life, from the flame of love to the dangers of fire, is suggested by the proximity of the straw nest to matchboxes that could catch fire, if we imagine an amusing chemistry experiment that, given these materials, turns into tragedy. Finally, the cycle of the shipwreck and the funerals is suggested by the oblong aquarium rising above the composition, like a transparent coffin for the two fish lying in a kind of sea cemetery, which might be interpreted as an allegorical figure of the two heroes. The monochrome blue surroundings, by turns virginal and sealike, are modulated by Cornell through different shades in the sky of the diorama, the covers of the match boxes and the colored glass of the aquarium, in harmony with the yellowing pages of the old book.

This third metamorphosis of the box transforms it into a portable and private altar dedicated to the memory of the protagonists, a funerary monument, in continuity with the final plate of the Didot edition of *Paul et Virginie* of 1806, with its tombs made of palms. In the final analysis Cornell is thus giving form to a personal myth, and the aquarium *funerarium* perhaps induces a trans-Atlantic reflection on the past of an Old Europe and the future of a New World, or even a transcontinental one following the Second World War, the attack on Pearl Harbor, and the atomic bombing of Hiroshima that inspired Alain Resnais to make *Hiroshima mon amour* (1959).

Secret boxes and Pandora's boxes: Cornell's boxes in three dimensions offer themselves to the spectator as magical transformational objects. Their artist is the master craftsman and the signatory, but his system of naming them *untitled* is left open, even if the reference to a title given in parentheses is added on for the box constructions. Recourse to Romantic illustrations and vignettes, making possible new associations between picture and text, thereby adds an iconotextual dimension, while underscoring the link between Surrealism and Romanticism.

Notes

1 Jean-Paul Sartre, *Words,* trans. Irene Clephane (New York: Penguin Books, 1964; reprint 1966), 51.

2 Frédéric Lachèvre, *Bibliographie sommaire des Keepsakes et autres recueils collectifs de la période romantique: 1825–1848* (1825–48, reprint Paris: L. Giraud-Badin, 1929), 2 vols.

3 *Le Livre de Beauté: Souvenirs historiques* (Paris: L. Janet, 1834); *Les Beautés de l'Opéra* (Paris: Soulié, 1845).

4 See New York 1980, nos. 59, 92, 110.

5 Ibid., no. 268.

6 Ibid., no. 95.

7 Ibid., no. 93.

8 Ségolène Le Men, "Le livre blanc," in Emmanuelle Brugerolles, ed., *L'oeil et la plume: Caricatures de Charles Garnier*, exh. cat. (Paris: ENSBA, 2010), 7–18.

9 Henry Monnier, "La manie des albums," in *Paris, ou le Livre des cent-et-un* (Paris: Ladvocat, 1832), vol. 5.

10 *Christine's Picture Book: Hans Christian Andersen and Grandfather Drewsen* (New York: Holt Rinehart Winston, 1985) (facsimile).

11 Among the figurines in Cornell's boxes can be found the little girl used by Menier Chocolates, reading an inscription backward behind a cafe window, after the picture poster by Steinlen (*Variétés Apollinaris (for Guillaume Apollinaire)*, 1953, fig. C 27), exp. 1980, no. 114. See also *Untitled (Chocolat Menier)*, 1952, ibid., no. 139.

12 Françoise Heilbrun and Michael Pantazzi, eds., *Collages et photomontages de l'Angleterre victorienne*, exh. cat. (Paris: Musée d'Orsay and RMN, 1997); Elizabeth Siegel, *Playing with Pictures: The Art of Victorian Photocollage*, exh. cat. (Chicago: Art Institute of Chicago, 2009).

13 Walter Benjamin, "Unpacking My Library," in *Illuminations*, ed. Hannah Arendt, trans. Harry Zohn (New York: Schocken, 1978), 66.

14 Ibid., 67.

15 Hartigan, in New York 1980, p. 93.

16 Ibid., 99.

17 Arthur Good, known as Tom Tit, in *La Science amusante* (3 vols. repeating the articles appearing in a newspaper for children, *Les Petits Français*) (Paris: Plon and Nourrit, 1889, 1891, 1893). See for example New York 1980, cat. 27. Arthur Good, *Magical Experiments or Science in Play*, trans. Camden Curwen and Robert Waters (New York: Worthington Co., 1892). Lyon 2013, cat. 57 (*Untitled*, early 1930s) has an image drawn directly from *Magical Experiments*, p. 55. I thank Matthew Affron for this information.

18 *Story without a Name—For Max Ernst* (cats. 64–79), collages from the 1930s, appearing in *View* in April 1942, ibid., cats. 36–51.

19 Joseph Cornell Papers, General Correspondence: Tanning, Dorothea, 1945–1965, undated, box 6, folder 54, Url:www.aaa.si.edu/collections/container/viewer/Tanning-Dorothea—190924.

20 Ibid., Reigel, Anne, 1968–1969, undated, box 3, folder 32, Url: www. aaa.si.edu/collections/container/viewer/Reigel-Anne–190902, fols. 12, 13, 14.

21 See *Untitled (Rosalba: Book with Marble)*, c. 1945, in New York 1980, no. 59; and *Untitled (Book with Window)*, c. 1945, ibid., no. 62.

22 Ibid., no. 58. See also above (cat. 39).

23 Ibid., no. 57.

24 Roger Laufer, *Introduction à la textologie* (Paris: Larousse, 1972).

25 Charles Rosen and Henri Zerner, *Romanticism and Realism: The Mythology of Nineteenth-Century Art* (New York: Viking, 1984), 81.

26 Ibid., 81, 84.

27 *Toiles de Nantes des XVIIIe et XIXe siècles*, exh. cat. (Nantes: Musée des Arts Décoratifs, Château des Ducs de Bretagne, 1978), 74–75, no. 46.

28 Charles Baudelaire, "Of the Essence of Laughter, and Generally of the Comic in the Plastic Arts" (1855), in *Baudelaire: Selected Writings on Art and Artists*, trans. P. E. Charvet (Harmondsworth: Penguin, 1972), 144.

29 Valéri Davd, "Sur l'iconographie de *Paul et Virginie*," in *Etudes sur* Paul et Virginie *et l'œuvre de Bernardin de Saint-Pierre*, ed. Jean-Michel Racault (Paris: Publications de l'Université de La Réunion, distribution Didier Erudition, 1986), 238–47.

30 Paul Toinet, *Paul et Virginie. Répertoire bibliographique et iconographique* (Paris: Maisonneuve et Larose, 1963).

31 Carpeaux worked on this uncompleted group at the Villa de Medici in 1859.

32 Paris, Musée du Quai Branly, inv. 75-4331.1–3, 75-4330.1–2.

33 Paris, Musée du Quai Branly, inv. 75-8387, 75-8393.

34 Jacques-Henri Bernardin de Saint-Pierre, *Paul and Virginia* (London: W.S. Orr and Co., 1839).

35 Jules Brivois, *Bibliographie des ouvrages illustrés du XIXe siècle* (Paris, 1883), 390.

36 Tony Johannot often drew the people and Louis Français the landscapes. See Bernardin de Saint-Pierre, *Paul et Virginie* (*Précédé d'une notice historique par Sainte-Beuve et suivi d'une Flore de l'Ile de-France et de l'Inde, par Th. Descourtilz*) (Paris: I. Curmer, 1838).

37 See Renée Riese Hubert, *Surrealism and the Book* (Berkeley: University of California Press, 1988), 331–40; Lorraine Piroux, "Illegibility and Grammophobia in *Paul et Virginie*," in *Visible Writings: Cultures, Forms, Readings*, ed. Marija Dalbello and Mary Shaw (New Brunswick, NJ: Rutgers University Press, 2011), 99–111.

38 Gustave Flaubert, *Madame Bovary*, trans. Raymond N. MacKenzie (Indianapolis: Hackett, 2009), 31.

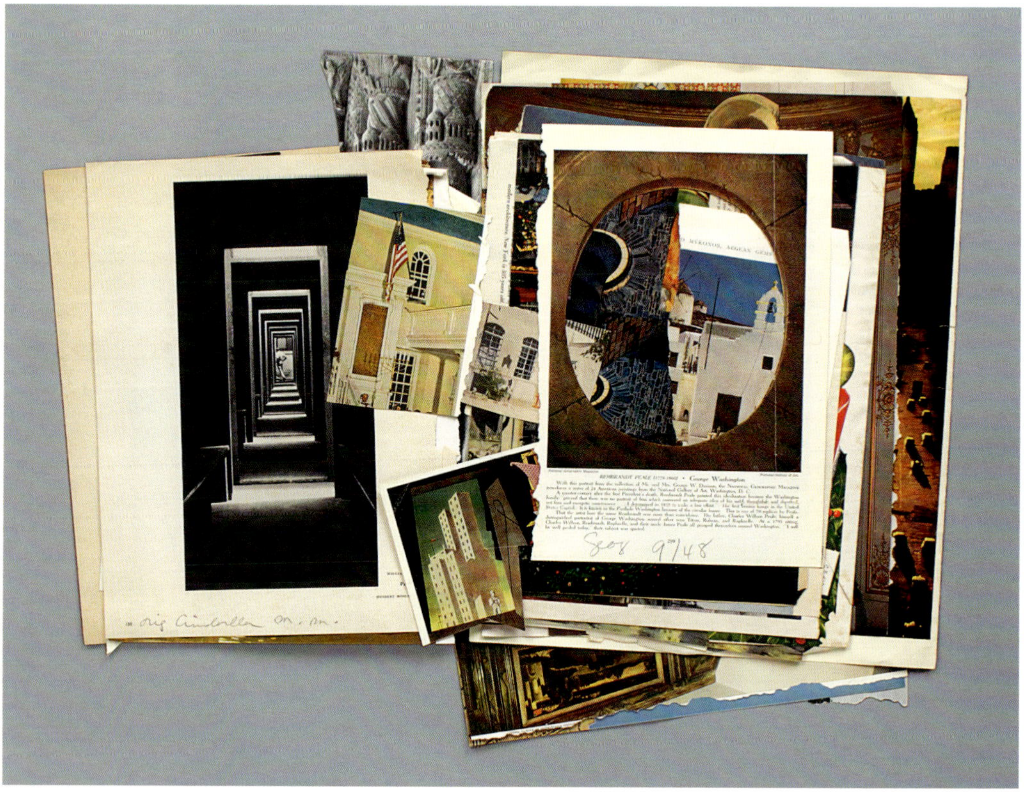

5.01 Joseph Cornell, *Windows* dossier (detail), c. 1950–60, Joseph Cornell Study Center, Smithsonian American Art Museum, Washington, DC

Joseph Cornell, Le Chasseur d'Images

Lynda Roscoe Hartigan

To glorify the cult of images (my great, my only, my earliest passion).

—Charles Baudelaire, "My Heart Laid Bare," 1964[1]

The adjectives "original" and "unique" have kept frequent company in assessments of Joseph Cornell's multifaceted achievements since he emerged as an artist in the 1930s. Cornell owes his inventiveness to a host of factors, most notably the conflation of his intense emotional and intellectual need to make sense of humanity and spirituality as complementary rather than polar-opposite states of being. This foundational motivation differs dramatically from the formal, cultural, and personal concerns of many of his peers from the 1930s into the early 1970s. Yet Cornell effortlessly earned the mantle "artist's artist" during his lifetime, and he has continued to evoke this kindred-spirit admiration among subsequent generations of visual and literary artists. Being true to oneself and to the act of making art rather than following trends and seeking success—these are some of the hallmarks of the artist's artist. Put another way, this concept implies that one artist recognizes in another artist the commitment to originality as the expression of independent inventiveness.

An inescapable irony, however, attends Cornell's originality: reproductions, multiples, quotations, and excerpts dominate his process, materials, and imagery (fig. 5.01). Some of these elements are of his making, while many are by the hands of others; all navigate along a spectrum that runs from the mechanical to the appropriated. Around 1940, in one of his rare self-assessments, Cornell described his aspiration and process as "image-making akin to poetry."[2] Almost twenty years later, in his ongoing construction of a cohort of peers, he acknowledged his admiration for John Singleton Copley as "one of the first and greatest of the 'Coonskinners'—that is, American artists who worked out their own style of seeing."[3] Considerations of Cornell as a visual poet and as an "American" artist are valid lines of inquiry, but ones set aside in this essay in favor of exploring the concepts of "seeing" and "images" as keys to parsing this irony.

The physical sense by which the eye receives and the brain constructs light stimuli into a representation of an object's position, shape, scale, brightness, and color: this is the working definition of our sense of sight (fig. 5.02). Sight, or vision, however, is not simply an optical or physiological phenomenon.[4] Although we assume that our perception of the visible occurs immediately and unmediated, sight involves cognitive and psychic processes that operate in time and space. We do not look at anything all at once or in isolation. Instead we go through a form of exploration or visual searching that integrates successive but non-sequential fixations, or points of information. Through this piecing and assimilation we identify what we are looking at and understand that something is both a whole occupying space and a fragment of a larger space.

Among these wholes and fragments are images that, in their broadest sense, are objects with physical characteristics that make them visible. As such, images represent and mediate our discovery of the visual world as projections of its three-dimensional reality. If we subscribe to the estimation of the visual as the most intellectual of our senses, then images are also gateways to knowledge, thought, language, and action as they communicate information, stimulate curiosity, and generate emotion. Inherently, images are also connective, social, and relative in nature because our physiological and cognitive processes operate and interact in particular environments, contexts in which images become historical, cultural, and symbolic objects. This is true even of images considered imaginary or abstract, the externalized expressions of the mind's eye—the imagination.

Our capacity to see the visible means that we bring images into existence in a cognitive and emotional partnership that includes our prior knowledge, experiences, and expectations. Our relationship to images—how and why we recognize and make use of them—is highly situational and subjective because a particular moment, culture, belief system, or lifestyle shapes our identity and ability as viewers, whether images are made for collective or individual purposes. This is, for example, why images produced in a time and space unrelated to our own are often not readily understood or are misinterpreted. Just as different societies develop different ways of seeing, understanding, and valuing images, so do individuals. Although artists, especially in Western cultures, have traditionally been considered more sensitive to images, each of us is a visual searcher, collector, and interpreter, regularly modifying or creating different images because of the impact of experience and emotion.

So, temporarily, let's consider Cornell as a viewer rather than a maker or inventor of images. In many respects, his activities as a viewer and as a collector are not easily separated because they existed in tandem at least a decade before he began making art around 1928 or 1929. His collection of images, more often described as his studio effects, media, and source materials, represents various typologies, outlined here without any intent of being complete.

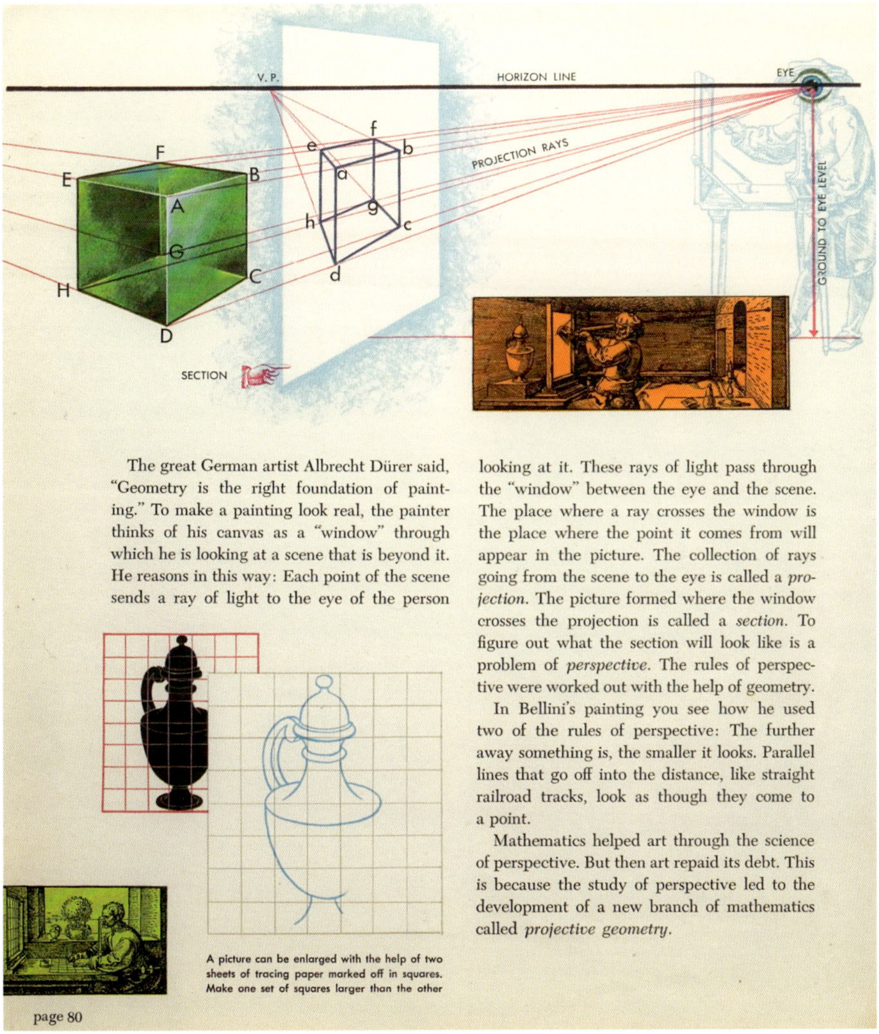

The great German artist Albrecht Dürer said, "Geometry is the right foundation of painting." To make a painting look real, the painter thinks of his canvas as a "window" through which he is looking at a scene that is beyond it. He reasons in this way: Each point of the scene sends a ray of light to the eye of the person looking at it. These rays of light pass through the "window" between the eye and the scene. The place where a ray crosses the window is the place where the point it comes from will appear in the picture. The collection of rays going from the scene to the eye is called a *projection*. The picture formed where the window crosses the projection is called a *section*. To figure out what the section will look like is a problem of *perspective*. The rules of perspective were worked out with the help of geometry.

In Bellini's painting you see how he used two of the rules of perspective: The further away something is, the smaller it looks. Parallel lines that go off into the distance, like straight railroad tracks, look as though they come to a point.

Mathematics helped art through the science of perspective. But then art repaid its debt. This is because the study of perspective led to the development of a new branch of mathematics called *projective geometry*.

page 80

5.02 Text about the relationship between mathematics and perspective from Irving Adler, *The Giant Golden Book of Mathematics*, 1958, Joseph Cornell Study Center, Smithsonian American Art Museum, Washington, DC

Physical

Flat: unprinted and colored papers; pages from books, magazines, and newspapers; prints, paintings, watercolors, drawings, photographs, films, photomechanical reproductions
Three-dimensional: objects (soap bubble pipes to piston rings); publications especially books; sculpture, toys, mechanical apparatuses
Natural: botanical and zoological specimens, representations of terrestrial, physical, astronomical, and scientific phenomena
Manmade: art, functional objects, ephemera, duplicates, multiples
Fragments: for the significance of details, glimpses, and hints
Wholes: as compendiums and, ideally, distillations of associations and forms.

Temporal

Historical/old: from ancient civilizations through the first two decades of the twentieth century, with an overwhelming emphasis on the nineteenth century, the passage of time, and the ideal state of childhood
Contemporary/new: from the 1920s, the decade of his first efforts to make art, to his death in 1972, with a preference for the 1950s and 1960s
Forgotten: people and places, above all
Topical/timely: current local and international events, especially conflicts, losses, disappearances, and scientific developments; natural phenomena, performances, street scenes, people/faces.

Cultural

Artistic: from the visual to the performed, privileging the capacity for emotional and spiritual uplift over the expression of style and technique.
Nationalist: American and European in fierce competition for his attention; Chinese and Japanese underestimated sources of inspiration
Fine: an unabashed reverence for old masters and iconoclastic pioneers
Vernacular: in recognition of the humanitarian, sentimental, and humorous aspects of the everyday, communal, and anonymous.

Conceptual

Ordinary: mass-produced, from the Woolworth's/five-and-dime realm
Rare: frequently, the only known example or version
Used/discarded: valued for the imprint of time and humanity

Found: whether hunted for or accidentally discovered, powerful candidates for repurposing and reinterpreting
Real: actual two- and three-dimensional objects
Metaphorical/symbolic: evoking the intangibles of experience, memory, emotion, and idea.

Certainly, these typologies correspond to the images that Cornell incorporated and created in his boxes, collages, and films. First and foremost, however, they index his preoccupations as someone who enjoyed looking at and consuming images. Much of the pleasure that he derived from these acts can be traced to a childhood filled with the fruits of the nineteenth century's technological advances in printing and photography. Images abounded in inexpensive illustrated books, magazines, and mass-produced prints, trade cards, and sheets of die-cut "scraps" to decorate scrapbooks and letters. Whether created for educational, recreational, or advertising purposes, all were humble in character and intimate in scale, designed to stimulate mass consumption.

Cornell's childhood engagement with reading was obsessive, so much so that it is not unreasonable to suggest a constellation of influential impressions that he derived from the printed images in his formative environment, from books to photographic albums to framed calendar reproductions of famous artworks. Many shared a strikingly similar visual vocabulary: disruptions in scale, a sense of the fragment or cutout, and unexpected combinations of typeface, text, and imagery. Reproductions in publications, in particular, were so abundant that they acquired the same weight as the printed word, like texts to be read. One of the principal lessons garnered from this type of reading related to scale. Printed images are generally small, and as a result they can be considered mobile or something to be manipulated: turned on a page, carried from one context or setting to another, cut out for saving, sharing, or changing. The potential to tempt a viewer or reader to engage in manipulation is all the more real because images in prints, books, and other media have already altered the dimensions and spatial relationships of what they represent. Similarly, small things like a book or photograph project a sense of intimacy and the ability to see close up and in detail, as they invite curiosity and the desire to look, touch, and possess. The scale of Cornell's collages and boxes is not accidental. Instead, it emulates the field of vision traditionally occupied by the realm of images in books (vertical closed, horizontal open) and other printed materials, even more so than the modest scale of the domestic and commercial containers he also loved.

Reading is a form of visual scanning or gleaning that can yield multiple meanings. Cornell favored this word "gleaning," an invocation that echoes a sphere

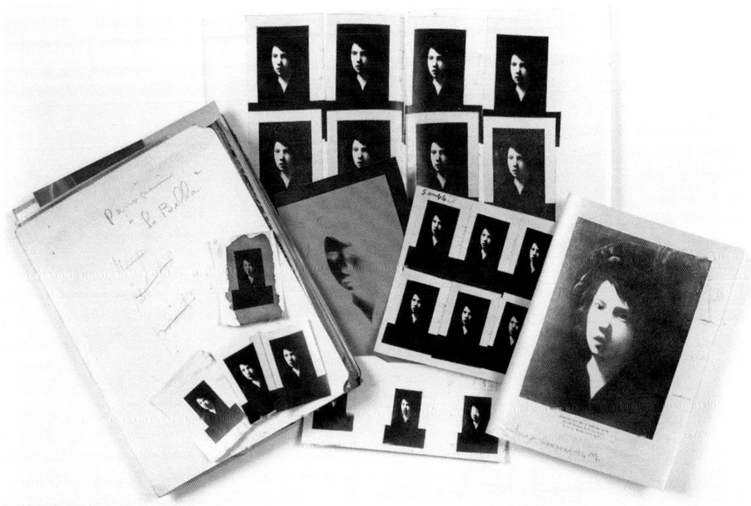

5.03 Photostats of a portrait once attributed to Caravaggio, extract from Joseph Cornell's *Medici Slot Machine Variants* dossier, condensed c. 1966, documents collected by Cornell from the end of the 1930s, Joseph Cornell Study Center, Smithsonian American Art Museum, Washington, DC

of activity engendered by the explosion of images in the nineteenth and early twentieth centuries. Caught between considering mass-produced, widely circulated publications as disposable or valuable, numerous readers turned to an already existing cultural value: the idea of saving and re-using scraps as good housekeeping and a demonstration of the concepts of survival and usefulness. Crazy quilts and memory jugs were not the only products of this attitude. Clipping scrapbooks—compilations of quotes and sayings from newspapers and magazines—abounded as highly individual and private compendiums of how and what someone read and saved. In creating a clipping scrapbook, a reader became an editor and self-publishing author through someone else's words, often unattributed, thanks to the act of cutting. Connections among the various clippings were usually clear only to the reader/clipper, but the scrapbooks were often shared with friends and family, creating a collective appreciation of recirculation and the belief that all media, no matter how ephemeral, were renewable resources.

Inspired by his mother's example especially, Cornell joined this gleaning circuit some time in his teens and early twenties, as he compiled a group of clipping scrapbooks that relied heavily on excerpts from publications such as *The Christian Science Monitor* and *The Dial*. His choices ran the gamut: poetry; criticism of the arts;

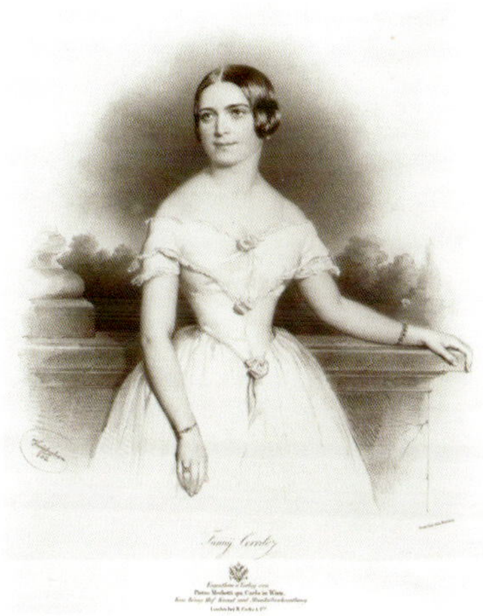

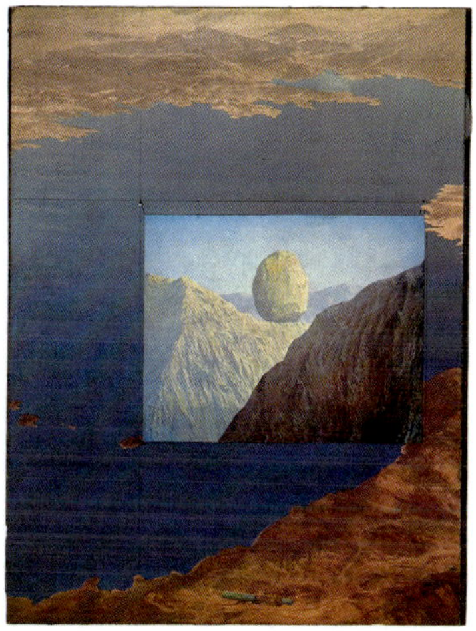

5.04 Joseph Kriehuber, *Fanny Cerrito*, 1842, Lithograph, Joseph Cornell Study Center, Smithsonian American Art Museum, Washington, DC **5.05** Joseph Cornell, *Untitled (After René Magritte, "La clef verre" [The Glass Key], 1959)*, c. 1965, collage, 12 × 9 in., Peabody Essex Museum, Salem. Gift of The Joseph and Robert Cornell Memorial Foundation

commentary on spiritual, social, and civic values; editorials on world events and other cultures and traditions; and an abundance of mottoes and aphorisms. It is virtually impossible and even unnecessary to determine which came first: compiling his clipping scrapbooks or collecting the first of what gradually became tens of thousands of printed images and publications. The more significant point is that Cornell's reading-based exposure to the cult of images and the act of clipping not only inspired him to make art but also empowered him to embrace reproducing, multiplying, and altering images and words.

Historically, the value and authenticity we have attached to an art work has been predicated on experiencing an "original" rather than a copy and by limiting production. Yet the acts of quoting, excerpting, copying, and borrowing have time-honored roots going back to printmaking in the sixteenth century and, today, are widely accessible and acceptable means of acquiring, expressing, or questioning information and meaning among artists and nonartists alike.

So where does Cornell fit into this spectrum of activity, based on how and when he acquired his love of images? The concept of the original mattered to him, but primarily from two perspectives: inspirational images or experiences, and images that enabled him to make reproductions. His diaries, for example, contain numerous descriptions of the visceral impact of discovering an original and rare nineteenth-century print of the Romantic ballerina Fanny Cerrito, which became the leitmotif for a family of works dedicated to the dancer and the world of dance (fig. 5.04). Cornell's relationship with images, as a viewer and as an artist, revolved around translating emotional responses into action. He also inscribed the word "original" on hundreds of reproductions from books and magazines that he regularly sent to a photostating service with instructions to make copies that actually represent variations in positive or negative versions, enlarged or reduced sizes, and as full or partial images. Statistically, no two copies are ever alike (fig. 5.03). Photostating, coupled with subsequent silhouetting and excerpting through clipping, enabled him to eliminate differences in elements such as scale or material among the range of images he worked with. Many of these images were drawn from his very personal survey of art history, chosen in appreciation of the personal or formal connotations the artists or specific works held for him. Yet even in the midst of these acts of borrowing and reproducing as homage, Cornell had episodes of guilt. The most notable one involved the work of the Belgian Surrealist painter René Magritte (fig. 5.05). Well into making several series of collages in the 1960s that featured details from reproductions of Magritte's paintings, Cornell consulted a lawyer because he feared that this famous living artist would find the collages objectionable.[5]

Pragmatism is not a quality generally associated with Cornell, but he was exactly that when it came to the use of reproductions and multiples of images. Compiling and stockpiling can connote being prepared with enough materials at hand, eliminating the need to stop and start in order to find or make a particular element, and having access to an eclectic assembly of forms and images. From an emotional or psychic perspective, compiling and stockpiling can also suggest that some sense of totality or completeness is elusive. Conceptually, Cornell very consciously gave himself permission to pick and choose from multiple images and to reproduce them, all in the spirit of considering originals and reproductions as equally effective intermediaries in the gleaning and image-making processes. His understanding of found or copied images was such that he isolated, framed, and created a context in which the image became an honorary or symbolic original in individual works and across multiple examples in a series. Although Cornell appropriated images made by others as his own, he did so without the critical edge or embrace of simulation for the sake of simulation that we associate with artists in the 1980s.

Instead, Cornell's engagement with images was highly idealistic, reflecting his quest to represent events, moments, and ideas by means of images. His emphasis on the pregnant moment assumed that it could be reconstituted, and he therefore assigned holistic significance to every part of every image that he associated with that moment because of the possibilities they represented. Yet he also viewed images as fragments, each with their own spatial, temporal, and metaphorical logic. His compositional talent lay in bringing fragments together in persuasive juxtapositions within the same frame or container, and the cohesiveness that this represents is the core concept of vision, editing, and cinematic montage as structural and expressive processes. His love of looking at film, again an experience originating in his childhood, communicated the significance of the framed image as a discrete field of vision and as part of a larger, unitary space that we can construe as his accumulation of series and variations.

We applaud the fact that Cornell's complex mediation of images, ideas, forms, and textures creates multiple paths to interpretation. We also continue to be uncomfortable with how he bypassed the mastery of traditional techniques of painting, drawing, and sculpting. At the heart of his "own way of seeing" is an approach to making images that incorporates subtle layers of reference and composition without relying on traditional materials and techniques. Visual and tactile, resonant and flexible, original and copied, the image was never ordinary to his eye. What does it mean to see an image? This is a question that Cornell invites us all to consider.

Notes

1 Cornell used the phrase "le chasseur d'images" (loosely, "image chaser" or "image hunter") to describe his process of assembling his dossier project, *GC 44* (1944–70, Smithsonian American Art Museum, Washington, DC), as well as for the title of one of the image-based sections in the dossier. The epigraphic is from Charles Baudelaire, "Mon coeur mis à nu" (My Heart Laid Bare) (1864) in *Journaux intimes* (1864–67; published 1887). Charles Baudelaire, *Intimate Journals*, trans. Christopher Isherwood (New York: Dover, 2006 [1947]), 96.

2 This phrase appears in Cornell's pamphlet "Portrait of Ondine Continued" in his exploration *Portrait of Ondine* (c. 1940–late 1960s, Smithsonian American Art Museum, Washington, DC), and in numerous drafts of this statement in the Joseph Cornell Papers, Archives of American Art, Smithsonian Institution, Washington, DC.

3 Cornell made this notation on the verso of his collage *Fountain of Youth* (1959, private collection).

4 Cognitive, aesthetic, and psychoanalytical studies offer a plethora of definitions and interpretations of seeing, images, and the relationship between the two realms. Cornell was equally aware and unaware of such studies dating back to the Renaissance, and he may or not have been attracted to post-1972 developments in these fields.

5 Harry Torczyner, a lawyer, friend, and art collector involved with René Magritte, in an interview with the author, 1978.

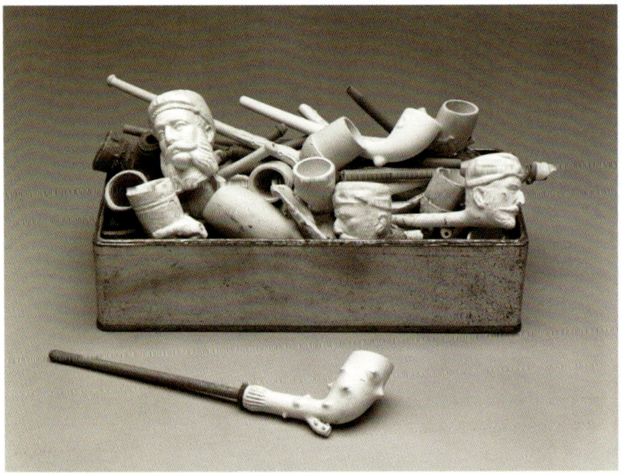

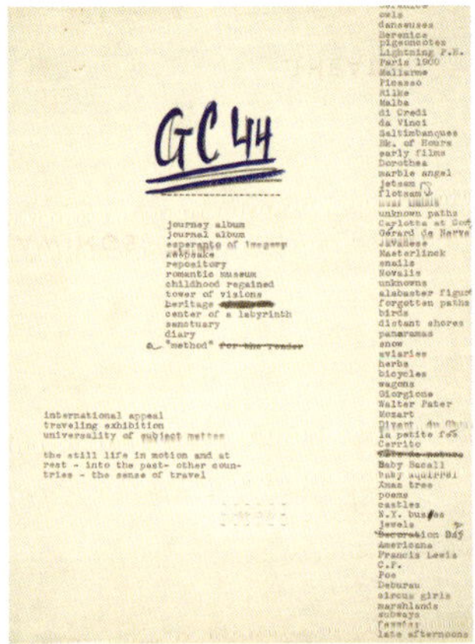

GC 44

journey album
journal album
esperanto of imagery
keepsake
repository
romantic museum
childhood regained
tower of visions
heritage
center of a labyrinth
sanctuary
diary
a "method"

international appeal
traveling exhibition
universality of subject matter

the still life in motion and at rest - into the past- other countries - the sense of travel

owls
danseuses
Berenice
pigeoncotes
Lightning P.H.
Paris 1900
Mallarme
Picasso
Rilke
Malba
di Credi
da Vinci
Saltimbanques
Bk. of Hours
early films
Dorothea
marble angel
jetsam
flotsam
unknown paths
Gérard de Nerval
Javanese
Maeterlinck
snails
Novalis
unknowns
forgotten paths
birds
distant shores
panoramas
snow
aviaries
herbs
bicycles
wagons
Giorgione
Walter Pater
Mozart
la petite fée
Cerrito
Baby Bacall
baby squirrel
Xmas tree
poems
castles
N.Y. busses
jewels
Americana
Francis Lewis
C.P.
Poe
Deburau
circus girls
marshlands
subways
late afternoons

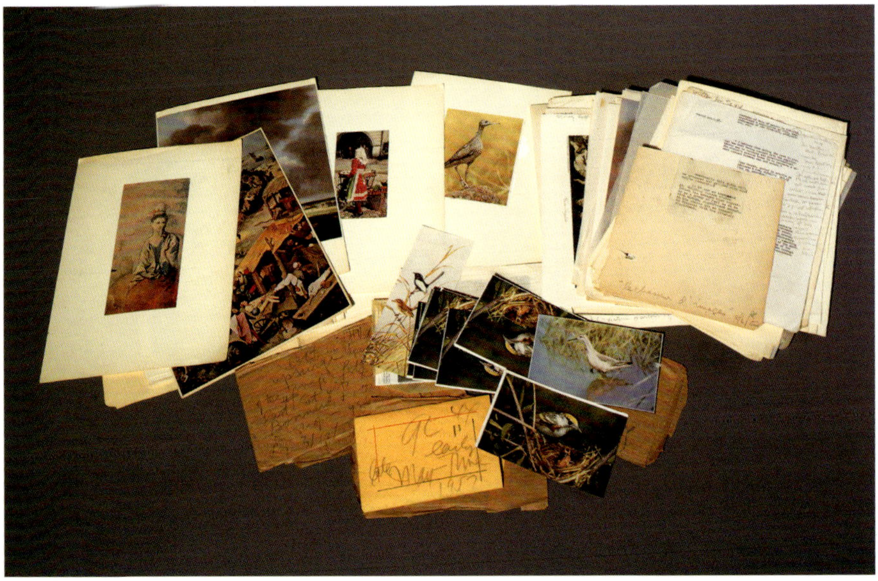

6.01 Metal box with clay pipes, Joseph Cornell Study Center, Smithsonian American Art Museum, Washington, DC **6.02, 6.03** Joseph Cornell, *GC 44*, notes 1944–61, and dossier, 1944–70, Joseph Cornell Study Center, Smithsonian American Art Museum, Washington, DC

Sweepings

Jodi Hauptman

Feb. 4. 1947
the recol. Of Fourth Avenue Book Stall Browsing 2nd Hand section
develop

the peculiarly "enriching" experience from the endless diversity of second hand books
flooding the stores & outside stalls
sense of refreshment from *ever changing* stock
anti-chronological

Max Ernst "Femme Cent Têtes" period
early morning sunlight* etc.
joy of discovery

my own Baedeker "inserts"

"the golden age" before W. War II
1¢ tables...
Prints etc.

the exploring that became creative
Cerrito—montage etc.

lunch hours Traphagen (escape) element

feelings aroused by Argosy albums
carte-de-visite
Radiguet quote[1]

Looking back at the reception of his oeuvre at the end of his life, Joseph Cornell expresses surprise that the works he had been making and exhibiting for almost four decades—his "so-called 'objects' (from Surrealist lingo)," he said, had "become so typecast as sculpture."[2] This doubt and discomfort with a single descriptive term for his work—he is not so sure about the use of the word *object*, either—is typical of Cornell, whose practice, based on collecting and juxtaposing, accumulating and assembling, is itself an argument for multiplicity and miscellany, one that had important consequences for the art of the twentieth century. Whether in collecting or naming, his evasion of singularity, along with life-long struggles with completion, is part and parcel of his approach, from his tendency to work in series to his return, years later, to cherished subjects; from his enormous and ongoing collection and storage of source material—boxes in all shapes and sizes, clay pipes (fig. 6.01), copies of magazines, to name just a few of the vast assortment—to enlarged and reduced duplicates of beloved images made via the Photostat machine; from his propensity to inscribe multiple titles on the backs of his boxes to his penchant for writing and rewriting, typing and retyping in his life-long journal. Though his deployment of multiplicity and accumulation can be seen in his famed box constructions and collages, it is in his less-known "explorations" where we find its most radical form.

Cornell's explorations are ever-expanding collections of paper ephemera: photographs from magazines and reproductions of works of art, sometimes mounted on cardstock and labeled by the artist, sometimes left loose; postcards; newspaper clippings; scrawled notes on scraps of paper and carefully typed text—all collected in the service of explicating, describing, and evoking a subject of the artist's choosing.[3] Over the course of his career, these topics included the romantic ballet, stars of opera and cinema, an imaginary child (*Collage from the Crystal Cage* [*Portrait of Berenice*], c. 1943–61, private collection), the night sky. Stored in cardboard or wooden boxes, paper folders, suitcases, or brown shopping bags, each fragment is itself a collection within a collection, as the texts were compilations of carefully copied quotations and the photographs, lithographs, and engravings were multiples of a single image or were grouped according to subject matter (species of birds or types of clouds, for example).

The label "exploration" seems fitting for a project that requires travel in the service of discovery and foregrounds process over permanence, wandering over stasis.[4] The making of the explorations, in fact, depended on what Cornell would describe as "city wandering" while viewing them was meant, he explained, to take the spectator on a virtual journey through time and space. Even so, Cornell expressed doubt about the word's suitability. In diaries, letters, or accompanying commentary, Cornell often surrounded the word *exploration* with quotation marks, perhaps a clue to the visual and verbal citations with which these projects trafficked, but also an indication of the word's contingency. Demonstrating that language was not immune to his voracious accumulation, Cornell had a list of other terms at the ready, including portfolio, dossier, file, scrapbook. And even though he may have used these words interchangeably, Cornell would have surely noted the subtle distinctions between them and what such differences would imply: more or fewer pictures, more or less permanently organized, and so on.

Cornell's uncertainty regarding nomenclature reflected his ongoing ruminations, doubt, and rethinking about what exactly these explorations could or should be: their function, conditions of creation, and format as well as the roles of artist and viewer. A key point of consistency within their ever-fluctuating content is his own self-conscious reflections on their making. Though Cornell is typically described as a romantic, a magician, a self-taught savant, or an alchemist, the thinking that we see in these explorations, along with related diary entries, notes in source files, and letters to friends and colleagues, proves that Cornell was a sophisticated and imaginative thinker and theorist about the creation and display of works of art. Taking a cue from his declaration that the exploration's "method is more important than subject matter," my task here is to extract Cornell's theoretical ambitions to more closely explicate his method.[5]

Though Cornell had collected clippings and other paper ephemera since at least 1926, his most elaborate exploration was sparked around 1944.[6] That spring he took a temporary job at a nursery near his home in Flushing, Queens. The experience at the garden center and, even more, the journey to and from work resulted in "a never ending series of surprises connected with flowers, forgotten paths, experiences on bicycle through fields heavy with summer and mellow with autumn."[7] Struck by certain images ("the passing of the delivery truck [small auto type] with its enseigne of the fish and smoked meats")[8] and enamored with seeing Queens by bike ("Walking to places inevitably produces fatigue. . . . Riding by car one takes too much for granted . . . . A bicycle affords a happy medium between the advantages of the two"),[9] Cornell was determined to capture, share, and communicate these visions and sensations, to "hold fast that overflowing 'bouquet' before the 'full flavor faded.'"[10]

He immediately realized that his own skills were woefully inadequate—it "would require the englamoured pen of a de la Mare"[11]—and that the tools at hand—brush, pigment, canvas—would be equally insufficient. Cornell sought alternate means, "devis[ing]" what he called a "method." "What could ever express those [orig] feelings in their felicity, depth, supreme happiness and wonder," he wrote. "Rather than ever expect to do so by a passage of written words or of a picture that might be painted, these experiences find an endless fulfilling in literature, painters' images, items found unexpectedly in newspapers, any sundry stray item that might bring an 'extension,' a renewal of the original magic."[12]

Cornell began to accumulate objects, articles, quotations from literary sources, and cut-out images, combining them with his own commentary: descriptions of related experiences, recordings of his dreams, and meditations on his own efforts. He lists, for example: "Maeterlinck 'Old Fashioned Flowers,' snails May 30, 1946 near Lawrence farm 50 Ave . . . . swaying with antennae outstretched like a ballet, pie wagon with sign and shelves of wares inside, De Quincey 'Glory of Motion' essay."[13] Cornell describes his collecting as both frenzied ("At first the material was gathered in the same spirit as one hoards souvenirs of every description of an especially precious journey")[14] and fortuitous (it "evolved in spite of myself, overwhelmingly completely 'accidentally'").[15] He referred to these materials and his commentary as *GC 44* (Garden Center 44) for the date and place of its beginnings, but with almost three decades of additions, the collection expanded well beyond the initial spark. From the beginning there was tension between expansive accumulation and careful editing, between organization and disarray, between focus and sweep. Aspiring to a form that could encompass a multimedia collection (this in itself was a way to restrict and focus), Cornell turned, as we see in a key note for the project (fig. 6.02), to the institutional purveyors of cataloguing and salvaging (the museum, the sanctuary, the library, the repository, the laboratory, the observatory)[16] and tools of organization: the list that seeks to capture multitudes in single file; the folder, a form of housing to systematize large fields and break them down into their constituent parts; the book, with its table of contents, chapters, and footnotes; the album, with its sequence of images; the travel diary that collates the world; the scrapbook that saves the past from disappearance; the portfolio that offers a neat display of images (fig. 6.03). His desire for more; his ability to see yet another connection, affinity, or association; his unearthing of still another quotation or image perpetually disrupted these structures and means. Taking into consideration Cornell's own (often frustrated) thinking on this subject,[17] can we see his inability to find closure in form or content less as a failure and more as the essence of his method? Could unfinish and contingency—the core of accumulation—be the crucial ingredients?

In seeing unfinish and accumulation as generative, as itself a practice or a method, my point of reference is the work of Walter Benjamin, specifically his *Passagen-Werk,* or Arcades Project. Like Cornell, Benjamin's "medium" in addressing his subject, the Paris arcades and, more generally, the nineteenth century, was the file or dossier—known as the *Konvolut*—and the acquisitions within. Benjamin began his project in 1927 and over many years gathered material on such topics as iron construction (Convolute F), Charles Baudelaire (Convolute J), the *flâneur* (Convolute J), including texts by Marcel Proust, Karl Marx, Honoré de Balzac, Louis Aragon, and Theodor Adorno, among many others, and illustrations such as *Glass Roofs and Iron Girders, Passage Vivienne, The Paris Stock Exchange, Mid-Nineteenth Century, The Sewers of Paris, by Nadar.* In each convolute the reader finds citations and commentary, much of which was written and rewritten,

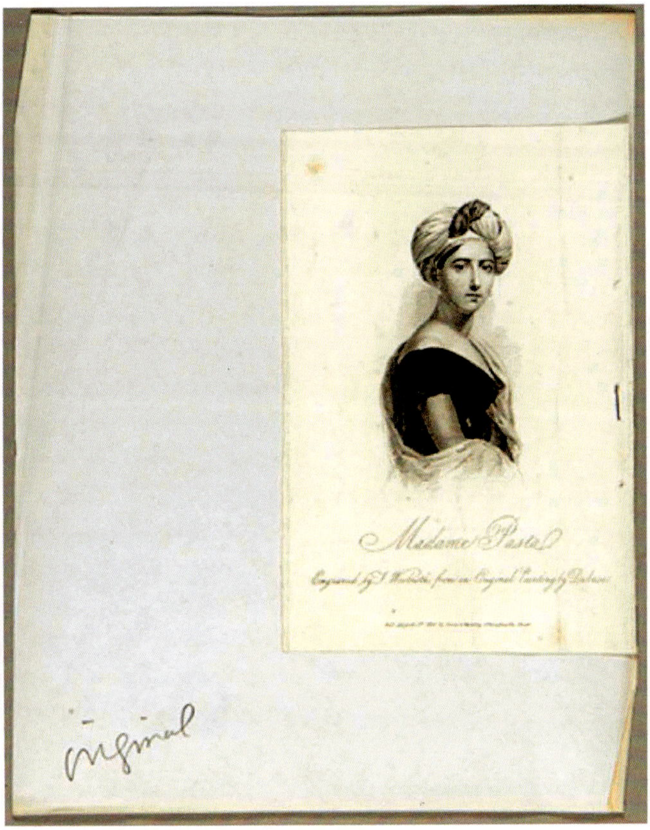

6.04 Portrait of Giuditta Pasta included in Joseph Cornell's *Guiditta Pasta Dossier*, 1940–60, Joseph Cornell Study Center, Smithsonian, American Art Museum, Washington, DC. Gift of Mr. and Mrs. John A. Benton

first in notebooks and then for the files. In the midst of these topic-based convolutes, Benjamin devotes one—known as Convolute N—to theoretical and philosophical reflections. Even more significant for us here is that the project, the research, the manuscript—whatever is the right word for this massive materialization of thought—remained unfinished. For Benjamin the "research project became an end in itself" its "elaborate organization" "might . . . bespeak a compositional principle," its "ostensible patchwork [can be regarded] as, de facto, a determinate literary form."[18] Resonant of Cornell's practice and prose, Benjamin writes, "Method of this project: literary montage. I needn't say anything. Merely show. I shall purloin no valuables, appropriate no ingenious formulations. But the rags, the refuse—these I will not inventory but allow, in the only way possible, to come into their own: by making use of them."[19]

Cornell's most explicit attempt to theorize his method can be found in the exploration devoted to the nineteenth-century opera singer Giuditta Pasta.[20] Sparked, like many of his other homages to female stars, by the discovery of a portrait (fig. 6.04), its goal was to make "this nostalgic subject of an opera singer of the past teem with present day applicability."[21] Cornell's exploration contains lithographic portraits of the singer, coins, pamphlets about the weather, a small collage joining Pasta to a white cockatoo, stamps, sheet music, pressed leaves, among myriad others. In his accompanying notes and commentary, Cornell maps the relationship of these items to his subject, some more direct than others. A chapter from Stendhal's book on Rossini is an obvious inclusion; in it the writer poses a question that Cornell's exploration seeks to answer: "Where should I find words adequate to describe the vision of celestial beauty which spread before us in dazzling glory when Madame Pasta sings, or the strange glimpses into the secrets of sublime and fantastic passions which her art affords us?" Other kinds of ephemera demonstrate Cornell's far-flung associations: "scurrying sailors," Baudelaire's discussion of crowds, clouds, and sky-scrapers. Fearing that he might lose himself in such redolent matter, Cornell warns of the "necessity of stating position and purpose and of presentation of something more than nostalgia."[22]

Certainly, a critical purpose is to reintroduce the artist/author (himself of course) not as a maker but as "a compiler." Culling his notes for the compiler's primary activities, we find an array of verbs: to correlate, to present, to consolidate, to compile, to appraise, to edit, to recognize, to bring to light, to search, to sort, to appropriate.[23]

These words are a glossary of possible actions to be used by the artist vis-à-vis his chosen medium, that is, found objects, images, and texts. Devoid of the hand, such "Creative filing" and "Creative arranging," the artist writes, are a form of "poetics . . . technique . . . [and] joyous creation," offering a vital chapter in the history of deskilling that begins with Postimpressionism and emerges, in various forms including here, as a persistent and prevalent tendency throughout the twentieth century.[24] Without the hand's implied dexterity and competence, these actions nonetheless demand the compiler's intervention as they imply such intrusions into the material as assembling, extracting, cutting, or highlighting.

Quotation was an essential aspect of Cornell's compiling practice. Quotations, painstakingly copied (and often re-copied) by hand or typewriter or cut from the pages of newspapers and magazines, comprise the majority of textual material in Cornell's explorations.[25] They also fill his journals as research or as additional description for something seen or felt when his own words were not enough. In the Pasta exploration, Cornell quotes extensively from Charles Lamb and Charles Baudelaire; note, for example, from the latter on crowds, as he records: "Not everybody has the gift of bathing himself in the crowd: finding pleasure in the masses is an art; and the only person who can indulge in a drunken spree of vitality, for which the human race itself foots the bill, is one to whom a fairy has breathed, in his cradle, a love of fancy dress and masquerades, a hatred of domesticity and a passion for travel."[26]

Cornell found the structural limitations of the box too restrictive and imagined, with explorations like that devoted to Pasta, "the realization, at long last, of the potentialities of fuller presentation of a given subject."[27] "A box," he explains, needs no "apologies" and "is something in itself, fully realized with its quality of 'architecture' or whatever element it is that gives the boxes a distinct appeal—sometimes a baffling simplicity that no words can communicate to one who has not had direct experience or confrontation with the box(es)."[28] Rather than a "'bolstering up' of the box" the "exploration" would offer "possibilities inherent in material of transcending original idea into paths further afield—where a surplus of material is on hand (or there is an opportunity of acquiring same."[29] So much research went into the making of each box—and Cornell was keenly aware of what was left behind: "Had satisfactory feeling about clearing up debris on the cellar floor—"sweepings" represent all the rich cross-currents ramifications etc that go into the boxes but which are not apparent (I feel at least) in the final result."[30] Thus, the explorations became a way for Cornell to repurpose his research.

From the role of the artist and the making of the work, Cornell's theorizing in the Pasta project takes on the hows and whys of presentation and display.[31] In his notes, we see him consider the work's format: Should it take the form of a landscape? A portrait? Might it have educational possibilities for students? As for its function, Cornell wonders how can one bring "to light . . . figures from the past hardly known"?

What are the "possibil[ities] of making this 'nostalgic' subject of an opera singer of the past teem with present day applicability"? Cornell also ruminates on how best to present a found image: Should it be simply clipped or should it be mounted? Should it stand alone or should it be seen as part of a group? Should it be left clean or should it have a caption? If yes to the latter, should it be placed on the mount below the image or farther away, on the verso? At one point he concludes that it would be better to have the image and caption on a "folded double mounting sheet" "so that the images may interpret themselves to the spectator in all their purity" and create "a kind of theme and variations." At one point, he considers making two separate files, in contrasting colors, one with images and the other with related text, to be kept together in a case in the "format of a newsboard cover." Cornell also borrows modes of scholarship in the service of order. In the case of Pasta, he suggests deploying footnotes as a way to provide a fuller context or make the viewer aware of relationships between and among elements. He also wonders how much of his own experiences—when the image was found and where, for example—should be revealed to the viewer. Does this enhance the experience or detract? One solution, he suggests, is to introduce another means of collecting data, the log book, writing that it may be kept "to preserve . . . their [his findings] original purity and flavor."[32]

In this context, it is useful to consider the book as a touchstone for Cornell's explorations—as well as a physical and conceptual *thing* with which Cornell continually engaged. Cornell collected books (at his death his library numbered in the thousands) and they served as critical sources for his research. Even as a devoted bibliophile, however, Cornell constantly challenged the book's architecture and authority as a container and custodian of knowledge, cutting into its flesh to create caverns for embedding objects within; depleting its innards so that it could be used as housing for his finds (see fig. 4.01); pasting playful paper ephemera onto its pages, wholly transforming a text's original purpose and meaning.[33] Though in the explorations Cornell exploits the structure of the book as a model for organization and presentation, he also resists its inherent constrictions. In the case of Pasta, Cornell considers the format of the scrapbook as it could encompass the "artist's working notes . . . possibly even making a completely personal such edition entirely done by self" while in *GC 44*, the novel—Alain-Fournier's *Le Grand Meaulnes* (Meaulnes the great, 1913)—is a prototype, with chapters organizing materials and imaginative titles inspiring equally evocative section headings. In the end, his ambitions for the explorations surpass the sequential rigor of the book form—even the scrapbook which he praises for its "impromptu quality—the freedom" is too restrictive.[34] Rejecting the idea of a prescribed beginning or end, he wants the viewer/reader to be "left to 'enter' the house on the hill [one of the sections in *GC 44*] via the plates of his own choosing.[35]

Wherever viewers/readers enter, they are Cornell's partners in plethora. In the Pasta exploration, he describes the "impromptu possibilities" of "plates, notes, etc." "so that students work along same time as compiler (self)" and argues that the "basic experience of the compiler (artist)" will encourage but not control the viewer's "own reaction & development or applying it to his own experience." The "stress" of the Pasta exploration, Cornell explains, should be less on the artist's take and should allow for an "ampler outlook" that a viewer may provide. The artist/compiler's job is thus to find the "pitiful relics"—here for example, "Scurrying sailors, Delacroix—diary not[e]s, love of city aspect, elab auto, Baudelaire—crowds, Lamb? London"—and the viewer has every opportunity to envision their own interpretation.

An essential component of the exploration is what Cornell calls an "extension," a concept of his own invention that relates to Baudelaire's notion of the correspondence, the Surrealist found object, and the way images are linked via association in forms of montage.[36] Mentioned and utilized in the Pasta exploration and most explicitly elucidated and theorized in *GC 44*, extensions are, Cornell explains, "evocations of experiences at unexpected times and places with such a force, significance & 'extension' or complement of the original inspiration & joy as to make of them worthy of being developed & evaluated."[37] For example, Cornell describes "a routine trip to the Fourth Avenue book-stalls with some of that 'after-glow' of *GC 44* in which something in a magazine might renew or 'extend' the original magic."[38] In addition to extending an experience, the extension links past and present or reawakens the past through a contemporary object or event. Even the most humdrum occurrence can "evok[e] something elusive (but real) of the past which made the present enjoyment of spectacle (scenery, people etc.)—a feeling that a *particular* moment of past was transmuting a pres[e]nt moment within 'unnamed but significant touch.'"[39]

Cornell wavers between foregrounding what is undoubtedly personal about what he finds and sees and communicating what he envisions as universal. His reflections on ways to publish his explorations and his sense that a few, like Pasta, would engage students demonstrates his ambitions for a wide reach, while more often than not the reasons he includes a particular item remain private, even intimate. He writes, for example, about the way the objects he "discovers" are "waiting" for him and "smiling lend themselves if wanted."[40] But he also frets over the diminution of his intentions ("consequent bric-a-brac aspect of such englamoured objects") when the associations become too personal.[41]

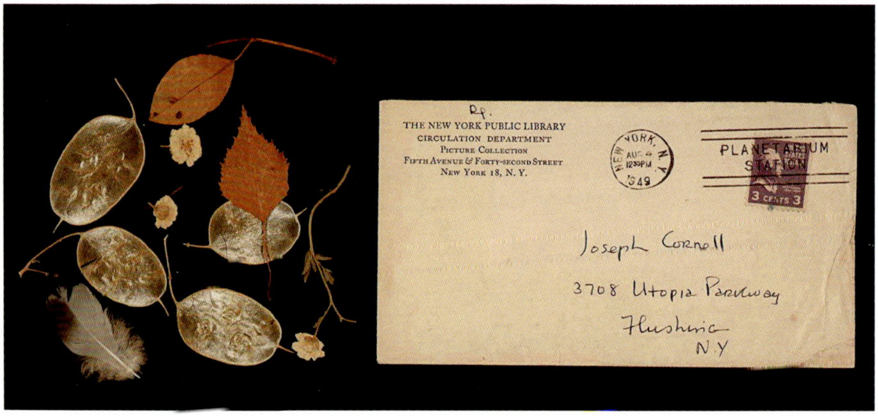

6.05 Envelope containing leaves, flowers, seeds, and a feather, collected on August 4, 1949, Joseph Cornell Study Center, Smithsonian American Art Museum, Washington, DC. Gift of Mr. and Mrs. John A. Benton

Cornell not only focuses on acquisition in his reflections on the practice of the explorations, he also shows a deep awareness of the need for limitation, admitting that compiling can easily tip into chaos: "so voluminously did thus pile up material bewilderingly diffuse,—prints, clippings, memorabilia etc etc," he writes, "that innumerable threshings have been imperative during the 10 years of accumulation."[42] Editing, he realizes, demands vigilance: "A discipline," he writes, "will also be acquired against the habit of too much piling up of unness. material."[43] Acquiring that discipline, however, would prove largely unattainable.

Bound or boundless, what are the sources that allowed Cornell's "sweeping," his "pil[ing] upon," and his "creative arranging," to become a full-blown technique? For someone who spent his career gathering and compiling, there are no doubt many sources we might turn to—the artist himself describes the influence of "modern French painting and music at least a dozen years before doing creative work"[44]—but I want to focus here on three that showed Cornell the creative possibilities inherent in association: his encounter with Surrealism, his experience at the New York Public Library's Picture Collection, and his engagement with cinema.

The first, of course, is well-trodden territory. In 1931 Cornell first visits the Julien Levy Gallery, where his own proclivities are reflected back at him in frames or on pedestals. Levy and the exhibitions he organized at his gallery showed Cornell that the found object could be deployed as a work of art, that cut and pasted images were as vital as painting. On this front, Cornell's encounter with Max Ernst's *La Femme 100 Têtes* (The Hundred headless woman, 1929), was crucial. As an extended

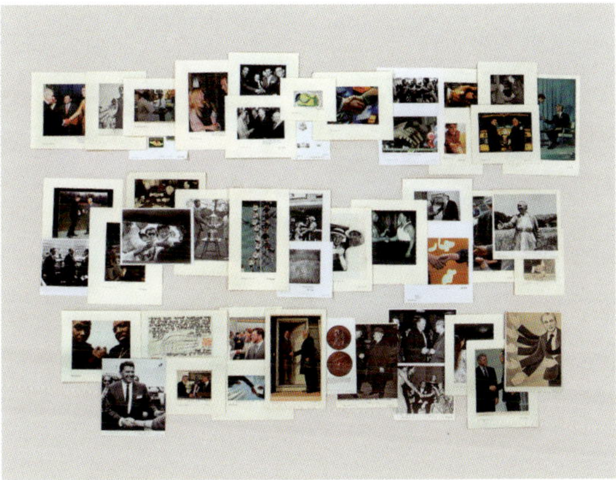

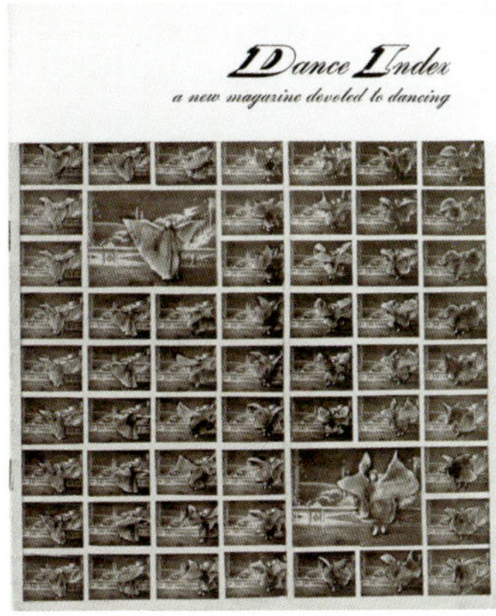

6.06 Taryn Simon, *Folder: Handshaking*, 2012, archival inkjet print, 47 × 62 in., Gagosian Gallery, New York **6.07** Cover of *Dance Index* 1, no. 3 (March 1942), designed by Joseph Cornell, Joseph Cornell Study Center, Smithsonian American Art Museum, Washington, DC

series of images, made of cut and pasted nineteenth-century wood engravings, it confirmed Cornell's nascent interests: in the outmoded, in the cutting and stitching together of disparate images, and the benefits of working in series. Cornell's *Story without a Name—for Max Ernst* (1942, artist's album containing reproductions of 16 preexisting collages by Cornell, published in *View* 2, 1 [April 1942]), is said to be a direct response, but what he would have described as the "white magic" variety.[45]

Even more crucial, the combinatory strategies Cornell exploits in his explorations, including the juxtaposition of chronological moments, material heterogeneity, shifts in scale, and varied relations between individuals and groups would have long been familiar to Cornell from his immersion in the files of the New York Public Library's Picture Collection (fig. 6.05). Though following certain taxonomic organizational principles derived from the library's own cataloguing practice—dividing material by subjects, alphabetical headings, cross referencing, for example—the files themselves were expansive interpretations, meant to enlarge an understanding of a topic rather than to focus it. The collection was founded in 1914 to serve the growing image-based media industry and recognized advances in reproduction technologies.[46] By the end of its first year, the library had made almost 18,000 images available for patrons and by 1926 the Picture Collection officially began. Today, with twelve million pictures on line, use of the collection is a far cry from Cornell's era, when patrons could physically flip through racks organized by subject—the pictures were clipped from various sources so "abacus," "birds," "moving pictures," or "men shaking hands," (fig. 6.06) would be filled with images of varying shapes, sizes, dates, mediums, resolutions, and sources. In 1934, when Cornell frequented the collection, there were 667,967 items to peruse. The Picture Collection demonstrated to him the expansiveness of association, the veritable stew of images and ideas that can find a home (if not harmony) together.

Above all, it was Cornell's engagement with cinema that most impacted the development of a theoretical apparatus for his explorations.[47] If the Picture Collection demonstrated expansiveness, cinema taught him ways to harness multiple and ever-accumulating images. As a collector and maker of films, Cornell had a deep understanding of the medium's materiality. On a small viewer in his basement studio, he would thread strips of celluloid through two sheets of glass and then hand crank the reel, allowing the image to be projected on a small illuminated screen. He could see that motion pictures are constructed from chains of individual images linked either as complements or contrasts (from this position the break between each may be just as significant as the image itself). He exploited the essence of film's one-after-another sequence in several key works. For the March 1942 cover of *Dance Index*, Cornell appropriated a landmark of early cinema, the 1895 film of Loie Fuller performing her famous Fire Dance (fig. 6.07). Cornell simply laid out strips of film in a grid across the magazine's cover, breaking down her choreography and the cinematic representation of it into its constituent parts: a sequence of bodily moves, a succession of stills. In box constructions like *Medici Slot Machine* (fig. 6.08), Cornell creates his own film strips without any film at all (proving something can be cinematic without celluloid), isolating critical aspects of the cinema, including movement and time. Cornell duplicates the faces of three different subjects and glues them onto blocks that are installed in stacks around the box's main figure. By making minute adjustments so that the blocks do not align and by slightly altering the cropping from image to image, the faces appear animated (seeming to run with the herky-jerky quality of early movies) as our eyes travel from top to bottom.[48]

As an avid student and true fan of the cinema, Cornell appreciated cinema's reach, its visual, narrative, and conceptual possibilities: from the bodily transformations and magic tricks seen in the films of Georges Méliès and Émile Cohl or access to far-flung territories and points of view provided in Ferdinand Zecca's travelogues, to name just a few of the pioneers of early cinema Cornell admired.[49] He embarked on his first forays into moviemaking in the 1930s using techniques of collage and montage that he was also deploying in works on paper (for himself and for commercial purposes) and in modest assemblings of found material, making the filmmaker, too, primarily a compiler. He joined together fragments of celluloid he had collected, creating a body of collage films that were extraordinarily influential

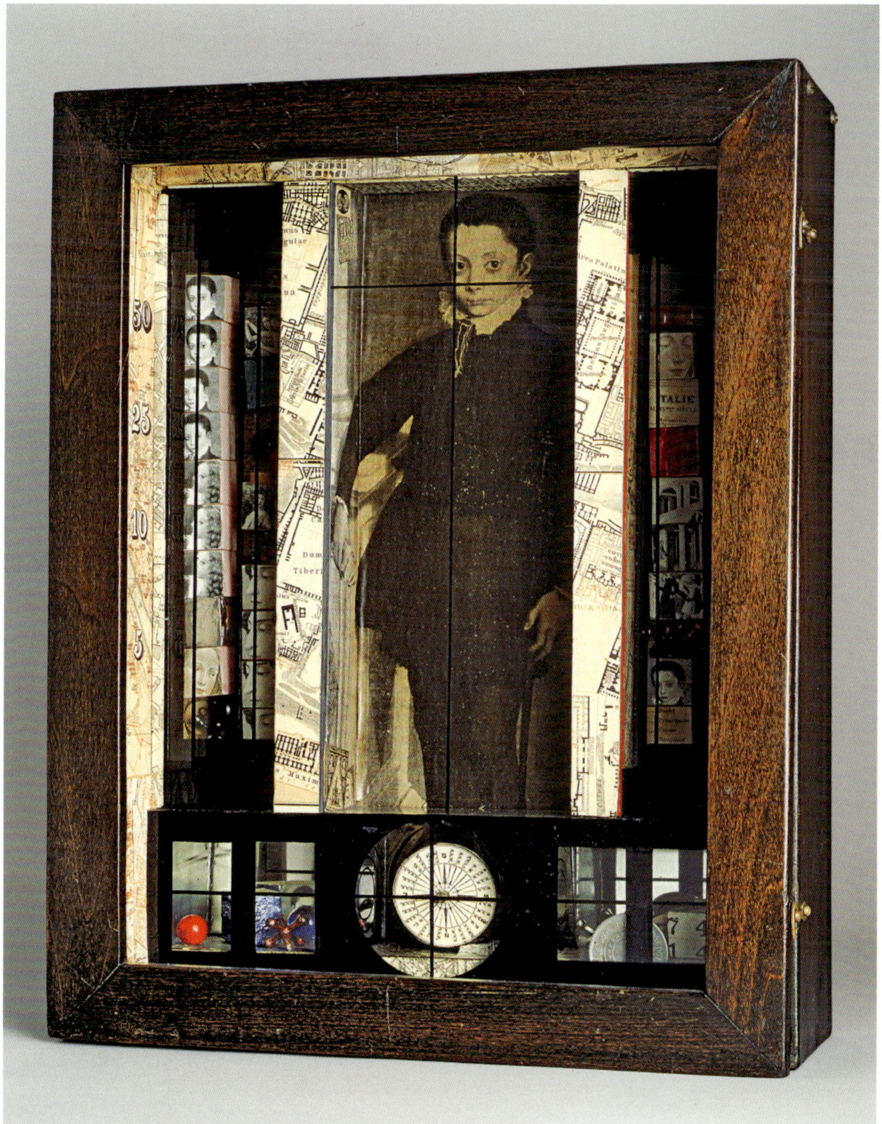

6.08 Joseph Cornell, *Medici Slot Machine*, 1942, box construction, 15 ½ × 12 × 4 ⅜ in., The Reis Family Collection

in the history of filmmaking in the twentieth century, despite their status as unfinished fragments.[50]

Although the technical possibilities were primitive, Cornell used what he had at hand, experimenting on his viewer with speeding up, slowing down, or reversing his footage or cutting and pasting each or groups of frames to create strange, uncanny shifts in scale, chronology, and point of view. The selection of film fragments, the recycling of lost and found images, is equivalent to—or even a form of—the quotation that, we have seen, was a key aspect of his compiling practice. While we think of quotations as purely textual, the film fragments serve as a kind of quote, an excision from one source used in another. Working with these pieces, these quotations, taught Cornell the explosive and evocative possibilities of montage, the way two images can meet and relate across the divide of the frame, as well as the way images can be ordered into sequences to build a story or break it down (it is the chain, the relation of one to another that remains essential).

Take a film fragment known as *Bookstalls*, for example (1940s). It is another example of Cornell's meditations on the book, but is also a canny take on cinema itself. The film opens with a view of the Paris skyline and then focuses on a boy among a group of men perusing the wares at a bookstall along the Seine in the shadow of Notre Dame. The boy opens a small volume and the film cuts to a still image that, given its position in the narrative sequence, seems to be what the boy sees inside the book (fig. 6.09). Placed in the position of the boy/reader, we see his/our fingers holding what now appears to be a large photo album. After a few turns of the album's pages, there is a cut to a scene in motion, as if the pictures in the album have now come to life. The footage has been cut from a travelogue, but Cornell jumbled the order of the intertitles and reversed the direction (and increased the speed) of the film at points to scramble the original structure. Finally, the film ends with a return to Paris, where we started, at the bookstalls with the same boy and, ultimately, his closing of the book. While the film argues for the wonders of reading, it also shows that cinema has surpassed the book, offering a far greater range of image and subject, movement, and a heightened experience of time.

Book and film, however, remain reliant on sequence: a one-after-another relationship of image to image, page to page, word to word. Even though the chains of images or text can extend indefinitely, this extension is in only two directions, backward and forward. With his explorations (and the manifold associations represented within), Cornell imagined a form that went beyond the sequential, that was less a chain and more of a web, ever-expanding in all directions and dimensions. This expansiveness can be seen in the Pasta exploration: in the multiple points of entry (no beginning and no end), in notes that stretch across sheets without a particular order

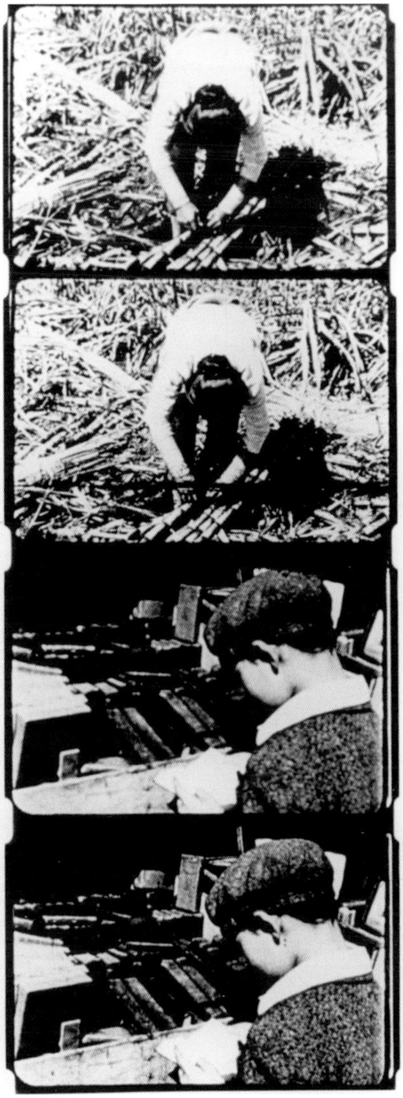

6.09 Frames from Joseph Cornell's film *Bookstalls*, 1940s, Courtesy of Anthology Film Archives, New York

("diary entries scattered"), in the compulsion to add and to link and to reveal and to find ("prolonged accumulation," the search for an "ampler outlook"), in the visual and textual quotations ("as a means of 'launching' this material"), in its temporality in which present is intimately linked to the past ("bringing to light . . . figures from the past hardly known or presented for the first time"). And though Cornell's notes often refer to a traditional final outcome for his research—"a view to feuilleton, brochure and/or magazine article"—what is most defining about Pasta and the other explorations is his ultimate resistance to such goals, his refusal of finish, finality, form. Instead, the explorations argue for a series of continuations: an extended elaboration of content, thus shifting the function of the artist from maker to compiler; a suite of enigmatic relationships among images based on association and joined by montage, thus transforming the role of the viewer; challenges to structure, nomenclature, and taxonomy, thus contesting traditional modes of museological presentation and display and setting acquisition as a perpetual state; accessing the past through the present, thus offering an alternate way to experience the historical people and events that are so often his subjects; proposing accumulation and unfinish as the material conditions of the work of art, thus allowing, as Cornell would put it, an alternate way of seeing.

In the notes from 1947 that serve as the epigraph to this essay, Cornell presents a constellation of what would remain his life-long passions and concerns: book collecting, the second-hand object, Surrealism, printed ephemera, old photographs, nineteenth-century literature, quotation. The list format in which these items are presented—the one after another that Cornell's explorations both seek to exploit and undermine—demonstrates the artist's propensity to collect while the relationships that may be plotted among them offer a microcosm of the artist's approach to objects and experiences: to connect through association. Embedded in the text itself is the word *montage*—an apt term, as we have seen, for Cornell's process of linkage and juxtaposition. Most important, Cornell offers a concise description summing up the methodology presented here, a practice that defies the finality that most art aspires to, and instead revels in continuation and contingency: "the exploring that became creative."

Notes

1 Joseph Cornell Papers, Archives of American Art, Smithsonian Institution, Washington, DC (hereafter abbreviated JCP), Reel 1076: Frames 0002–3. I am grateful to Matthew Affron and Maria Gough for their generosity and insight in discussing Cornell's practice and the subject of this text and to Anne Morra for essential help with Cornell's films.

2 Joseph Cornell, letter to Elizabeth Fairbank, Herbert F. Johnson Museum of Art, Cornell University, Ithaca, New York, March 12, 1967, quoted in Washington 2006, 103.

3 My understanding of Cornell's "explorations" is informed by Lynda Roscoe Hartigan's wonderful essay "Joseph Cornell's Explorations: Art on File" in Philadelphia 1998, 221–43. As the founding director of the Joseph Cornell Study Center at the Smithsonian American Art Museum, Hartigan's work on Cornell is fundamental to understanding the artist and his practice.

4 Hartigan also discusses what she describes as "a thicket of terms" in his explorations. See Hartigan, "Joseph Cornell's Explorations," 223–24.

5 Cornell's notes as part of the "Pasta Exploration," JCP, box 52.

6 His earliest exploration was probably *Portrait of Ondine*, a box of paper texts, lithographs, reproductions of works of art, etc., related to the ballerina Fanny Cerrito; its existence was recorded by the artist by 1941. See Hartigan, "Joseph Cornell's Explorations," 225–26; and my own discussion in Kynaston McShine, ed., *The Museum as Muse: Artists Reflect* (New York: Museum of Modern Art, 1999), 58–59 .

7 JCP, "Garden Center 1944" Source File, 1072: 0413, July 22, 1948.

8 Ibid., 1072: 0121.

9 "Random Notes, Garden Center '44," in Caws 1993, 107.

10 JCP, "Garden Center 1944," Source File, 1072: 0413.

11 Ibid.

12 JCP, "Garden Center 1944," Source File, 1072: 0466.

13 Ibid., 1072: 0121.

14 Ibid., 1072: 0508–11.

15 Ibid., 1072: 0123.

16 On artists and archives, see Sven Spieker, *The Big Archive: Art from Bureaucracy* (Cambridge: MIT Press, 2008).

17 See the discussion of Cornell's "frustration" in Hartigan, "Joseph Cornell's Explorations," 221–22.

18 Howard Eiland and Kevin McLaughlin, "Translators' Foreword," in Walter Benjamin, *The Arcades Project* ed. Rolf Tiedemann, trans. Howard Eiland and Kevin McLaughlin (Cambridge: Harvard University Press, 1999), xi. This volume is a full translation. Benjamin and Cornell share an uncanny similarity in interests and approach. They lived and worked under very different conditions, but born only just over a decade apart, they matured in a time when each of their cities and their respective image cultures were undergoing tremendous change—and their thinking reflected this. For both, however, their guiding enthusiasm was for the past, specifically the nineteenth century, and they had similar ideas about how to access that past; collecting its fragments was one fundamental aspect. For further discussion regarding the points of coincidence between these two figures, see Hauptman 1999, 37–40.

19 Benjamin, *The Arcades Project,* 460.

20 Cornell's notes for this project are stored in a wooden box, along with a host of other found objects and ephemera, in JCP, box 52, AAA.

21 Unless otherwise indicated, all quotations about the Pasta exploration can be found in these notes, JCP, box 52.

22 Though the Pasta exploration is never completed, Cornell did finish a number of boxes related to this subject, for example, *Planet Set, Tête Etoilée, Giuditta Pasta (dédicace)*, 1950. For a very interesting reading of this work and of Cornell's interest in Pasta, see Mundy, 2004.

23 These call to mind Richard Serra's *Verb List*, 1967–68 (The Museum of Modern Art, New York), an accounting of his engagement with material. With infinitives such as "to roll, to crease, to fold, to suspend, to support, to rotate, to impress," Serra offers a set of actions and reveals the artist's activities as doing something to something else—a far more aggressive lexicon of operations than those registered by Cornell.

24 Cornell Papers, in Caws 1993, 254. For deskilling as a thematic, see Benjamin H. D. Buchloh, "Hans Haacke: Memory and Instrumental Reason" (1988) in his *Neo-Avantgarde and Culture Industry* (Cambridge: MIT Press, 2000), 203–41.

25 Here again in the case of quotation and citation, we see a striking similarity with Benjamin's Arcades Project: "To write history thus means to *cite* history. It belongs to the concept of citation, however, that the historical object in each case is torn from its context." Benjamin, *The Arcades Project*, 476.

26 Pasta exploration, JCP, box 52.

27 JCP, Dürer File, AAA, box 17.

28 Ibid. Interestingly, in thinking about how to expand the boxes' potential, Cornell considers "the possib. or advisability of presenting one, 2 or 3 boxes in sketch form, semi-completed, in ADDITION to admitted variations"; ibid.

29 For "bolstering," see ibid.; for "possibilities," see Caws 1993, 177.

30 Ibid., 128.

31 See notes in Pasta exploration, JCP, box 52.

32 JCP, Garden Center 1944 File, 1072: 0464.

33 Cornell's most elaborate engagement with a single book is his *Untitled Book Object (Journal d'agriculture pratique et Journal de l'agriculture)* (1933-45), Philadelphia Museum of Art, in which he cut into, pasted onto, and added snippets of text. See the facsimile and accompanying essays, Leppanen-Guerra and Tashjian 2012.

34 JCP, Garden Center 1944, 1072: 0499.

35 Ibid., 1072: 0464.

36 Baudelaire and the idea of correspondence loom large in Cornell's imagination, appearing frequently in his journals. An interesting comparison, beyond the scope here, would be to think through Cornell's ideas about associating images vis-à-vis Roman Jakobson's concept of the metonymic. See Roman Jakobson, "Two Aspects of Language and Two Types of Aphasic Disturbances" in *Language in Literature* (Cambridge, MA: Belknap Press, 1987), 95–114. As for montage, Cornell would have known Sergei Eisenstein's films, but there is no significant discussion of them in his journals. Importantly, there is a letter from Cornell to Jay Leyda, dated April 17, 1935, now in the archives of Anthology Film Archives, in which he reveals his knowledge and interest in the European avant-garde cinema. He tells Leyda–who had studied with Eisenstein in the Soviet Union and then worked as a curator at the Museum of Modern Art—that he is interested in stills from Eisenstein and Dziga Vertov, among others. My thanks to Matthew Affron for bringing this letter to my attention.

37 JCP, 1072: 0148.

38 Ibid., 1072: 0379.

39 Ibid., 1072: 0158.

40 Ibid., 1072: 0495.

41 Ibid., 1072:0508–11. In the Pasta exploration, Cornell notes the need for "consideration of possibly losing purely individual flavor."

42 Ibid., 1072: 0508–11.

43 Ibid., 1072:0123–25. Another expression of defeat in the face of too much accumulation: "so that now before a bulging chaos of notes and souvenirs and engulfing futility at the thought of formulation, a hopelessness of adequate expression and recapture of countless moments and longer periods"; ibid., 1072: 0389. Hartigan calls frustration "a powerful motivational force in Cornell's work." See Hartigan, "Joseph Cornell's Explorations," 223.

44 JCP, 1059: 0833. This is a draft of a letter explaining his work.

45 Cornell classed his involvement with Surrealism as "white magic" as opposed to the "black magic" of mainstream figures like Salvador Dalí and André Breton. See, for example, Cornell's letter to Charles Henri Ford, September 25, 1940, Getty Research Library, Charles Henri Ford Papers, 1920–1989, archival acc. 900194.

46 For the history of the New York Public Library Picture Collection and the statistics cited here, see Anthony T. Troncale, "Worth Beyond Words: Romana Javitz and The New York Public Library's Picture Collection," originally published in *Biblion: Bulletin of the New York Public Library* 4, no. 1 (Fall 1995); see http://www.ypl.org/locations/tid/45/node/62019.

47 For a more extensive discussion of Cornell's engagement with cinema, see Hauptman 1999.

48 The hand-made film strips seen here echo similar efforts in other projects: small games like his *Jouets surréalistes*, optical toys that offer the illusion of movement through persistence of vision, and boxes and collages that allude to the time-motion studies of Étienne-Jules Marey and Eadweard Muybridge or seek to recreate the experience of viewing images through protocinematic machines like the zoetrope and arcade gadgets like kinetoscopes and mutoscopes.

49 See excerpts from program notes for various film screenings he would organize during the 1940s reproduced in Washington 2006, 69.

50 His *Rose Hobart*, 1936, is a different case, a wholly finished work.

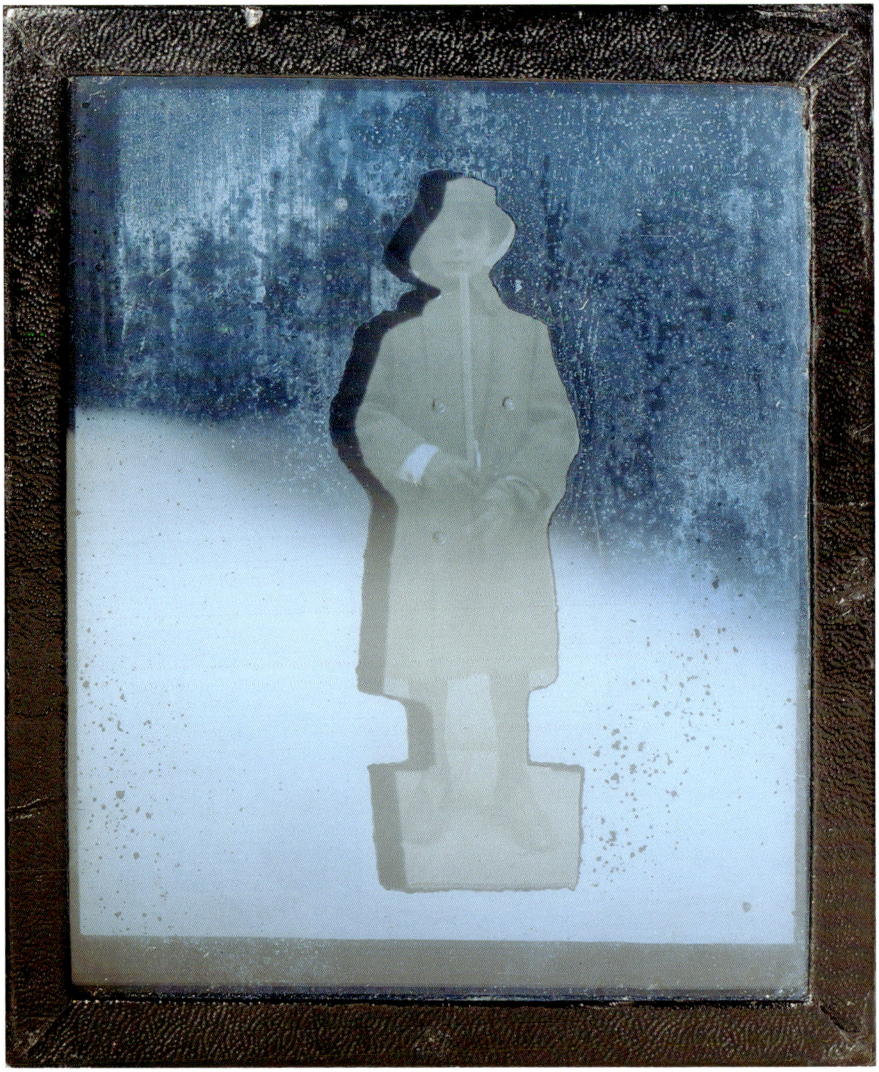

7.01 Joseph Cornell, *Portrait of Julien Levy, Daguerreotype-Object*, c. 1938–39, box construction, 5 3/16 × 4 3/16 × 1 in., Philadelphia Museum of Art. 125th Anniversary Acquisition, The Lynn and Harold Honickman Gift of the Julien Levy Collection, 2001

Joseph Cornell's Optical Toys

Matthew Affron

In late March 1941, André Breton and his family departed Marseille for the Caribbean on a small steamer called the *Capitaine Paul-Lemerle*. They boarded another vessel in mid-May for the journey from Martinique to the United States, and in July arrived in New York. There Breton quickly resumed his various activities as writer, cultural organizer, and propagandist of Surrealism. New York, the home of a burgeoning Surrealist network, would serve as his base of operations during five years of wartime exile.[1]

Among Breton's first public statements in this American period was an interview with Charles Henri Ford, the poet, artist, and editor of *View* magazine, published in that journal's October–November 1941 "Surrealist Number." Breton discusses the meaning of France's defeat, gives his initial impressions of the American scene, and offers his thoughts on the manner in which poets and artists might respond to the European conflict. He also affirms the continued relevance of a Baudelairian conception of the modern and speaks of the imperative to "seek the new" as a point of resistance against all forces that would restrain freedom. Finally, he names a roster of friends and colleagues who stand with him for this principle. The list includes many poets and painters who had been associated with the Surrealist group in Paris; some of these were already or would soon be fellow exiles. Breton also makes reference to a few younger artists from the Americas. One of these is Joseph Cornell.[2]

Breton mentioned Cornell a second time, adding a few morsels of commentary, in an essay entitled "Genesis and Perspective of Surrealism," composed in the second half of 1941 and published a year later as a preface in the inaugural catalogue of Art of This Century, Peggy Guggenheim's hybrid museum and gallery on New York's 57th Street, which served as a gathering place for the European avant-garde in exile. Breton begins this essay by invoking the first European navigators to the New World as ancestors of the paradigm-shifting modern artist: "Like Christopher Columbus who, on the verge of discovering the Antilles, believed he was on the road to India, so in the twentieth century the painter found himself confronted by a new world before it occurred to him that he could depart from the old." He then launches into a survey of leading artists and European art movements represented in the Art of This Century collection, whose assembly he had helped advise.[3]

He discusses the overthrow of mimesis in Cubism and abstract art and touches on the machine aesthetic in Futurism and Dada. His main topic, however, is the emergence and development of Surrealist art. Toward the end of the essay, he highlights two painters, the German Richard Oelze and the Belgian Paul Delvaux, and two makers of sculptural constructions, the German Hans Bellmer and the American Cornell, as artists in whose work "the sap of *Surrealism* also rises from the great root-system of dream-life."[4]

It is understandable that Breton would have thought of Cornell in this instance, since his work was being featured at Art of This Century. Moreover, Cornell would have been on Breton's radar screen since 1933, when the artist sent him a photograph of one of his early bell jar objects.[5] Further traces of Cornell's work would reach Breton over the next several years—the period in which the writer laid out, in such essays as "Équation de l'objet trouvé" (Equation of the found object) of 1934 and "Crisis of the Object," published in the wake of the May 1936 *Exposition surréaliste d'objets* (Surrealist exhibition of objects) at the Galerie Charles Ratton in Paris, much of his theory of the found object as a catalyst for unconscious desire (see figs. 3.02–.04).[6] Breton possessed a copy of the publication that accompanied the 1936 *Surréalisme* exhibition at the Julien Levy Gallery in New York, with cover image by Cornell. He would have been familiar with George Platt Lynes's photograph of components from Cornell's 1936 *Untitled* (*Soap Bubble Set*) (The Wadsworth Atheneum Museum of Art, Hartford) as reproduced in Alfred H. Barr's book accompanying the exhibition *Fantastic Art, Dada, Surrealism* at the Museum of Modern Art in the same year.[7] *Minotaure*, the Parisian Surrealist journal, had published Cornell's early object *Untitled* (*Glass Bell*) (c. 1932, see fig. 3.05) in its winter 1937 issue.[8] Finally, Cornell was the sole American artist represented at the 1938 *Exposition internationale du Surréalisme* (International exhibition of Surrealism) that Breton organized and staged at the Galerie Beaux-Arts in Paris. Reproduced in the publication accompanying that exhibition was an early collage by Cornell depicting a flattened cutout of a lady of fashion being run through a sewing machine in the setting of a garment factory. The exhibition checklist also lists unspecified objects by Cornell that, according to gallery records, had been consigned by the artist Max Ernst.[9]

But if Breton's remarks on Cornell in "Genesis and Perspective of Surrealism" reward our attention here, it is because they do more than simply show that the founder of Surrealism had an interest in the American artist's work. They are useful because Breton puts his finger on a key feature of Cornell's sensibility: his fascination with optical illusions and the tricky toys used to create them. Here is Breton's often cited and rarely understood sentence about Cornell: "And at the extreme limits of a point of view which may be characterized as stereotypical and anaglyphic, or of the stereotyped vision of things, Cornell has devised an experiment which completely overturns the conventional use of the object."[10] The key words—*stereotypical, stereotyped,* and *anaglyphic*—require some clarification. The first two should not be taken in the familiar sense of stereotype, a preconceived mental representation that we project onto others. Instead, Breton was drawing on the specialized vocabulary of psychoanalysis, where stereotypy refers to the symptoms of a psychological disorder: the involuntary repetition of apparently meaningless words and gestures that express the unconscious fixations of the schizophrenic patient. Breton had begun pondering the meaning of the phenomenon during his time as an orderly at the Saint-Dizier army psychiatric center in 1916, just as he was coming to understand the perturbed mind as a free mind and madness as a creative resource. In a well-known letter of that era to his friend Theodore Fraenkel, Breton referred to verbal stereotypy as a form of poetic expression.[11] Stereotypy would continue to hold his interest. In a 1933 essay entitled "The Automatic Message," he associated it with the basic Surrealist principle of psychic automatism, or the creation of works of literature or art in a trancelike or dream state.[12]

Did Breton think of stereotypy as a descriptor for sculptural constructions? The best evidence is in a well-known passage from the 1934 essay "Équation de l'objet trouvé" (Equation of the found object), which was reworked by Breton in his 1937 novel *Mad Love* (*L'Amour fou*), where he had used the concept in discussing the Surrealist found object as a material projection of associations in the mind of the viewer. Breton recalls a visit with the sculptor Alberto Giacometti to the Saint-Ouen flea market in the northern part of Paris, where they hoped to chance upon mysterious, eloquent objects. Breton comes across a large wooden spoon with a handle in the form of a little shoe. Once he has brought the object home, he is hit by its latent associations. The entire spoon seems to change before his eyes, assuming the silhouette of a dancer's slipper. Breton describes the enchanting effect as one of infinite recursion: "In fact the slipper-heel presided over the spell cast, containing in itself the very *source* of the *stereotype* (the heel of this shoe heel could have been a shoe, whose heel itself . . . and so on)."[13] A similar effect of *mise en abyme* (mirror construction)—for Breton the sign of the existence of an alternate reality—is frequently found in Cornell's work.

If Breton uses the concept of stereotypy to characterize the poetics of Cornell's art of the found object, his second key term opens up a rich Surrealist context for that art. He refers to Cornell as an artist with an "anaglyphic" point of view. The anaglyph process is a method of producing three-dimensional appearances from simple linear diagrams, photographs, or moving pictures. A given image is printed twice in different colors (red and a contrasting tone) and superimposed with a slight lateral displacement corresponding to the viewpoints of the right and left eye. The viewer looks through lenses in the same two colors. As with other stereoscopic technologies, what results is an immersion in the illusion of tridimensionality.[14] With this discussion of the anaglyphic image, Breton in effect connects Cornell to a broader Surrealist engagement with both the aesthetics of optical illusion and a rich visual tradition of devices that are used to duplicate visual reality, and simultaneously, to generate unreal fantasies. Two well-known examples can be cited as standing for this line of inquiry. In an image from his 1929–30 collage novel *A Little Girl Dreams of Taking the Veil*, Max Ernst presents an image of a zoetrope, the mechanical device that consists of a rotating cylinder containing a series of images representing the stages of a body in motion, in this case a sequence of figurines representing a seagull in flight, as originally published by Étienne-Jules Marey, the physiologist and pioneer of chronophotography, in *La Nature*, a French magazine of popularized science, in 1877.[15] Following his usual practice, Ernst uses collage to make the source image strange. He takes a separate illustration from Marey's article, an image of a pigeon in flight, and pastes it in. In its new context, the additional bird seems to come alive—and seems to be in the process of flying the coop. Also through collage, Ernst places the eponymous young girl of his novel in a strange place: not the usual spectator's position, looking into the rotating device through the slits as repeated images come into lifelike motion, but instead literally within the gyratory drum and therefore within the scene of illusion, where she swoons.[16]

The second example is Marcel Duchamp's *Anémic Cinéma* of 1926, a film composed of alternating shots of disks printed with flat spiral diagrams that seem to pulse forward and backward in space when rotated and disks printed with sentences filled with sexualized puns that spiral on a plane. Some of the underlying themes of the film are the relationship between real flatness and the illusion of embodied form and the interaction of image and language in cinema. *Anémic cinéma* had come on the heels of an abortive experiment with true anaglyphic film that Duchamp undertook in collaboration with Man Ray in 1925, and it belongs to a longer line of experiments in optical illusion that go back to 1918, with Duchamp's glass painting *To Be Looked at (from the Other Side of the Glass) with One Eye, Close to, for Almost an Hour* and his *Handmade Stereopticon Slide*.[17]

Breton, as it happens, would have had an opportunity in 1941 or 1942 to contemplate a work that strongly affirmed Cornell's attraction toward technical and aesthetic aspects of optical illusion. One of the two objects by Cornell listed in the Art of This Century catalogue is a *Thimble Box* of 1938 (now lost), part of a series that also includes *Beehive: Thimble Forest* from 1943–48 (private collection), a drum-shaped wooden box lined with mirrors and filled with thimbles.[18] When we look through the peephole in the box's wall, the spring-mounted thimbles multiply infinitely in the mirrors. When the box is shaken, they wobble into motion. Given their drumlike form and their effect of animating the inanimate, the *Beehives* can be considered Cornellian variation on the zoetrope precedent. But there are many other traces in Cornell's work of his deep engagement with the history of mechanical devices that demonstrate the principles of optics and feed our fascination with illusion. Such devices, which belong to princely cabinets of curiosity in the seventeenth century and in the penny arcades of the twentieth century, make up a tradition that the film historian Laurent Mannoni has aptly named "deceptive art."[19] They include magic lanterns and optical peepboxes, the stereoscope and the stereograph, photography and chronophotography, zoetropes and other early machines for making pictures move, and the cinema.

Among the mythical points of origin for Cornell's involvement with deceptive art are the stereoscope that artist reportedly treasured and studied throughout his life and his childhood visits to his hometown cinema (later he remembered being much impressed by *Cabiria*, Giovanni Pastrone's silent epic, which played at the Broadway Theater in Nyack, New York, in December 1914, just before Cornell's eleventh birthday).[20] But in order to see how Cornell incorporated this tradition into his own work, and to what effect, one might begin with his involvement with photography. He collected photographs in all manner of outmoded nineteenth-century processes—ambrotype, daguerreotype, *carte-de-visite*, cabinet card, and tintype—and he exemplified a modernist appreciation for the work of both anonymous and master photographers of the previous century. Cornell, for example, was an admirer of Nadar's portraits and Eugène Atget's scenes of Paris, just like his contemporaries the photographer Walker Evans and the dealer Julien Levy, who had paired the two French masters in a December 1931 exhibition.[21] Cornell also collected works by modern photographers whom Levy featured in his gallery, including Berenice Abbott, Brassaï, Henri Cartier-Bresson, George Platt Lynes, Lee Miller, and Clarence John Laughlin. And Cornell put together large collections of modern snapshots and film stills and production shots.[22] Photographic materials began finding their way into Cornell's work in 1932 and 1933. He started by incorporating photographic elements into collages and by making shadow box constructions with central compartments sized to accommodate cabinet card portraits of performers.[23] These early efforts would lead to such complex statements as the "exploration" or archive-box entitled *Untitled (The Life of Ludwig II of Bavaria)* (c. 1941–52, Philadelphia Museum of Art), among whose assorted printed materials and objects are postcards, *cartes-de-visite*, and other photographs relating

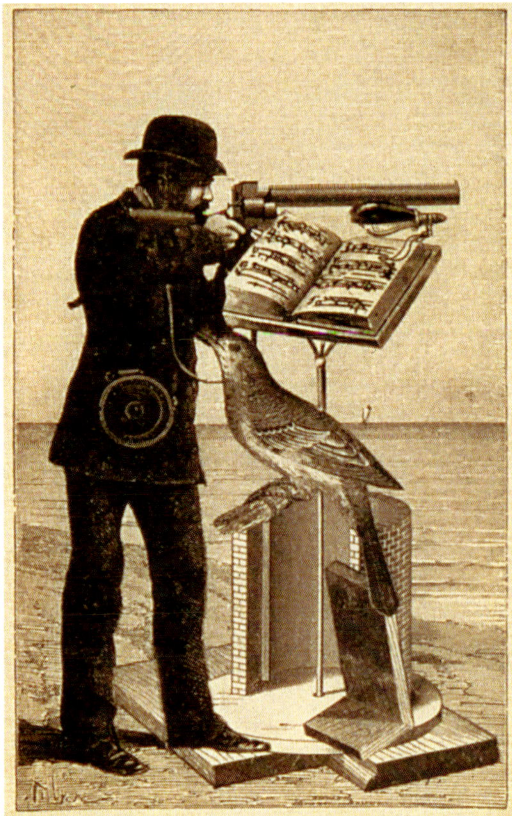

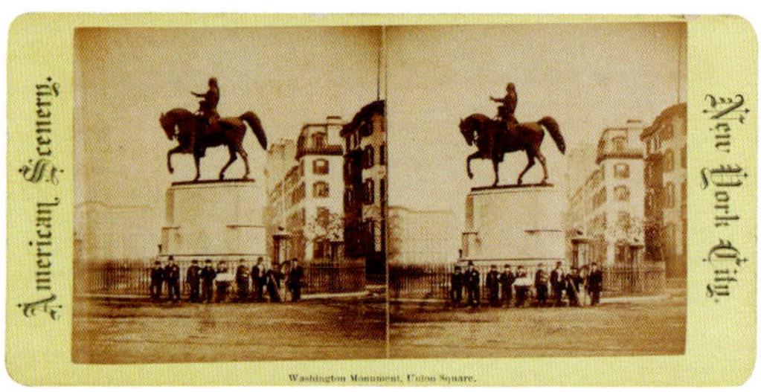

7.02 Joseph Cornell, *Untitled (Man Shooting)*, 1930s, collage, 5 5/8 × 3 9/16 in., Collection of Satoshi Yokota **7.03** *American Scenery. New York City. Washington Monument, Union Square*, c. 1870–1900, albumen silver print stereograph, 3 1/2 × 6 7/8 in., Collection of the author

to both the nineteenth-century Bavarian monarch and the fervent Wagnerism with which he is associated, and to many boxes in homage to female film stars and dancers that incorporate photographic materials.[24]

Beyond the use of photographs as fodder for his boxes, Cornell also demonstrates in certain works of the early period his interest in the history of the medium. An untitled collage of the 1930s presents an illustration of a man operating the gunlike camera that Marey, the French pioneer of chronophotography, developed in the 1880s to follow the flight of a bird and record its movements in very small increments of time.[25] By means of collage, Cornell adds to the source image a music stand that seems to sprout a treelike perch for a bird (fig. 7.02).[26] And if a certain degree of identification with early photographers as ancestors or alter egos is suggested in the collage with image of the operator of the Marey rifle, it comes through unmistakably in *Monsieur Phot*, Cornell's illustrated typescript scenario for an imaginary film, realized in 1933 in numbered copies—each enclosed in black kraft paper covers—like an editioned work of art. The story concerns the comical and poetic misadventures of a photographer of the Victorian era and a shifting cast of characters that includes a band of New York street urchins, a hotel maid, a pianist, and various animals, among them an unruly group of pigeons and a pheasant with dazzling plumage. The script's five scenes are illustrated with single photographs (perhaps copy photographs) from old stereographs. Each image provides a visual cue to the action but also serves as the basis for a dreamlike episode that Cornell develops in writing. For example, the scenario opens with Cornell's fairly straight description of a photograph of the 1850s equestrian monument of George Washington at Manhattan's Union Square with a group of boys posed along the circular enclosure at its original location in the square's southeast corner (fig. 7.03). "New York City about 1870. A park on a winter afternoon. In front of a large equestrian statue, the base of which is protected by an iron picket fence, stands a row of nine street urchins facing the camera." At this point Monsieur Phot enters the scene with his old-fashioned tripod-mounted view camera. Oneiric invention takes over the narration.[27]

Monsieur Phot has been called Cornell's first completed cinematic work.[28] It is no less a testament to Cornell's interest in historical forms of photography and in their specific aesthetic effects, types of materiality, and presentational formats. One of the striking features of Cornell's encasement of cabinet cards, which are photographs attached to thick cardboard supports, is to play up their inherent plasticity. A whole group of small pocket objects of the 1930s are related in their construction to the nineteenth-century practice of putting miniature images of deceased family members (often tintype portraits) into wearable lockets or pendants.[29] We might also point to more intricate translations of photographic and optical forms in certain boxes of the

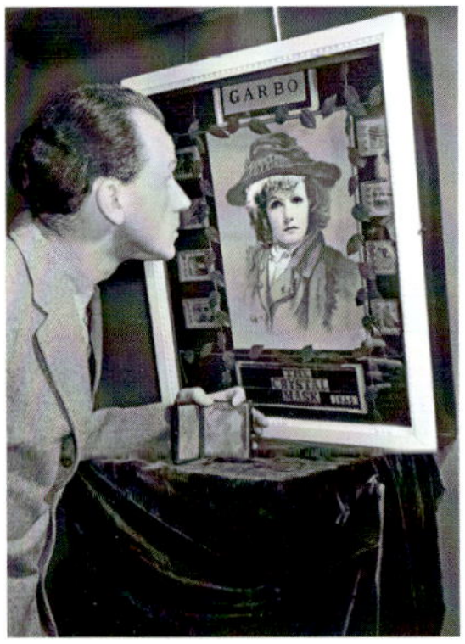

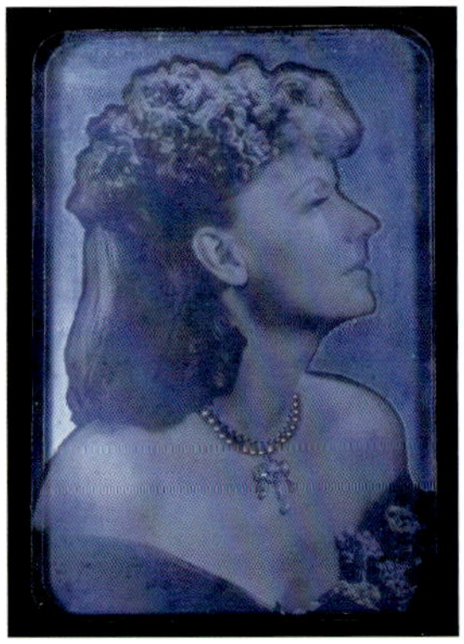

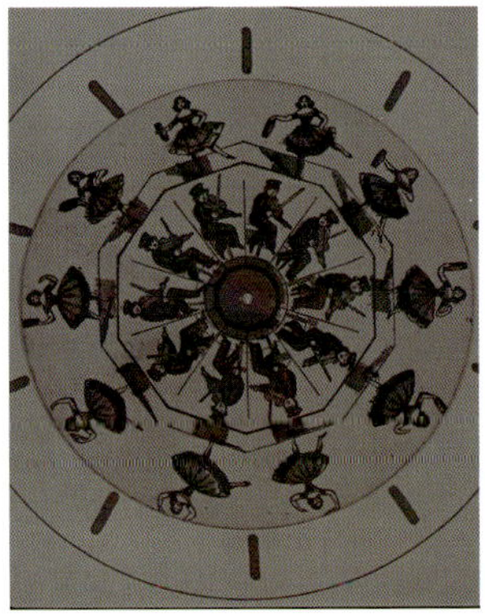

7.04 Cornell with his *Construction Garbo* (*Greta Garbo in the Legendary Film* The Crystal Mask, *c. 1845*), in his *Exhibition of Objects* at Julien Levy Gallery, New York, 1939, Joseph Cornell Study Center, Smithsonian American Art Museum, Washington, DC **7.05** Joseph Cornell, *Untitled* (*Greta Garbo*), c. 1939, box construction, 13 ½ × 9 ½ × 3 in., Collection of Richard L. Feigen **7.06** "Colored phenakistoscope disk from THE MAGIC WHEEL," published in *Dance Index* 3, no. 7/8 (July/August 1944)

1930s that use double images or image sequences to refer to the binocular workings of the stereoscope (e.g., *Variétés de Minéralogie Object*, 1939), the multiple images of chronophotography (*Untitled* [*Black Hunter*], 1939), or historical processes, such as the *carte-de-visite* (*Object* [*Hotel Theatricals*], 1940).[30]

The outstanding demonstration of Cornell's interest in the material forms of photography is the remarkable set of assemblages dated 1938 and 1939, called "daguerreotype-objects," three of which remained in Julien Levy's collection before going into the collection of the Philadelphia Museum of Art.[31] These boxes use photographs as the basis of complex, layered illusions. Beholding "*Imperious Jewelry of the Universe*" (*Lunar Baedecker*)*: Portrait of Mina Loy* (1938), we find ourselves peering at the source image, an early photographic portrait (1920) by Man Ray of Cornell's friend, the poet and artist Loy, through layers of tinted glass and other mobile, light-refracting or reflective materials. *Portrait of Julien Levy, Daguerreotype-Object* (c. 1938–39, see fig. 7.01) is a small box or case faced with blue-tinted glass. Immediately below is a layer of silvered or mirrored glass whose coating has been partly scraped away to create the silhouette of a standing figure, and visible through this silhouette, residing in the shadowy bottom of the box, is a gelatin silver print of a man in a topcoat and hat. Small metal balls roll across the image of the man in the coat, when the object is handled; with some skillful manipulation, they can be brought to rest in small hollow indentations corresponding to the coat's buttons.

What attributes drew Cornell to the daguerreotype—and inspired him to adopt it as a visual and conceptual model? The physicality of the image is certainly one important quality. Daguerreotypes present richly detailed images on polished copper plates with surfaces of silver iodide. So sensitive and fragile is that surface that the image must be encased for its protection in a metal mat, under a glass covering, and in a hinged, covered, and velvet-lined container. The importance of physical handling for the meaning and effect of the daguerreotype is a second, related issue of importance for Cornell—it is confirmed by the manner in which he constructed his daguerreotype-objects. A true daguerreotype bears a negative image. To see it as a positive, the viewer must angle the object in his or her hand until the image aligns properly in relation to ambient light. With its rolling balls and incised dimples, *Portrait of Julien Levy, Daguerreotype-Object* displays a masterful Cornellian translation of the true daguerreotype's inherent toggling effect. His version produces something new: the photographic object as a motion trick game.

It is also quite clear that the peculiar mystique of the daguerreotype image was of the highest significance for Cornell. Their very special optical properties make daguerreotypes poetically ambiguous images. They are encased, like relics. They flicker between ghostly absence and hallucinatory presence. They blur the boundary between the spiritual and the material, the distanced and the immediate, death and life. This confusion gives rise to strange and uncanny feelings. But empathy, or the viewer's projection of feeling onto the object, also comes into play, since the beholder's active mediation, through the look, is an indispensable factor in the image's existence as image.[32] All of these associations are factors in a remarkable photograph that was taken on the occasion of *Exhibition of Objects* (*Bilboquet*), Cornell's second one-artist show at the Julien Levy Gallery, in 1939 (fig. 7.04). It shows Cornell in the act of gazing intently at a portrait-homage box entitled (*Greta Garbo in the Legendary Film* The Crystal Mask, *c. 1845*) (1939). His largest construction up to that time, it consisted principally of a charcoal portrait of a member of the artist's own family with the figure's face cut out to reveal a photograph of Garbo's face. This Garbo construction engages with the logic of the relic on two counts. It presents the film actress, whom Cornell had adopted as one of his muses, as an object of devotion. And through its complicated title, it also frames her in terms of an imagined Romantic past, and thus (for him) as an object of sentimental longing. The effect of nostalgia is further intensified by the setup of the photograph showing Cornell with his work. It echoes a theme of importance in nineteenth-century photographic portraiture: depictions of people looking at images of other people, either encased in holders or inserted into albums. As depicted in the photograph with the Garbo portrait, Cornell holds in his left hand an old-fashioned cased photograph, perhaps a daguerreotype or a tintype, as if to judge the effect of the larger image against it, or vice versa. The photograph, in other words, shows Cornell doubly spellbound, in the grip both of Garbo's face and the mystique of the old cased photograph. Another version of the same conceit is the work *Untitled* (*Greta Garbo*) (c. 1939, fig. 7.05), which consists of a publicity image of the actress in her 1935 *Anna Karenina* role under blue glass and in a velvet-lined box with a wooden frame. This smaller work is replete with the charisma that seems lacking in the strangely deglamorized presentation of Garbo in the larger construction.[33]

Photography was, though, just one wellspring of Cornell's inquiry into deceptive art. It was paralleled by his deep interest in devices for putting the image in motion. Just as he collected still images, Cornell was also a collector both of artifacts related to early technologies of the moving image—the so-called optical toys that preceded the advent of the cinema—and of film. In the July–August 1944 issue of *Dance Index* devoted to the dance of the Romantic period, Cornell reproduced an 1860s phenaskisticope disk from his own collection, with sequential images of a dancer and her violin accompanist (fig. 7.06). The caption in the magazine suggests that he was as interested in the beguiling workings of the device, also known as the "wheel of life," as he was in the dance imagery on the disk. "Colored phenakistoscope disk from THE MAGIC WHEEL, an American philosophical toy of the Civil War period. One of a series boxed with holder and mask, the effect of motion being obtained by spinning disk on holder and viewing through apertures in mask the reflection of the figures in a mirror. Same principle as the better known zoëtrope."[34] Or, to take another example, Cornell owned a toy of French manufacture of circa 1900, the *Cinématographe-Jouet*. The toy contains a miniature flip-book mechanism analogous to the Edison Mutoscope. A tiny hand crank rotates a sequence of images seen through a peephole.[35]

Cornell also began adapting and making optical toys of his own. In the early 1930s he altered several commercially available thaumatrope sets with images of his own choosing. For example, the set that he named *"Le Voyageur dans les Glaces:" Jouet Surréaliste* (1935, Mark Kelman Collection) presents black-and-white photographs and illustrations drawn from Cornell's repertoire of favorite images: astronomical marvels, a gesturing woman (perhaps a performer), and images of long jumpers, pole vaulters, and horseback riders. Some of the latter he took directly from illustrations of Marey's work of the 1880s and 1890s.[36] Just as with ordinary thaumatropes, when the disks spin, the images on their two sides fuse in the viewer's eye: lunging fencer/shooting star, pole vaulter/the firmament of the heavens, a runner/flashes of lightning. This produces, in effect, an animation of Surrealist automatism, based in the juxtaposition of more or less distant realities at the intersection of contradictory planes, with an arbitrariness that resists translation into practical or commonsense language.[37]

Cinema was the inevitable next step. Cornell, having been an avid filmgoer from an early age, assembled by the end of the 1930s a large collector's library of cartoons, travelogues, documentaries, newsreels, and early silent films. In a 1939 letter to the writer and art historian James Thrall Soby (Cornell was offering some items from his film collection for sale), Cornell pitched himself as a collector of "interesting old movies," of classics and rarities.

> Regarding subject, I have things from the very early topical shots through about 1922. The things that I imagine would appeal to you would be possibly my own favorites, primitive comedies such as "The Man with the Calf"s Head' (this reminded Dalí of Gérard de Nerval in sections), "The Lightning Paper Hanger," "The Automatic Moving Van," Emil Cohl's early cartoons from "Phantasmagoria," Max Linder, many Chaplins, Keystones (the wild kind), W. S. Hart, Pearl White (pre-thriller), fake African Game Hunt of Colonel Roosevelt, "Les Six Soeurs Dainef," MÉLIÈS, and many others of the early days.[38]

Cornell also presented film soirées with projections of items from his collection.[39] The unsigned program description published on the occasion of a 1949 screening of Early Films from the Unique Collection of Joseph Cornell at Cinema 16, a New York film society devoted to experimental cinema, captures his basic sensibility as a collector: "The magic, free abandon and creative imaginativeness of the early cinema are fully revealed in these unique and charming films, some of them not seen for 30 years . . . slapstick at its unspoiled best, unbridled trick photography, Gallic wit, and unconscious avant-garde techniques."[40]

Cornell made his public debut as a filmmaker at a now-celebrated December 1936 screening at the Julien Levy Gallery. According to Levy, the evening started off with two films by other artists: Duchamp's *Anémic Cinema*, and Man Ray's *L'Étoile de mer* (The Starfish, 1928), based on Robert Desnos's poetic scenario about a haunting erotic encounter and partly filmed through distorting lenses, like some of Man Ray's still photographs. Cornell's *Rose Hobart* (1936) and some unidentified items from his collection of historical films closed the proceedings.[41] Cornell had constructed *Rose Hobart*, a work now considered a landmark in the history of the avant-garde collage film, by recutting *East of Borneo*, a 1931 Universal picture directed by George Melford and starring Charles Bickford and Rose Hobart, with additional elements drawn from other sources. In Cornell's adaptation, this feature-length sound movie was reordered and condensed to some twenty minutes, run at the slower sixteen-frames-per-second projection speed of silent cinema, projected through a dark blue filter, stripped of its original soundtrack, and given a new musical accompaniment Latin-American nightclub music. We see the film's protagonists in its principal settings of the jungle and the ruler's palace in an imaginary Southeast Asian principality called Marudu, but Cornell's disjunctive editing undoes the narrative, temporal, and spatial flow of the source film. The looks and gestures of Rose Hobart, now disengaged from their original context like other Surrealist found objects, acquire an aura of dreamlike and poetic mystery not anticipated by the original filmmakers.[42]

Cornell's contributions to that now-celebrated evening of films set the pattern for his subsequent filmmaking in the 1930s and 1940s. These films would draw on the artist's collection of documentaries, nature films, fairy tales acted out by animated puppets, movies of old vaudeville routines, animal and acrobat acts, and child performers. Some are silent and others incorporate soundtracks made up of snippets of musical material, including American folksongs, circus organ tunes, and ballet and piano music.

As a collector, the Cinema 16 program notes inform us, Cornell valued early cinema for its unspoiled sense of fun, unrestrained visual trickery, and unconscious, organic destabilization of dominant narrative conventions. He applied the same ideas in his own collage filmmaking. Certainly he played up the early cinema's roots in the older entertainment traditions of the fairground, the circus, vaudeville, and the magic show.[43] It is notable, in this regard, that his collage film *Thimble Theater* (c. 1940s) incorporates footage from *Addition and Subtraction*, an 1899 Méliès film of a whirling, dancing conjurer who, through the magic of the cinematic jump cut, causes people to appear and disappear out of thin air. But looking back in time past the era of Edison, Méliès, the Lumière brothers, and other pioneers of early cinema, Cornell also engaged with a set of formal principles and optical characteristics of the earlier tradition of optical toys and devices that had preceded the development of cinema itself. The repetitive rhythms of Cornell's collage films, their nonlinearity, their tendency toward bursts of action and visual agitation—these were simultaneously the fruit of Cornell's contemplation of early cinema and of the optical devices that prepared the way for its development.[44] The circularity of *By Night with Torch and Spear* (c. 1940s), some of whose elements appear upside-down and backward, and of *The Children's Party* (c. 1938 or 1940s–1969), which begins with the upside-down title "THE END," is related to the looping, repetitive structures of optical toys.

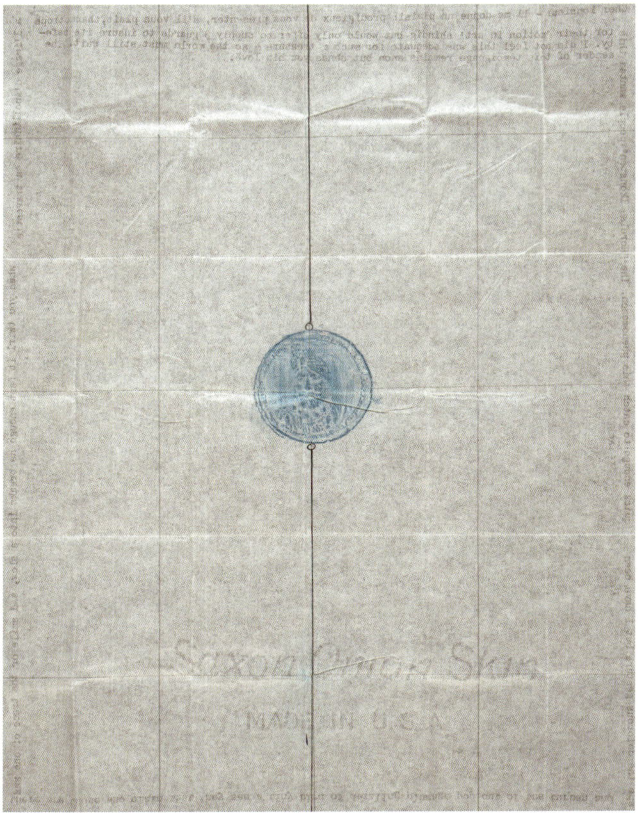

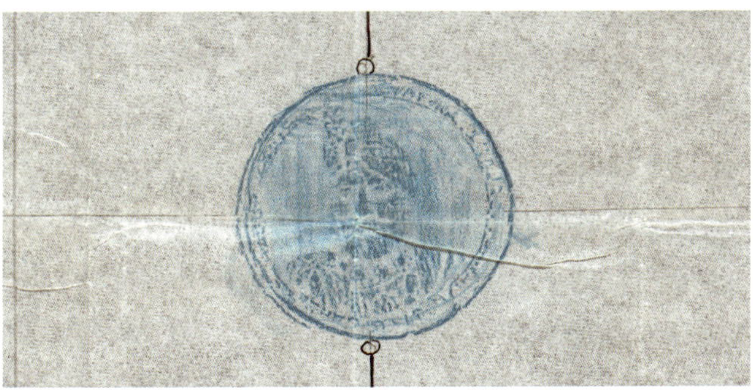

7.07 Joseph Cornell, typescript letter to Marcel Duchamp, between 1955 and 1968 (verso and detail), Joseph Cornell papers, Archives of American Art, Smithsonian Institution, Washington, DC

So is the effect of repetition—of cuts and of images—across the films in the so-called Children's Trilogy (*The Children's Party, Cotillion*, and *The Midnight Party,* c. 1938 or 1940s–1969).

What Cornell prized in both early cinema and the broader tradition of deceptive art was the visual strangeness of the image: its ephemerality, elusiveness, and ambiguity. This type of fantastic image would never lose its hold on his imagination. In the early 1960s, Cornell sent a playful message to Duchamp, his friend and fellow experimenter in optical illusions. "Cher Monsieur," he wrote, starting with a sentence in French before reverting to English, "It gives me great pleasure to present to you, if you please, a thaumatrope with an image of [Guillaume] Apollinaire in disguise. When you twirl it fast enough he breaks into a slow, sad smile or the trace of one. There are those who claim that they see a tiny bird of dazzling plumage pop out of the turban and ape the dolorous gesture but I have not been quick enough so far to catch this phenomenon."[45] The verso of the page bears a rubbing of a circular medallion or disk embossed with the picture of a bearded and turbaned man. It is the very image of the magical device Cornell describes in his letter (fig. 7.07).

A concluding remark: Breton's comments on Cornell in "Genesis and Perspective of Surrealism" serve in the present discussion as the jumping-off point for an examination of the artist's involvement with the flickering, intangible, tricky images of deceptive art. But Breton had a different discussion in mind. He was actually referring to Cornell's art a broader sense. And he made an implicit connection between Cornell's art in general—including, certainly, the classic boxes containing found objects—to parallel uses of optical illusion for philosophical, poetic, or oneiric representation in the work of such Surrealists and Surrealist fellow travelers as Duchamp, Ernst, and Man Ray. In this connection, it is worth recalling Cornell's famous March 1960 diary entry in which he compares his own work to a "kind of 'forgotten game,' a philosophical toy of the Victorian era, with poetic or magical 'moving parts.'" Cornell was drawing here on an idea that Baudelaire had brought forth in his essay "The Philosophy of Toys" (1853). Baudelaire's specific examples of scientific toys that "develop in the mind of a child the taste for marvelous and unexpected effects" had been, precisely, optical toys: the stereoscope and the phenakistoscope.[46] The same point can be made with a final consideration of Cornell's *Beehive: Thimble Forest* of 1943–48, where mirror play produces a dizzying effect of *mise en abyme*, and a strange tension between miniaturization and enlargement develops when the eye is put to the peephole. Cornell's poetics flow from the workings of optical illusion.[47]

Notes

1 The voyage on the Capitaine Paul-Lemerle was described by one of Breton's ship companions, the anthropologist Claude Lévi-Strauss, in *Tristes Tropiques*, trans. John and Doreen Weightman (New York: Atheneum, 1974), 24–26. For a chronology of Breton's years in exile, see Breton, *Oeuvres complètes*, vol. 3, ed. Étienne-Alain Hubert with Philippe Bernier, Marie-Claire Dumas, and José Pierre (Paris: Gallimard, 1999), xxi–xxx.

2 "Interview with *View* Magazine" (1941), in Breton 1978, 204.

3 Alfred H. Barr, Jr., "Introduction," in Peggy Guggenheim, *Confessions of an Art Addict* (New York: Macmillan, 1960) 13.

4 Breton 1941, 26.

5 Lee Miller, *Objet by Joseph Cornell (Glass Dome)* (1933); Cornell put the following inscription on the back of the print: "A Andre Breton en Hommage Joseph Cornell November 9, 1933." See *1936 Surrealism: Objects, Photographs, Collages, Documents* (New York: Zabriskie Gallery, 1986), 21.

6 André Breton, "Equation de l'objet trouvé," in *Documents 34* (June 1934; reprint Brussels: Didier Devillez, 1998), 17–24, and republished in revised form in Breton 1998, 25–34; and André Breton, "Crisis of the Object" (1936), in *Surrealism and Painting*, trans. Simon Watson Taylor (New York: Harper & Row, 1972), 275–81.

7 Both books were inscribed to Breton by their authors. See *André Breton: 42 rue Fontaine* (Paris: Calmels Cohen, 2002), vol. 2, cats. 1539, 1556.

8 *Minotaure* 3, no. 10 (Winter 1937), n. pag.

9 *Dictionnaire abrégé du surréalisme* (Paris: Galerie Beaux-Arts, 1938), 70 and cat. 42, and Exposition internationale du surréalisme, Archives Expositions Wildenstein, Paris, 2004–5 (11), "Surréalisme, prêt / assurances oeuvres." The collage is reproduced in Hartigan, Vine, Lehrman 2003, cat. 2.

10 Breton, "Genesis and Perspective of Surrealism," 26.

11 See Marguerite Bonnet, *André Breton: Naissance de l'aventure surréaliste* (Paris: Librairie José Corti, 1975), 109, and Jacqueline Chénieux-Gendron, "L'Expérience vive du récit dans le surréalisme," in *André Breton ou le surréalisme, même*, ed. Marc Saporta with Henri Béhar (Paris: L'Age d'homme, 1988), 68.

12 Breton, "The Automatic Message" (1933), in Breton 1978, 104.

13 Breton 1998, 33–34.

14 An often-cited English version mistranslates "vue stéréotypique, anaglyphique" as "stereoptic and anaglyphic perspective," in effect intensifying the link to optical toys but not helping to clarify the psychoanalytic resonance. See Breton, "Artistic Genesis and Perspective of Surrealism" in *Surrealism and Painting*, trans. Simon Watson Taylor (New York: Harper & Row, 1972), 81.

15 É[tienne]-J[ules] Marey, "Le mécanisme du vol des oiseaux éclairé par la photochronographie," *La Nature* 16, no. 757 (Dec. 3, 1887): 8–14.

16 Max Ernst, "*… you won't be poor anymore, head-shaven pigeons, under my white dress, in my columbarium. I'll bring you a dozen tons of sugar. But don't you touch my hair!*" ("… sous mon blanc vêtement, dans mon colombodrôme, vous ne serez plus pauvres, pigeons tonsures. Je vous apporterai douze tonnes de sucre. Mais ne touchez pas à mes cheveux!"), 1929–30. This collage was owned in the 1930s and 1940s by the Julien Levy Gallery. It was published as plate 34, chapter 2, in Ernst, *A Little Girl Dreams of Taking the Veil* (Rêve d'une petite fille qui voulut entrer au Carmel) (Paris: Editions du

Carrefour, 1930). See *Max Ernst Oeuvre-Katalog: Werke 1929–1938*, vol. 4, ed. Werner Spies, Sigrid Metken, and Günter Metken (Cologne: DuMont Schauberg, 1979), cat. 1621.

17 See, on these works by Duchamp and Ernst, Jean Clair, "Opticeries," *October* no. 5 (Summer 1978): 101–12.

18 *Art of This Century*, 149. The 1938 work was subsequently given away by Guggenheim; see Susan Davidson, "Chronology," in Philadelphia 1998, 283.

19 See Laurent Mannoni, "The Art of Deception," trans. Richard Crangle, in *Eyes, Lies, and Illusions* (London: Hayward Gallery, 2004), 41–52.

20 The family stereoscope is reproduced as fig. 77 in Washington 2006. See also David Saunders, "Joseph Cornell's Steropticon," *Turtle Point Press Magazine* (Spring 2013), http://www.turtlepointpress.com/mgzne/joseph-cornells-stereopticon/. (I thank Jodi Hauptman for referring me to this essay.) On the artist's early filmgoing, see Hartigan, "Joseph Cornell: A Biography," in New York 1980, 93.

21 Walker Evans, "The Reappearance of Photography" (1931), in *Classic Essays on Photography*, ed. Alan Trachtenberg (New Haven, CT: Leete's Island Books, 1980), 185–88. On Levy's appreciation of Atget, see Peter Barberie, *Looking at Atget* (Philadelphia: Philadelphia Museum of Art, 2005.

22 See Washington 2006, 27, 44.

23 For an example of a shadow box with cabinet card, see *Mlle Faretti* (1933): Washington 2006, plate 3.

24 See ibid., plate 2, fig. 37, plates 3, 51, 75.

25 Étienne-Jules Marey, *Le Mouvement* (Paris: G. Masson, 1894), fig. 784, "Le Fusil photographique."

26 This collage is reproduced in New York 1980, cat. 30.

27 Cornell, "Monsieur Phot," in Cornell 1936, 77–88.

28 Annette Michelson, "Rose Hobart and Monsieur Phot," *Artforum* 11, no. 10 (June 1973): 51. One might also say that Cornell approached the cinema through the genre of the scenario text and that he used the conventions of the screenplay to suspend the ordinary laws of causality and logic in his story, like numerous Surrealist writers in the late 1920s and early 1930s. See Richard Abel, "Exploring the Discursive Field of the Surrealist Film Scenario Text," in *Dada and Surrealist Film*, ed. Rudolf E. Kuenzli (New York: Willis Locker & Owens, 1987), 58–71.

29 See Jeffrey Batchen, *Forget Me Not: Photography and Remembrance* (New York: Princeton Architectural Press, 2004), 66–68.

30 On *Untitled* (*Black Hunter*) (1939), see Ades 1997, 36–37. On *Variétés de Minéraologie Object* (1939) and *Object* [*Hotel Theatricals*] (1940), see New York 1982, 9–13 and 14–20.

31 These are reproduced in Philadelphia 2006, plates 206, 208, and 209.

32 See Alan Trachtenberg, "Likeness as Identity: Reflections on the Daguerrean Mystique," in *The Portrait in Photography*, ed. Graham Clarke (London: Reaktion Books, 1992), 173–92, Elizabeth Edwards, "Photographs as Objects of Memory," in *The Object Reader*, ed. Fiona Candlin and Raiford Guins (New York: Routledge, 2009), 331–42, and Laura Mulvey, "The Index and the Uncanny: Life and Death in the Photograph," in *Death 24 x a Second: Stillness and the Moving Image* (London: Reaktion Books, 2006), 54–66.

33 See Washington 2006, 74–75. On the two Garbo constructions and Cornell's creative paraphrase of daguerreotype aesthetics, see Hauptman 1999, 117–39.

34 *Dance Index* 3, no. 7/8 (July–Aug. 1944): 104.

35 This toy is preserved in the Joseph Cornell Study Center, Smithsonian American Art Museum.

36 See, for example, the 1890–91 image of the pole vaulter reproduced in Marta Braun, *Picturing Time: The Work of Étienne-Jules Marey (1830–1904)* (Chicago: University of Chicago Press, 1992), 117.

37 See Breton's definition of the Surrealist image in the "Manifesto of Surrealism" (1924), in *Manifestoes of Surrealism*, trans. Richard Seaver and Helen R. Lane (Ann Arbor: The University of Michigan Press, 1972), 38.

38 Cornell to James Thrall Soby, July 23, 1939, James Thrall Soby Papers, Getty Research Institute. For clarity, these are the titles and dates of some of the films Cornell mentions: *The Man with the Calf's Head* (Ferdinand Zecca, 1908); *The Automatic Moving Company* (Émile Cohl, 1910); *Fantasmagorie* (Cohl, 1908); *Hunting Big Game in Africa* (Francis Boggs, 1909); *The Six Sisters Dainef* (Zecca, 1902). The film Cornell calls *The Lightning Paper Hanger* may be *On Demande un tapissier* (Pathé Frères, 1912).

39 See Cornell's letter of Jan. 14, 1940 to Charles Henri Ford, in Caws 1993, 89; and his letter of Jan. 19, 1948 to Amos Vogel, in Scott MacDonald, *Cinema 16: Documents Toward a History of the Film Society* (Philadelphia: Temple University Press, 2002), 99.

40 MacDonald, *Cinema 16*, 135.

41 See Levy 1977, 229–31, and P. Adams Sitney, "The Cinematic Gaze of Joseph Cornell," in New York 1980, 77.

42 Michelson, "Rose Hobart and Monsieur Phot," 56.

43 See Tom Gunning, "'We are Here and Not Here': Late Nineteenth-Century Stage Magic and the Roots of Cinema in the Appearance (and Disappearance) of the Virtual Image," in *A Companion to Early Cinema*, ed. André Gaudreault, Nicolas Dulac, and Santiago Hidalgo (Malden, MA: John Wiley & Sons, 2012), 52–63.

44 On the concept of a field of animated pictures that comprises both optical toys and early cinema, see Nicolas Dulac and André Gaudreault, "Circularity and Repetition at the Heart of the Attraction: Optical Toys and the Emergence of a New Cultural Series," in *The Cinema of Attractions Reloaded*, ed. Wanda Strauven (Amsterdam: Amsterdam University Press, 2007), 227–44.

45 The French text reads: "Il me donne un plaisir prodigieux de vous présenter, s'il vous plait, [un] thaumatrope à l'image d'Apollinaire en travestie." Joseph Cornell, New York, NY [*sic*], letter to Marcel Duchamp, Flushing, NY [*sic*], between 1955 and 1968. Joseph Cornell papers, Archives of American Art, Smithsonian Institution. This letter is probably from c. 1961. His use in several works of the early 1950s of "Apollinaris" (a brand of mineral water) as a pun on Apollinaire's name was one of the ways Cornell signaled his keen interest in the poet. That Apollinaire had spoken of the cinema as a creative opportunity for poets is certainly also relevant to the present discussion. See Guillaume Apollinaire, "The New Spirit and the Poets" (1917), in *Selected Writings of Guillaume Apollinaire*, ed. Roger Shattuck (New York: New Directions, 1971), 228. See also Abel, "Exploring the Discursive Field of the Surrealist Film Scenario Text," 59.

46 Charles Baudelaire, "The Philosophy of Toys" (1853), in *The Painter of Modern Life and Other Essays*, ed. and trans. Jonathan Mayne (London: Phaidon, 1995), 202. See Dawn Ades's discussion of Cornell's March 1960 diary entry and of the nineteenth-century precedents for the ideas it expresses, in "The Transcendental Surrealism of Joseph Cornell," in New York 1980, 29–32.

47 Max Kozloff makes a related comparison between the illusion of the stereoscope and pictorial space in Cornell's classic shadow boxes; see Kozloff, "Joseph Cornell" (1967), in *Renderings: Critical Essays on a Century of Modern Art* (New York: Simon and Schuster, 1969), 155–56.

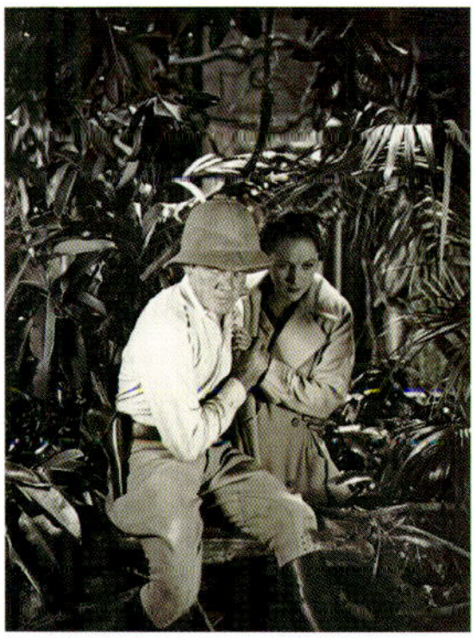
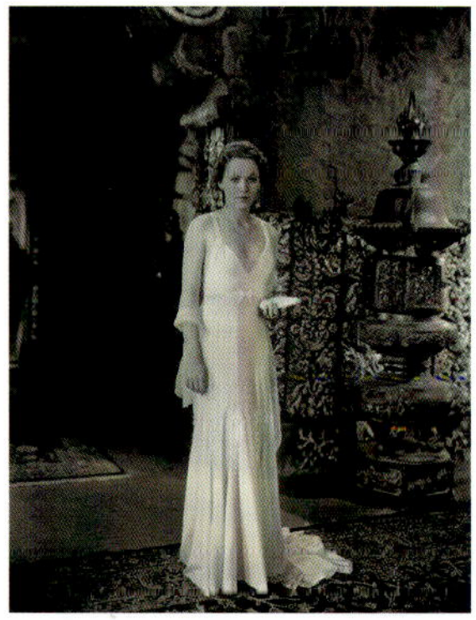
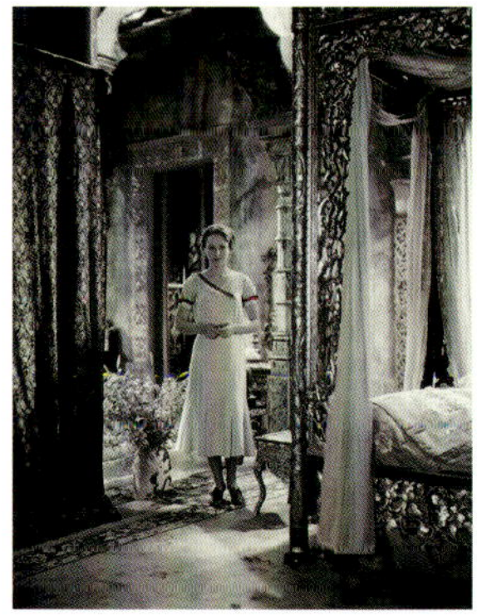
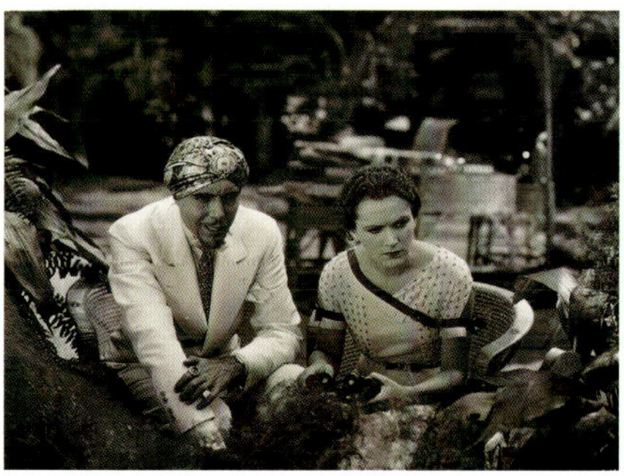
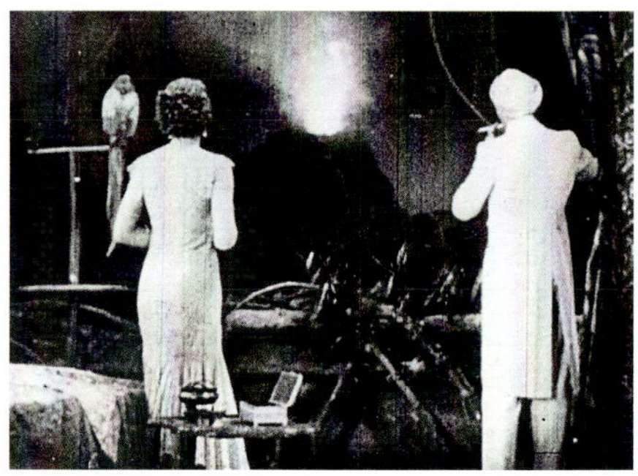

Left to right, top to bottom: **8.01** Charles Bickford and Rose Hobart, still from the film *East of Borneo*, 1931, Courtesy of The Museum of Modern Art, New York **8.02–.03** Rose Hobart, stills from the film *East of Borneo*, 1931, Courtesy of The Museum of Modern Art, New York **8.04** Rose Hobart and Georges Renavent, still from the film *East of Borneo*, 1931, Courtesy of The Museum of Modern Art, New York **8.05** Joseph Cornell, Rose Hobart and Georges Renavent in the volcano scene, still from the film *Rose Hobart,* 1936, Courtesy of Anthology Film Archives, New York

Unforgettable: How Joseph Cornell Wrested *Rose Hobart* (1936) from *East of Borneo* (1931)

Anne Morra

Joseph Cornell Goes to the Movies

East of Borneo is a middling adventure feature transformed into a paradigm of the experimental cinema. It was born of appropriating Universal Pictures stock footage photographed in Sumatra, with further appropriation by Joseph Cornell. In wresting select scenes of the actress Rose Hobart from *East of Borneo* and excising those of lead actor Charles Bickford, Cornell shrewdly twists and repositions the meaning of the film—and its star—in his compulsive fan's-eye view (fig. 8.01).

Joseph Cornell loved the cinema. According to his biographer Deborah Solomon, he spent many hours at the Bayside Motion Picture Theatre, a local movie house frequented by the residents of Bayside, Queens. The darkness of the theater wrapped him in a security blanket, allowing him to passively absorb the cinematic diversion while also envisioning himself as the triumphant hero. Solomon writes: "[T]he movies were pure illusion. Cornell could become the hero of his imaginings, the handsome suitor up on the screen who was loved by the quivering, spotless maidens and was worthy of their outpouring."[1] The movies and the notable men and women whose films he admired also permeated his dreams. In a 1942 diary entry, Cornell writes, "Night of Nov. 5, 1942 wonderful dreams of Lillian Gish."[2] His practice was also fueled by the films he saw and the glamorous actresses he admired and perhaps desired. He created the *Enchanted Wanderer* collage for Hedy Lamar in 1941–42 and a penny-arcade box construction featuring Lauren Bacall in 1945–46 (see fig. 1.03), not to mention works obsessively privileging images of Greta Garbo (see figs. 7.04, 7.05), Jennifer Jones, Deanna Durbin, and the most famous and fabulous of all screen idols, Marilyn Monroe. The pictures Cornell selected of these iconic women were generally gleaned from the screen fan magazines he bought at the newsstand or found in a dusty pile in a used book store on one of his frequent trips to Manhattan. Unlike Bacall, Lamar, Garbo, and the rest of their screen sisters, only Marilyn Monroe exuded raw, warm, and lush sensuality and a sexuality that was on display for both admiration and veneration. The artist fell into the latter category and when Monroe died in 1962 he became obsessed with the details of her story. Gleaning information from news reports of the day that documented her tragic death—the morbidly erotic mention of her being found in the nude after succumbing to a suicide by pills, as well as references to her youth spent shuttling between foster homes, an early marriage, and torrid relationships with many men—Cornell was compelled to become a guardian for Monroe's memory.[3] He put himself in a position to rehabilitate her reputation and memory, even if this cleansing was only for his puritanical moral code to feel better about the highly sexualized Monroe. In *Joseph Cornell: Stargazing in the Cinema*, Jodi Hauptman writes that Cornell "described his duty toward Monroe as the dedication to the better part of Monroe vs. false."[4] As his most epic gesture of admiration and rehabilitation, Cornell created the box *Construction II (Custodian, Silent Dedication to MM)* in 1963 (see fig. 8.06). Deciphering the iconography of the objects and images pasted inside the box, Cornell included a small red rubber ball, perhaps referencing the gifts good children received while studying the Friedrich Fröbel method of kindergarten education, as well as a celestial map of the Custos Messium constellation, featuring a small boy appearing to walk on a shelf of driftwood affixed to the back wall of the box by the artist. Scholars read this iconography as Cornell suggesting he is the boy symbolically accompanying Monroe (the constellation) to the afterlife.

Cornell established a regular practice of including celebrities—stars in the constellation of film, ballet, history, and literature—as subjects in his artistic production. In spite of his attraction to the most famous and glamorous performers of the day, it was a somewhat obscure, androgynous-looking film actress named Rose Hobart that cemented Cornell's name and artistic reputation to the unlikely and rarefied status of experimental film history.

The B Movie

George Melford's exotic jungle adventure *East of Borneo* was released to thrill audiences in September 1931. It was set in the mythological tropical kingdom of Marudu, where man-eating snakes wind themselves in the boughs of trees and crocodiles are kept at bay by spear-wielding sentries outside of the palace walls. Marudu is always dark and enigmatic; the hallucinatory action seems to take place only at night—which best takes cinematic advantage of the luminous eclipse and erupting volcano. The movie stars Charles Bickford, who as Dr. Allan Randolph, leaves his Western world and his wife, Linda Randolph (played by actress Rose Hobart); he becomes the personal physician to Prince Hashin, the Rajah of Marudu. For 1931, Linda is indeed an unusually brave woman when she follows her husband

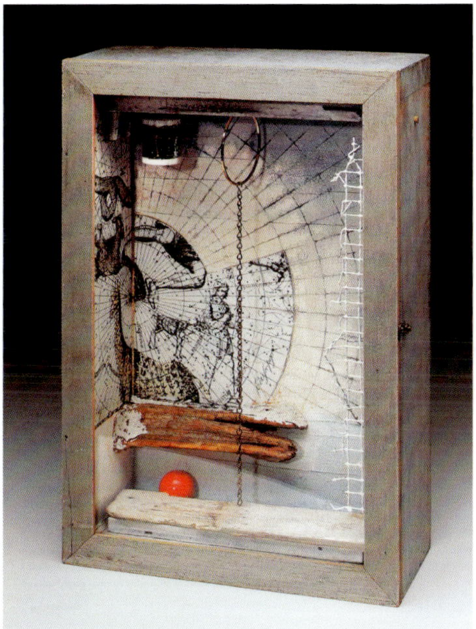

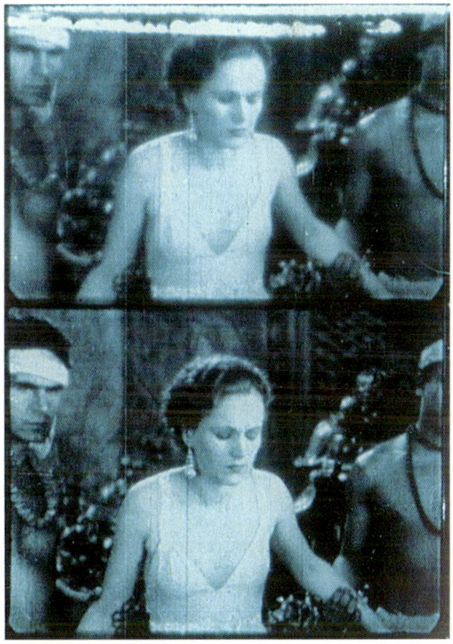

8.06 Joseph Cornell, *Construction II (Custodian, Silent Dedication to MM)*, 1963, box construction, 18 × 12 1/4 × 5 in., location unknown **8.07** Joseph Cornell, frame enlargements from *Rose Hobart*, 1936, Courtesy of The Museum of Modern Art, New York

to Marudu. The journey is arduous, and perhaps to avoid any perception of feminine weakness, Linda is wearing what appears to be a mannish suit and fedora while the natives greet her in not much more than loincloths in the tropical heat. As she draws closer to the kingdom, the dangers of the jungle reveal themselves; Linda is confronted with the savage nature of both man and beast. If the threat of snakebite, mauling by a rabid ape, or leopard are not enough, she must also fight off the unwanted advances of the prince. The *Los Angeles Times* called the plot something of a "Perils of Pauline type of film"[5] because Linda must endeavor to keep herself safe from the prince's wandering hands as well as try to snatch her husband back and escape Marudu. None of this is easy, especially when the prince is threatening to feed her husband to the crocodiles unless Linda succumbs to passion. *East of Borneo* reaches its narrative climax with Linda shooting the leering prince when one of his advances becomes all too real. Torn between escape and his duties to heal, her husband, who has since changed his name to Dr. Allan Clark, tends to the prince in spite of what was done to his wife. A perfectly timed *deus ex machina* arrives when the volcano erupts and sends Linda and Clark running to the docked river barge to find safety. As in the prophecy once told to the prince, the volcano will cover Marudu with lava and the kingdom will perish. Looking back on Marudu, Linda and Clark witness the horrific destruction and see the once frightening beasts running from the forest desperately looking for safety.

The critical reception to *East of Borneo* at its release in 1931 was overwhelmingly positive. *Harrison's Reports* wrote, "[T]his picture holds one in tense suspense from the beginning to the end, by reason of the fact that the danger to the life of the heroine is ever present" (fig. 8.03). [6] *The Film Daily* cheered: "A pop smash. Spectacular melodrama will wow 'em with sex, suspense and smashing thrills."[7] On June 20, 1931, *Motion Picture Daily* proclaimed: "An adventure picture, and based on audience reaction at a preview here, one of real entertainment value."[8] Needless to say, movie-going audiences in 1931 were eager to see Universal Pictures' *East of Borneo.* To ensure authenticity, the studio sent a second camera unit to Sumatra to photograph the dense rainforest and unfamiliar flora and fauna found only in Western Indonesia. Additional footage was pulled from the Universal Pictures archives, making *East of Borneo* something of a collage film itself before Cornell's intervention in 1936.

Leading man Charles Bickford (1891–1967) was best known for his bad-tempered character roles. In spite of his three nominations for an Academy Award in the category of best actor in a supporting role for *The Song of Bernadette* (1944), *The Farmer's Daughter* (1947), and *Johnny Belinda* (1948), Bickford concluded his career as a television actor in the Western series *The Virginian* from 1962 to 1967. Bickford's leading lady, Rose Hobart (1906–2000), made her screen debut in 1930 in the Frank Borzage version of *Lilliom.* After an early but brief career on the stage, the New York–born Hobart went West hoping to launch a film career. Known mainly for work as a character actress, Hobart found the transition from stage to screen a challenging process. In her autobiography *A Steady Digression to a Fixed Point,* Hobart writes that director Borzage reminded the actress "that emotion meant nothing on the screen, all that registered was what you were thinking. Of course I didn't believe him. I thought to myself, he's used to picture actors who don't know how to act. So I struggled along my way of doing things, getting used to the tremendous difference between the two mediums."[9] This spirit of independence and skepticism may have been the behaviors that kept Hobart from propelling into the highest levels of movie stardom. Hobart worked frequently but often in the second-tier pictures made by the top studios and especially at Universal Pictures, where she was a contract player.

Rose Hobart was eager to report to the set of *East of Borneo* (fig. 8.02) as her co-star Charles Bickford had also been on the New York stage, thus she anticipated an immediate kinship. This turned out to be hardly the case, as a minor slip of the tongue with an inconsequential remark put Bickford out of sorts with Hobart for the duration of the production. By the end of the picture, Hobart was disgusted with the long hours, dangerous sets, and what she called an "improbable story."[10] Hobart did not suffer her displeasure in silence, but rather was public with her feelings about Bickford and what she perceived as a hostile work environment created by Universal Pictures. As a Hollywood novice, Hobart thought she could demand freedom from Universal and walk away from her contract. Of course the studio was willing to let her go but with a price to be paid. In her autobiography, Hobart notes that while reading the exit papers, she found a clause prohibiting her from any work, at any studio or on the stage, until the natural end of her contract. The plucky Hobart didn't blink; she tore up the papers and proclaimed "I'm staying."[11] Nearly a year later, the studio did not renew her contract and Hobart was a free agent.

While Rose Hobart worked steadily in motion pictures through 1949, her career could not be called that of a true movie star. It was ironic though, how for Joseph Cornell, Hobart was more crushworthy than Marilyn Monroe, Greta Garbo, and all of the other iconic actresses for whom he created works. For Hobart, Cornell fashioned an über-creation of devotion, obsession, and fascination made from the flinty bones of the film *East of Borneo* to become one of the most important experimental films of the twentieth century. (Peculiarly, Hobart does not make any mention of Joseph Cornell or his film in the pages of her autobiography. There is a scant reference in the book's foreword, written by another author.) Cornell did not deliberately set out to make a film that critics and scholars would continue to study more than seventy-five years after its manufacture; *Rose Hobart* was the means by which Cornell could passively observe the actress Rose Hobart in a world of his own creation and whenever he wanted to engage in private voyeurism.

Rose Hobart Morphs into *Rose Hobart*

In the introduction to *Visual and Other Pleasures*, Laura Mulvey writes "the fate of the heroine who adopts an active relation to narrative space and resists the intimidating look of the camera in its role as sculptor of passive femininity" may be construed as powerful and in control of her depiction.[12] When the heroine relinquishes this authority, she allows an outsider to re-author her role. This is exactly how Joseph Cornell transformed the melodramatic Linda Randolph from a wife desperately trying to rescue her husband and fend off a lovestruck prince into a cool, indifferent, and distant object of desire. As Dr. Clark's wife, Linda is a fully formed woman and a part of a marital unit that has become fractured. She embarks on a precarious journey to parts unknown to rescue her husband and reestablish their marriage. In *East of Borneo* as directed by George Melford, Linda is loving and tender when she discovers her husband is safe and when the prince makes an unwanted romantic pass, she protests only as far as she can in order to secure a safe departure from Marudu. In the company of men in *East of Borneo*, Linda is glamorous, enchanting, and seductive. She moves slowly and sensuously in a slinky beaded gown and even when wearing a pair of masculine jodhpurs and a blazer, she never loses her inherent, powerful, and beguiling femininity. When Joseph Cornell edits, extracts, and sews together footage from *East of Borneo* he disregards the story, the flow of real time, removes the soundtrack, and imparts a "self-involved" circular narrative that returns over and over again to gazing, observing, watching and surveilling actress Rose Hobart.[13] The actress is no longer the character Linda Randolph, as Cornell has erased the context of the feature film and created a newly crafted and repurposed carrier. Also worth considering is that actress Rose Hobart was playing a character named Linda Randolph in *East of Borneo*—so how is it that Cornell comes to believe he is adoring the real Rose and not the fictitious woman the actress created? The words Rose speaks as Linda belong to the screenplay writer Edwin Knopf and are not tumbling out of Miss Hobart's consciousness. Perhaps this is why Cornell suppresses the soundtrack and adds a track of incongruous Brazilian popular music?

Cornell was not a filmmaker who wrote screenplays, cast actors, and went on location to shoot his movies. Rather, at first he was content with tearing and wresting images from silent newsreels, travelogues, and early trick films from cinema's nascent days to recombine these disconnected pictures into self-wrought narratives. This practice is seen in *Cotillion, The Children's Party,* and *The Midnight Party,* three collage films begun in the 1940s. Later Cornell engaged with filmmakers such as Rudy Burckhardt, Stan Brakhage, and Larry Jordan to go out and shoot his films. He would provide each filmmaker with a general set of guidelines of what to shoot and would select the footage he wanted to use. But how did Cornell come to connect with the practice of collage filmmaking when in fact the practice was scant or limited to certain avant-garde circles of which he was not a member? The answer to this is simple: Look at his boxes. Each box is filled with unrelated pieces of string, wire, children's toys, magazine clippings, feathers, and old maps. The practice may seem haphazard but is firmly rooted in earnest and precise predetermination by a consciousness acutely familiar with object iconography gleaned from readings in literature, religion, theater, and history. Biographer Deborah Solomon accurately comments that "there was something to be gained from visual dislocations" for Cornell.[14] By the persistent and sustained repositioning of Rose Hobart as an object of desire, he was able to construct an entirely new and brilliant work from the ordinary shreds of *East of Borneo*. For Cornell, the movie was the apparatus by which he could proactively participate in a private endeavor such as adoring a movie star. Deliberately creating an enduring and inventive collage film that even Salvador Dalí found exhilarating was not part of Cornell's internal or external work practice.[15]

Scissors and Tape

While some artists work in a light-filled studio surrounded by the tools of their medium, Cornell spent much of his time constructing his celebrated boxes and films such as *Rose Hobart* in the basement of his home on Utopia Parkway in Flushing, New York. Cornell's initial purpose for collecting film prints was to provide at home entertainment for his invalid brother Robert; the brothers enjoyed early silent French films and travelogues. There is no scholarship to support knowing exactly when and where Cornell found the 16mm print of *East of Borneo* that he eventually modified into *Rose Hobart*. Just across the Hudson River from Manhattan is the small town of Fort Lee, New Jersey, once home to numerous film storage facilities. Oftentimes these warehouses would sell off unwanted reels of film, usually to jobbers who would reclaim the silver content from the celluloid, or to quirky collectors like Cornell. There is no way to be certain that Cornell saw *East of Borneo* in a theater during its original release, but he was a enthusiastic filmgoer and definitely aware of Rose Hobart's movie career, much in the way he fervently followed the livelihoods of other movie queens, ballerinas, opera divas, and Broadway stars. Joseph Cornell was a fan. The ability to possess an object such as a 16mm print of *East of Borneo* brought him closer to Hobart than any breathless article in a movie magazine ever could. Working with scissors, editing tape, and a rudimentary rewind setup, Cornell fractured the narrative by removing nearly all of the action in the seventy-seven-minute feature film. Paring his work down to nineteen minutes (and run at silent speed), the loss of almost two-thirds of the original film leaves the viewer with little more than a flip book of actress Rose Hobart reacting, gazing, and hiding from and spurning the viewer. But who is the viewer in this now very personal and personalized film? Obviously it is Cornell, and in his fan-obsessed perspective, all of Hobart's actions are in response to him (see fig. 8.03).

For someone who appreciated the delicious hunt, eventual acquisition, and accumulation of objects, Cornell did not hesitate to repurpose these treasures.

He was a collector of books, art prints, records, magazines, and photographs, among other common objects routinely deployed in his boxes, collages, and dossiers. For Cornell the action of collecting was "not a material activity so much as an emotional one," notes Deborah Solomon, who also refers to Susan Sontag's romantic assessment "to collect is by definition to collect the past."[16] The possession of a thing, in particular one that may refer directly to an object of desire, makes that yearned-for but not attainable thing somewhat more real. For example, for a fan of the movie *The Wizard of Oz*, no amount of dreaming will put one back on the set in 1939, but perhaps owning the ruby-red slippers worn by Dorothy and the knowledge that they were used to dance on the yellow brick road may provide satisfaction. Possessing the next best thing may be sufficient for some people, but others may still have a yearning for the real thing. In Cornell's case, by proactively redirecting Rose Hobart's actions in *East of Borneo*, he was able to make her immortal and always in response to his disposition and desires. Although Hobart was the product of light-illuminating celluloid, her countenance was real to Cornell as he created this specific woman who could exist only due to his intervention.

Cornell's intervention involved concentrating on Hobart by excising the narrative, slowing the film in projection, muting the sound track, and showing the work projected through a blue glass filter with a soundtrack of alluring Brazilian band music. The once standard studio melodrama morphed into an unexpected cinematic work that not only delighted the maker, but also (consciously or not) included many of the iconographic tropes common to Surrealism. Gathering these disparate items together and reading them as a whole, they are marked in the spirit of Surrealism with their dreamy nature, fractured time, and, in particular, the ready-made as a work of art. Cornell was keenly aware of the work of the Surrealists and visited the Julien Levy Gallery in New York just a few weeks after it opened in 1931. There Cornell saw radical new works by Max Ernst, Man Ray, and Marcel Duchamp. And if outwardly the thirty-three-year-old bachelor who still lived in the familial home did not seem like an archetypal Surrealist, Cornell was sufficiently meditative, languorous, secretly obsessed by female erotic iconography, and quietly daring with his artistic product to connect with the principal works at the Levy Gallery.

The Blue Movie

The term *blue movie*—a film that has a titillating or sexual content—derives from seventeenth-century colonial American puritanism. Sanctimonious puritan attitudes and sumptuary restrictions were mocked by calling them "blue." Surely Cornell would have been familiar with the phrase. Indeed, viewing *Rose Hobart* drew Cornell closer to the actress and provided the titillation he was seeking as both fan and a man observing a desirable woman.

By the time Cornell stripped away the main action from George Melford's *East of Borneo,* he reduced the usable footage to a fraction of its seventy-seven-minute running time. He also made several eccentric additions. Perhaps in order to reinforce the otherworldly nature of *Rose Hobart*, Cornell's practice of projecting the 16mm film using the dark-blue glass filter imbued the images with a pervasive sense of night, illicit voyeurism, and, more importantly, all that is mysterious (see fig. 8.07). While *East of Borneo* followed a traditional narrative trajectory and cinematographic style of establishing shot, close up/reaction shot and then back to the establishing shot, with facile scissors Cornell turned *Rose Hobart* into an avant-garde, kinetic shrine to his beloved actress. In less than twenty minutes there are more than seventy disconnected shots of Hobart, in addition to a minimum of filler shots drawn from *East of Borneo*. Cornell is not wedded to the natural flow of time in *Rose Hobart*; he allows ellipses to form and fold back on themselves throughout, creating a disconnect in the action. For example, there seems to be only nighttime in Marudu, during which Rose is either tossing about in her sleep, walking around the palace with insomnia, or dressed for a cocktail party.

Providing a synopsis of *Rose Hobart* is a thorny task for the writer, as the narrative appears elusive and embedded in Cornell's own profound psyche. A general read of the film begins with a group of men and women on a hillside gazing skyward. These observers are shielding their eyes from what one presumes is the eclipse that occurs later in the film. Rose/Linda arrives in Marudu hoping to rescue her husband. In short bursts of quick editing, Rose/Linda walks, paces, lounges, frets, smiles, and fends off the advances of the prince. She drinks wine, carries a small pistol in her evening bag, and watches a far-off volcano spew molten lava. At the conclusion of the film, she looks somewhat defeated. The movie ends. If this brief summary leaves the reader perplexed, it seems Cornell intended to keep much of the essence of the film private so that only he could find pleasure in the viewing. This is much like the blue movie, which was often viewed surreptitiously and in private.

As Cornell has consciously edited out much of Dr. Clark's role, he made judicious choices about retaining select frames that contain the prince of Marudu. Inside the kingdom, the prince is the master of his destiny as well as all of his subjects and guests. In Marudu's elemental world, the sea, the winds, the lunar eclipse, fire, and a volcano all threaten the existence of the natural realm. The urgency with which the prince longs to consummate his desire for Rose/Linda seems to be on some predetermined agenda. Did he surreptitiously lure Dr. Clark to Marudu hoping that Rose would follow? Has he brainwashed Dr. Clark to keep him from returning home with Rose/Linda? Perhaps the only event not orchestrated by the prince is the threat of the volcanic eruption (see fig. 8.05). As the film draws to a close, Rose/Linda does not recoil when the prince touches her. She may now realize that her only position of power is in succumbing to the prince in order to eventually steal away with her husband. This gloomy realization of sacrifice may be the rationale for her expression of misery at the conclusion of the film (see fig. 8.02).

Rose Hobart Endures

In the 1931 *Variety* review of *East of Borneo,* comments included "not much in the way of a dramatic film"[17] and addressed the "awful literary treatment"[18] as well as the "general script quality [as] Jules Verne in its lowest terms."[19] George Melford's film was described as "a European invention, a place of romance, exotic beings, haunting memories and landscapes, remarkable experiences,"[20] but ultimately the work proves uninspired and relegated to another mediocre release in 1931. Remarkably, Joseph Cornell's intervention with the existing film created an innovative, enduring, and treasured work. In 2001, sixty-five years after its initial screening at the Julien Levy Gallery, the Library of Congress National Film Preservation Board added *Rose Hobart* to the National Film Registry. According to the Library of Congress National Film Preservation Board website, films are added to the registry using the following criteria: "films deemed culturally, historically or aesthetically significant [that] are earmarked for preservation by the Library of Congress. These films are not selected as the 'best' American films of all time, but rather as works of enduring importance to American culture. They reflect who we are as a people and as a nation."[21] Art historians and critics agree that no one could have predicted that Cornell—reserved, taciturn, and decidedly unfashionable—would give homage to an unexceptional actress in this critical shift of cinematic history. In the 1980 catalog accompanying The Museum of Modern Art's exhibition *Joseph Cornell*, critic P. Adams Sitney cannily concludes in response to *Rose Hobart*: "nothing like it occurs in the history of cinema until thirty years later."[22] Cornell remained humble and unassuming throughout his life, even when his boxes, collages, and films entered museums, archives, and private collections. He once commented to Julien Levy, "I am nobody at all."[23]

Notes

1 Solomon 1997, 41.

2 Archives of American Art, Joseph Cornell Papers, Diary Entries, 1941–44.

3 Establishing a pattern of honoring women he felt met a tragic end, Cornell made the 1965 film *Flushing Meadows* in memory of teen runaway Joyce Hunter, who was murdered by an ex-boyfriend.

4 Hauptman 1999, 209.

5 "Jungle Invaded for Film," *The Los Angeles Times,* Sept. 21, 931, 11.

6 "*East of Borneo* with Rose Hobart and Charles Bickford," *Harrison's Reports*, Sept. 15, 1931, 143.

7 "*East of Borneo*," *The Film Daily* 6, no. 46 (Aug. 23, 1931): 18.

8 "*East of Borneo*," *Motion Picture Daily* 30, no. 18 (June 20, 1931).

9 Rose Hobart, *A Steady Digression to a Fixed Point* (Washington, DC: Scarecrow Press, 1994), 76.

10 Ibid.

11 Ibid., 77.

12 Laura Mulvey, *Visual and Other Pleasures* (Bloomington: Indiana University Press, 1989), ix.

13 Hauptman, 90.

14 Solomon 1997, 86.

15 In December 1936 Cornell projected *Rose Hobart* at the Julien Levy Gallery in Manhattan. In attendance was Salvador Dalí. Cornell scholars reiterate the anecdote that a boisterous Dalí accused a sheepish Cornell of stealing his idea for a similar type of collage film.

16 Solomon 1997, 48.

17 "East of Borneo," *Variety*, Sept. 29, 1931.

18 Ibid.

19 Ibid.

20 Edward Said, *Orientalism* (New York: Vintage Press, 1979), 1.

21 The Library of Congress, National Film Preservation Board, www.loc.gov/film/faq.html.

22 P. Adams Sitney, "The Cinematic Gaze of Joseph Cornell," in New York 1980, 77.

23 Solomon 1997, 89.

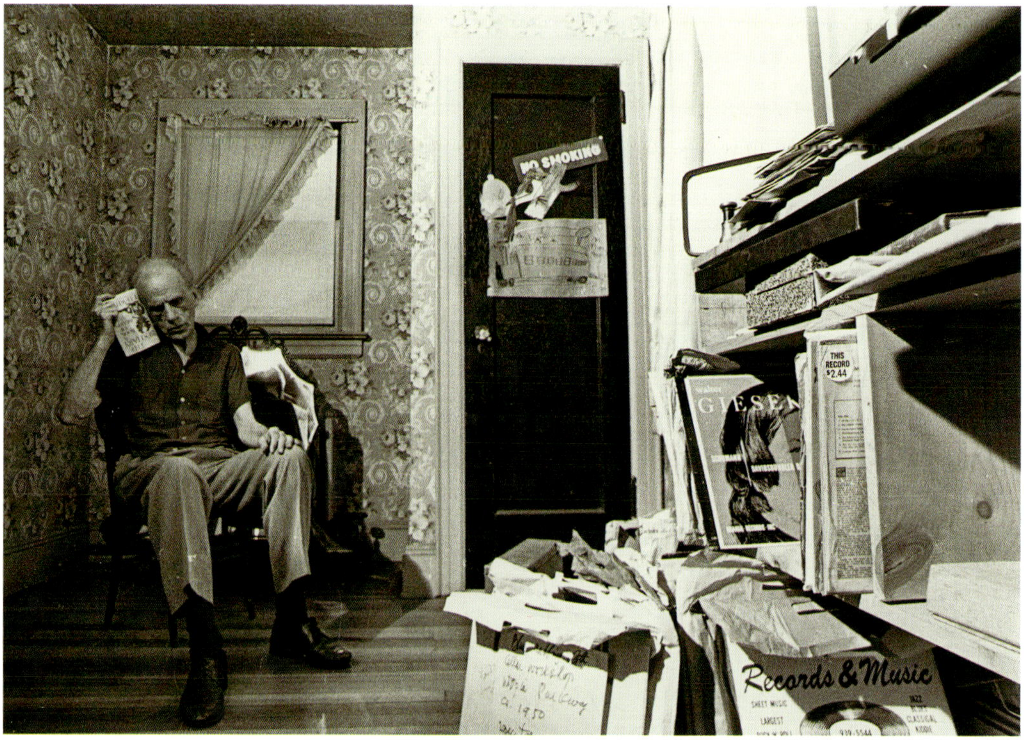

9.01 Hans Namuth, Joseph Cornell with his record collection, "Listening" to a Book, 1969, Courtesy of Center for Creative Photography, University of Arizona, Tuscon

Joseph Cornell's Music Box

Camille Lévêque-Claudet

Written by Jean Cocteau, choreographed by Léonide Massine with sets and costumes by Pablo Picasso, to the music of Erik Satie, the ballet *Parade* was staged at the Théâtre du Châtelet in Paris in 1917. Guillaume Apollinaire (1880–1918) used the word *surrealism*—the first time it was ever used—to describe this revolutionary alliance between the plastic arts, poetry, dance and music.[1] Like *Parade*—a total work of art to which Cornell refers many times in his diary—the work of the American artist makes the multiplicity of forms and media of the cultural and artistic world his very own. Cornell in his art summons both the great names and the little-known figures of painting as well as music, the celebrities of the world of dance, theater, and cinema, multiplying evocations and convergences, comings and goings between past and present and leaps between the genres.

In the field of performance arts, Cornell devotes a set of works to ballet and the figure of the ballerina, a deeply felt object of his fascination. Titles and iconographies make these references to dance relatively explicit.[2] References to the world of music, however—to composers, works, and musical interpreters—are less easily identifiable. Implicit, often allusive, they show up clearly only in rare boxes, a few essentially late collages and inside two small pamphlets, *Maria* (1954) and *Bel Canto Pet* (1955).

Writings, Listenings

Music, while only periodically perceptible in his work, is on the other hand omnipresent in his "papers," rich in references to titles of works, sometimes supplemented by references to a recording or an interpretation. The artist was receptive to all sorts of music, with no limit as to style, time, or space. Symphonies, operas, and chamber music appear in his writings following random listening to the radio—notably on WQXR and WNCN, two New York stations for classical music—or to recordings from his own rich record library of about three hundred LPs,[3] or from attending a concert at some New York music hall. The artist makes daily notes of his musical impressions, and they are particularly numerous because, as we are told by Howard Hussey, his assistant between 1966 and 1972,[4] Cornell constantly listened to music when he worked, day and night.[5]

Cornell's taste for music came from his parents, both of whom were amateur musicians. As a child he had been cradled to the sounds of melodies played on the piano by his mother, sung by his father's baritone voice, and by selections played on their turntable. Cornell later began to set up his own record collection with purchases made at Manhattan record shops, and he attended free concerts given in the auditorium of Wanamaker's Department Store on Broadway.[6] He regularly attended the Metropolitan Opera's Saturday matinees, in the standing room section. After spending the day working at his job at the William Whitman Company, the realm of opera, as well as the magic of dance, became a source of escape for him.

Diaries, printed material, and recordings allow us a glimpse into Cornell's eclectic musical interests and tastes: opera, ballet music, symphonies, chamber works, tunes, traditional music, and song, etc. Certain names appear repeatedly: Wolfgang Amadeus Mozart and Ludwig van Beethoven and their string quartets and quintets, concertos for piano and symphonies, the Romantic composers Franz Schubert and Robert Schumann, but also Emmanuel Chabrier, Claude Debussy, Erik Satie, Maurice Ravel, and the lesser known Marie-Joseph-Alexandre Déodat de Séverac, names that reveal his attachment to French culture: "I feel that in a more subtle manner (and a healthier one) I was more influenced by the work of the modern French School in painting and music, at least a dozen years before doing creative work," he wrote on July 20, 1953.[7] His infatuation with these composers also more generally reflects the interest of the United States in European music, in particular modern French music, the first recordings of which had become available only shortly before.

Cornell's record collection, moreover, contains pieces by the Russian composer Alexander Scriabin, the Hungarian Béla Bartók, the Frenchman Francis Poulenc, along with traditional Spanish and French songs, popular American music, as well as blues and jazz standards. To judge from the list of recordings left in his archives, he seems to have owned little ballet or opera music. With the exception of *Le Calife de Bagdad*, a comic opera by François-Adrien Boieldieu (1775–1834), the title of which he would use for one of his boxes, Cornell evokes these two musical genres in particular in the context of the figures of *prime donne* and *prime ballerine* that he admires.[8] His taste for the opera and the ballet seem to touch more on visual spectacle than on technical skill, hence the predominance of his visits to the Metropolitan Opera House over concert halls.

The borders between elite and popular culture disappear for Cornell, as in his boxes in the *Medici Slot Machines* series (see figs. 1.02, 6.08). Listening to Renaissance fanfares, German symphonies, French tunes, and world music was also a way for him to allow his imagination to escape and find new opportunities to travel without leaving New York (fig. 9.01).

Explorations

Beyond its presence, music is foremost, as he writes on several occasions in his diary, an "experience." He explores the field of music the same way he does for dance, painting, cinema, or even astronomy and ornithology, accumulating materials and information, notes, printed documents (brochures, books, programs, articles, etc.) that he cuts out, attaches, pastes, and sometimes puts away in his files.

Going beyond the simple pleasure of listening, Cornell gathers material on music, composers, their works, and their interpreters. At the Flushing and College Point libraries and the New York Public Library, he reads popularized and other works on music, and sometimes copies certain passages.[9] From second-hand bookstalls, bookstores, and specialized dealers such as Music Masters and Music Room, he purchased, among other things, books on French music,[10] biographies,[11] and writings by composers,[12] as well as magazines and lithographed portraits. Cornell started collecting these in the early 1920s, as he notes in his diary in January 1970: "21st second hand book (of at least 3 or 4 thousand to come) ever bought in N.Y.C. was in 1921 'MUSICA' for 1921 year of [Déodat] De Séverac's passing, 1st year of working, just out of prep. school."[13] He was guided in his readings and his record purchases by the works he heard on the radio and at the broadcast and recorded concerts organized by the New York Public Library (he saved and annotated the programs)—but also by his intuition.

Cornell shared his discoveries, readings, and what he listened to. Robert Motherwell remembers having an exchange with him regarding Hector Berlioz and Satie. In a letter from 1957, Cornell advises Charles Henri Ford on the "Solfèges" collection at the publisher Seuil: "I think that the new 'Solfèges' series at the Editions du Seuil will please you. I have the book on Schumann and on Schubert; there are only 4 for the moment."[14] John Ashbery recalls one of the musical moments he shared with Cornell: "He had us listen to a few records, music for piano by Fauré, I think, and we talked about French music for piano and regretted that so little of it was recorded. I told him that I had just seen a recording of piano music by a little known composer that he said he particularly admired, Déodat de Séverac. He seemed totally stunned and amazed to hear of it. I offered to buy him the record and send it to him because it is particularly hard to find, but he politely declined my offer, hinting that he knew very well where to get this rare kind of merchandise."[15]

An enlightened amateur, curious for new experiences, Cornell was interested in contemporary European music: Olivier Messiaen—Cornell owned a recording of his *Vingt Regards sur l'Enfant-Jésus* [Twenty contemplations on the Infant Jesus]—Darius Milhaud, who drew his syncopated rhythms from folk music and jazz, Paul

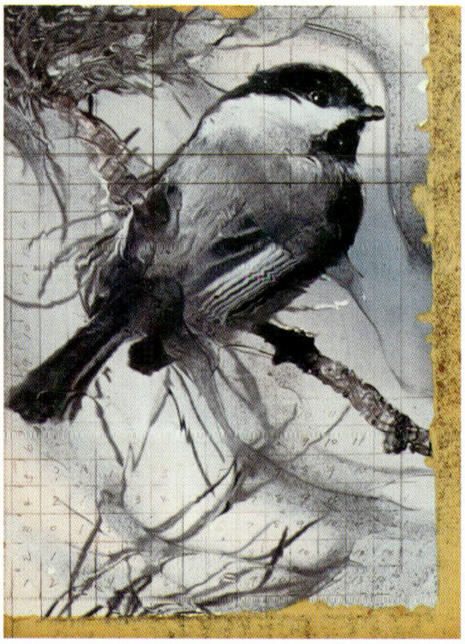

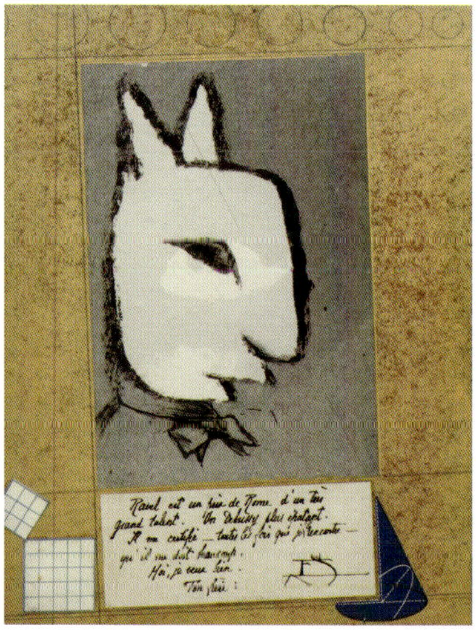

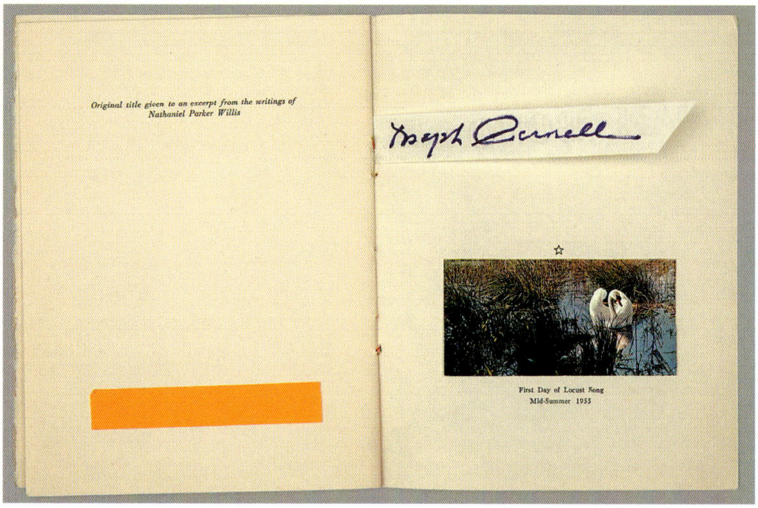

9.02 Joseph Cornell, *Webern's Room: Mathematics and Music*, 1964–67, collage, 12 × 9 in., Private collection **9.03** Joseph Cornell, *Untitled* (*Satie and Ravel*), March 14, 1968–early September 1969, collage, 11 3/8 × 8 3/4 in., The Art Institute of Chicago. Lindy and Edwin Bergman Joseph Cornell Collection **9.04** Pages from Joseph Cornell, *Bel Canto Pet*, 1955, booklet with collage, Private collection

Hindemith and Igor Stravinsky, and the twelve-tone music of Austrians Alban Berg, and Anton Webern (fig. 9.02).[16] Yet Cornell does not often evoke contemporary American music, works by Elliott Carter on atonality, the alternative notation forms of George Crumb, the symphonic music of Aaron Copland, Charles Ives, and Leonard Bernstein, the non-Western harmonic research of Lou Harrison, chance in the music of John Cage or the electronic music of Edgard Varèse. Cornell could not, however, have been unaware of these names: New York had been at the heart of musical innovation since the 1920s and 30s.[17] The Columbia Record company participated in this by publishing an album of contemporary music each month. Magazines gave accounts of the dynamism of the new music, including *View*,[18] to which Cornell also contributed. Keeping his art at a relative distance from experimentations on the contemporary New York scene, Cornell was an artist who was above all steeped in and passionate about European culture.

Composers and Singers

Reading biographies offered Cornell an immersion experience in the life of composers, and he jotted down notes from their lives in his diary. Likewise, he drew upon them for personality traits that attracted him particularly or to which he felt drawn and which could give substance to his work. Three composers in particular left their mark on him: Satie, Ravel, and Debussy.

Cornell was intrigued by Ravel's dandyism, his cane, gloves, and the suits he wore. In the collage *Untitled* (*Satie and Ravel*), 1968–69 (fig. 9.03), we can find the figure of Ravel the dandy, associated to an elegant rabbit wearing a detachable collar, drawn by his brother Robert, before the latter's death in 1965. Cornell would develop this association of the person of the composer with a rabbit in his series of *Ravel-Rabbit* collages, during the last years of his career. Dandyism of another sort, in Satie, attracted Cornell: "Satie at that time was a perfect Bohemian, he had a beard, wore a top-hat, wide bow-tie that flopped over," one can read in the book by Rollo Myers that was in his library.[19] Cornell wrote a letter to the "Velvet Gentleman" on May 4, 1956,[20] more than thirty years after Satie's death, and just as he had done for Chabrier, he dedicated a collage to him in the *Dedication* series (Smithsonian American Art Museum). As for Debussy, he stands out due to a painful event in his biography, the loss of his young brother Eugène-Octave in 1877; Cornell had himself had to face the same ordeal.[21]

Both Cornell and Ravel conceived of "intermittent escapes from reality and from life" through the presence of a multitude of objects.[22] According to the descriptions of their respective contemporaries, the studio of the American artist must have shared certain traits with the home of the French composer. And at the sight of the photograph of a boat under a glass bell sitting on the piano of the house at Montfort-l'Amaury, found in Jankélévitch's book,[23] how could Cornell not have thought of his own objects under glass, done in the 1930s and photographed by Lee Miller (*Object by Joseph Cornell* [*Glass Dome*] and *Object by Joseph Cornell* [*Glass Dome with Metronome*], both 1933, Lee Miller Archives, Chiddingly, East Sussex)?

Of these three composers, it is the name of Debussy that recurs most often in his writings. Debussy even appears in the artist's dreams on several occasions.[24] Beyond the atmosphere emanating from the composer's work, which transported Cornell, the American artist shared with Debussy the same sources of inspiration: night and the sky (*Nocturnes*, *Jeux* [Games]), the inducement to travel and to dream (*Préludes*), and childhood (*Children's Corner*). Cornell also finds the magic world of childhood in Satie and Ravel (*Mother Goose Suite*, *L'Enfant et les sortilèges* [The child and the spells]), for whom this was also a favorite theme.

The ideas and documents that Cornell gathered on music were organized by him into files. Composed in part of pages from books containing general information on the life and work of a composer and in part of articles bearing on more precise points in the composer's work and biographical details, and reviews of recordings or concerts, the sheer quantity of documentation gathered by the artist for the *Mozart* file makes this one a separate work in itself.[25]

The same can be said of the *Rossiniana* file, composed notably of a lithographed portrait of Gioachino Rossini based on an 1861 photograph, and of opera scores transcribed for piano (excerpts from *William Tell* and *The Barber of Seville*).[26] These documents were intended to serve as the idea for a pamphlet "in the spirit of a 'bouquet' of scrap pix such as the pages of a Victorian album plus modern overtone of collage,"[27] in homage to the Rossini vogue in fashion under the Restoration: "Our intention, in the space that is allowed to us, is to propose some Rossini presentation of our vintage," "a little collection stemming from the acquisition of a carte-de-visite original of the composer,"[28] Cornell states in his draft for an introduction to the pamphlet. Rossini and his lively music, the powerful orchestra with its booming percussions and basses, dominated the musical world of Paris of that period and played a part in the current vogue for Italy.[29]

Although this work never came about, Cornell did bring to fruition two other pamphlets with musical subjects: *Maria* (1954) and *Bel Canto Pet* (1955). These are little books composed of interspersed excerpts of texts, reproductions, bits of paper or colored cloth, and cut-out and pasted papers. Each was published at one hundred copies, and the artist offered them to his friends. Prepared respectively from a file in which Cornell includes information and ideas, they render homage to two famous sopranos of the nineteenth century: Maria Malibran (1808–1836) and Giulia Grisi (1811–1869). Their beauty and the emotional power of their performances constituted a creative stimulus for the American artist, who expressed his fascination by means of these very peculiar little pamphlets.

Cornell admired the Romantic diva he found in Maria Malibran, the first to sing Italian opera in New York, in 1825. Her physical presence had as great an effect on the public as her powerful voice, her particularly lengthy tessitura and her passionate acting.[30] She was applauded for her interpretation of the role of Desdemona in Rossini's *Otello*, one of the title roles she incarnated to perfection, and which is justly evoked in the excerpt of the text by the German writer Elise Polko (1823–1899), used by Cornell for this pamphlet.

The idyllic framework of a peaceful and luxuriant nature in which Elise Polko imagines an episode in the childhood of an anonymous diva, the story of a wonderful song of a nightingale transmitting its gift to the child—these could not fail to charm Cornell and induce him to dream: "The ever-beautiful world of blossoms and free luxurious nature became the wise and beloved preceptors of the susceptible child. . . . The child trembled with delight at the tones, which she heard for the first time. The bird sang on, and the little girl's whole soul hung upon the voice, and soared and floated with it far away into the infinite."[31]

In *Bel Canto Pet* (fig. 9.04), Cornell takes up the text "Loiterings of Travel" by American writer and newspaperman Nathaniel Parker Willis, published in issue no. 140 of *The Parterre of Fiction, Poetry, History, and General Literature*, which describes a private concert and a dinner given in London, where Giulia Grisi, another of the artist's muses, is the center of attraction.[32] The artist may have dreamed of attending this soirée and imagine here that he is its narrator. Beauty, gentleness, passion, the lyricism of the text, all partake in the fantasized image of the Romantic diva: "she sung [*sic*] with a rapture and a freshet of glory . . . which set all hearts on fire. . . . She reflected a moment or two with moisture in her eyes, and then commenced, low and soft, a poem which it would be difficult, nay impossible, to convey, in English, an idea of its music and beauty."[33]

There are other nineteenth-century divas who elicited Cornell's passion and to whom he makes reference in his diary. He envisaged writing a pamphlet on the life and musical career of the mezzo-soprano Pauline Viardot-Garcia (1821–1910): "Renewed feelings to do a brochure or article for MONITOR . . . almost (if not) unique quality of blending solid family life & children . . . and her full & rich musical career her inspiration to artists like Delacroix, Heine, Flaubert, St.-Saens."[34]

Cornell used a lithograph portrait of Giuditta Pasta (1797–1865) that he had found at a second-hand dealer in a work he presented for the exhibit "Romantic

Museum at the Hugo Gallery: Portraits of Women by Joseph Cornell" in 1946. She was the singer to whom he dedicated his box *Planet Set Tête Etoilée Giuditta Pasta (dedication)* in 1950 (Tate, London). Once again, Cornell "meets" the singer through the writings of her contemporaries and admirers, including Stendhal (1783–1842), who was one of the most fervent. Cornell added the English translation—fairly free compared with the original text[35]—of an excerpt from *The Life of Rossini*[36] in the file devoted to the singer: "Where should I find words adequate to describe the vision of celestial beauty which spread before us in dazzling glory when Madame Pasta sings, or the strange glimpses into the secrets of sublime and fantastic passions which her art afford us?" Is this the statement that gave rise to the artist's comparison between the singer's voice and the beauty of a starry sky, an association that he had already expressed on December 9, 1948 when he looked up at the zodiac on the ceiling of Grand Central Station in New York?[37] In addition, in his diary entry of August 30, 1956, he refers "to the anecdotes evoking the glistening crown worn by Pasta"[38] for the role of the diva in Rossini's opera *Tancredi*, her "Tête Etoilée." A crown of constellations, scintillating voices, a starry sky—all become inseparable in the sense of wonder felt by Cornell.

Cornell likewise associates Giuditta Pasta with a white parrot. It was certainly in discovering a lithographed portrait of the singer coifed in a plumed headdress, in the role of Tancredi, that this association arose. In his *Pasta* file, he wrote the words "PASTA'S PARROT" on the picture of one of these birds and dedicated to the diva one of the boxes in which a parrot figures, *Aviary (for Giuditta Pasta)* (c. 1953–57, in a private collection). As in his pamphlet *Maria* and his box *Untitled (Juan Gris)* (c. 1953–54, Philadelphia Museum of Art),[39] Cornell fashions his own plastic expression for the metaphor—current in nineteenth-century poems, texts and lithographs—between the feminine voice and the song of a bird. As an experienced music lover, Cornell was aware of the challenge certain composers present themselves to reproduce the song of birds through music, and, in parallel with his creation of boxes in the *Aviary* series, at the end of the 1940s, he extended his listening to works like *Le Rossignol en amour* (The nightingale in love) of François Couperin, *La Poule* (The hen) of Jean-Philippe Rameau, the String Quartet in D Major *The Lark* of Joseph Haydn or *The Birds* by Ottorino Respighi. In 1954–55, the artist sketched out the plan for a box entitled *Scarlatti Parrot*,[40] in homage to this composer who had tried his hand at transcriptions,[41] including for the parrot, and who was known for his imitations of the human voice.

Cornell dedicated several boxes to composers, such as Symphony in C (for Paul Dukas) (c. 1959, Collection Andrew Rosenfield and Betsy Bergman Rosenfield), and *A Pantry Ballet (for Jacques Offenbach)* (1942, fig. 9.05). Inspired by a

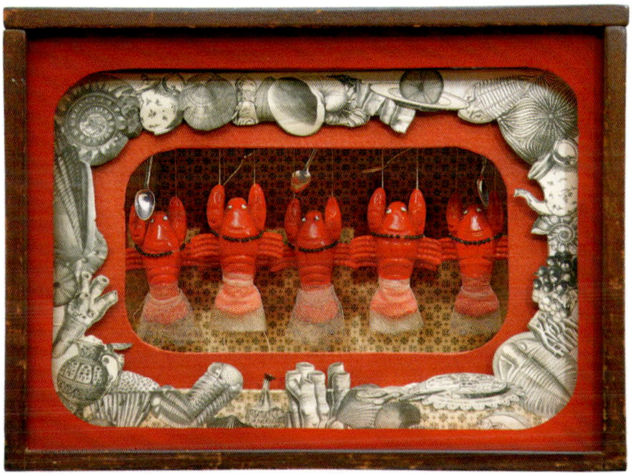

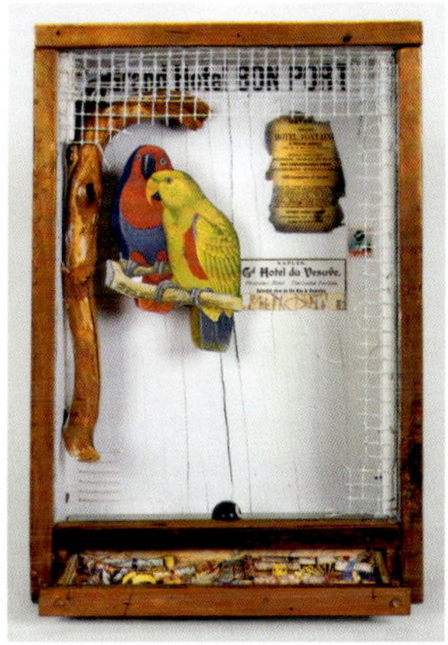

9.05 Joseph Cornell, *A Pantry Ballet (for Jacques Offenbach)*, 1942, box construction, 10 5/8 × 14 × 5 1/4 in., The Robert and Marguerite Hoffman Collection **9.06** Joseph Cornell, *Caliph of BagDAD*, 1954, box construction, 20 7/16 × 13 3/4 × 4 1/2 in., Collection of Carol and Douglas Cohen

kaleidoscope of pictures—elephants in tutus from the *Circus Polka* show presented at Madison Square Garden in the spring of 1942,[42] the lobster quadrille from Lewis Carroll's *Alice in Wonderland* or dancing crabs in J. J. Grandville's *Un autre monde* (1844)—the ballet of plastic lobsters dressed in tutus and hanging from strings like puppets in *A Pantry Ballet (for Jacques Offenbach)* makes innocent fun of the corps de ballet. As the title indicates, it is also a way of paying reverence to Jacques Offenbach, the composer of music for the ballet *Le Papillon* (The butterfly) in 1860, an important work for Cornell in that it was the only choreography for his muse Marie Taglioni. The American artist associates the French composer with this humorous evocation of dance, for he too, in his comic operas, knew how to carry off the art of caricature. The presence of Offenbach in this humorous evocation is also perhaps a bit of spitefulness on the part of a music lover toward this music; could the very unharmonious clashing of metal spoons that accompany the waddling crustaceans be the image that Cornell wanted to convey of Offenbach's music?

In the case of Boieldieu, rather than offer a homage to the composer himself and to the ensemble of his work, Cornell chose a specific work that he appreciated particularly,[43] *Le Calife de Bagdad*, his first triumph, as the subject of a file—containing several cut-outs from the contemporary press regarding the end of the war in Indochina[44]—and for one box, *Caliph of BagDAD*, 1954 (fig. 9.06). Why did he associate that conflict with the amorous adventures of Isaoun the Caliph and Zétulbé, as well as with the two parrots in the box perched on their branch? Once again,

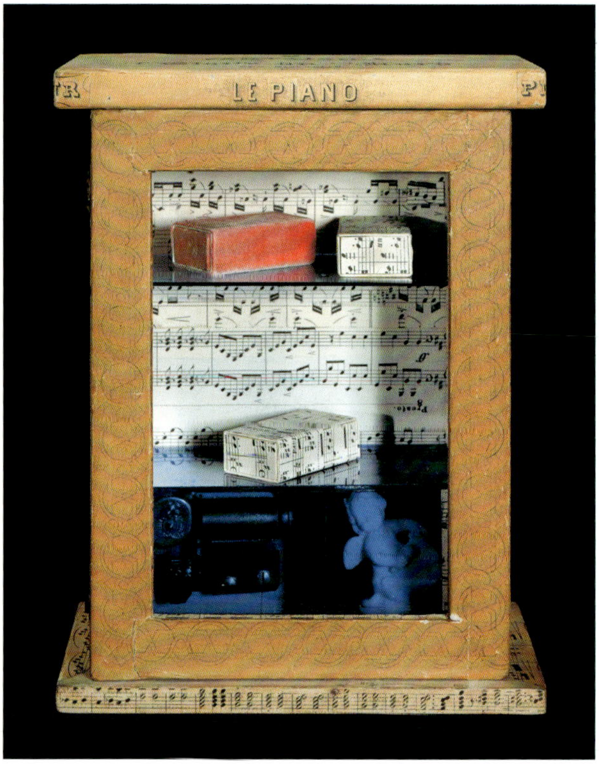

9.07 Joseph Cornell, *Untitled* (*Le Piano*), c. 1947–48, box construction, 11 1/8 × 8 3/8 × 4 3/4 in., Kawamura Memorial DIC Museum of Art, Sakura

Cornell's work, given the current state of our research, shows itself to be penetrable only with difficulty. It is, however, possible to suggest two hypotheses regarding the three last letters of the title, *DAD*, written in capital letters, one concerning the evocation of the artist's father, an amateur opera singer, the other concerning a play on phonemes, as was the case for *Ravel* and *Rabbit* (the *Ravel-Rabbit* series of collages).

From the Plastic to the Acoustic

The world of music and sounds, the object of perpetual personal explorations and associations for Cornell, allows him likewise to enrich the plastic vocabulary of his work and to try his hand at acoustical experimentations.

In 1947–48, Cornell conceived the idea for several small "cabinets," as he calls them. He carpeted the bottom or the exterior sides of several of them with piano arrangement scores for operas or for original piano pieces for four hands. To highlight the presence of the music, the artist set on the shelves of certain of these cabinets a porcelain sculpture representing a putto playing an instrument, for example a horn, in *La Favorite*, 1948 (Bergman Collection, Chicago). The musical dimension of these cabinets takes on material reality in *Untitled* (*Le Piano*) (c. 1946–48, fig. 9.07). In addition to the score covering the back of the cabinet, an excerpt from Mozart's Sonata for piano in C Major, K. 545 can be heard coming from a music box hidden behind blue glass in the lower part of the work, which could be activated by turning a key located behind the box.

Cornell had created an equivalent mechanism for others of his creations, notably for several boxes in the *Aviaries* series and for those with parrots and cockatoos. In *Untitled* (*Cockatoo and Corks*), around 1948 (private collection), the system of including a music box, which is visible in this case, serves at the same time as a decorative motif and as a way to play the music.

Just as in the case of the cinema, Cornell gives a key role to recorded music. With *Rose Hobart* (1936), a silent film accompanied by a separate soundtrack that is conceived in a very different spirit from the images projected on the screen, the artist takes a position in the debate over the use of sound in cinema.[45] By choosing the lively music of Nestor Amaral's record *Holiday in Brazil*, at odds with the strange atmosphere coming from the film's images, the artist shows how music can be not merely illustrative but can give an additional meaning to the image.

As in the case for *Rose Hobart*, the scenario for the film *Monsieur Phot* (1933)—left in the planning stage—tells us that "The voices will be silent and the rest of the picture will be in sound."[46] In this scenario, music—which accompanies the story of a nineteenth-century New York photographer—is omnipresent. Music is the protagonist of a storyline in which it finds itself as if challenged by a force that wishes to reduce it to silence: "The harp is lying over the rider with all its strings broken, so that it looks as if the rider's outstretched hand had just struck the last note on the wrecked instrument," one can read. The music returns, however, with chandeliers that "start jangling" and are supplemented with "incidental music from the orchestra," yet gradually fades into silence. This continues until "the camera lands in a drum, upsetting triangles, glockenspiels, etc., and causing false, bewildered notes by the frightened musicians."[47]

The balancing of the scenario between sound and silence—as between color and black and white—shows that Cornell had a knowledge of the new technologies and the debates over their usage, at a key moment in the history of the cinema.

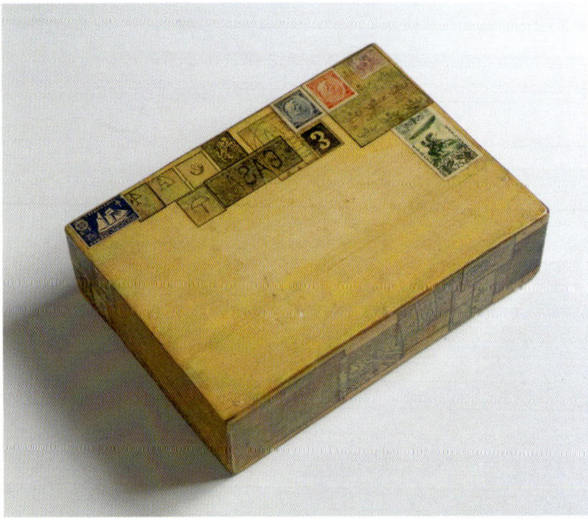

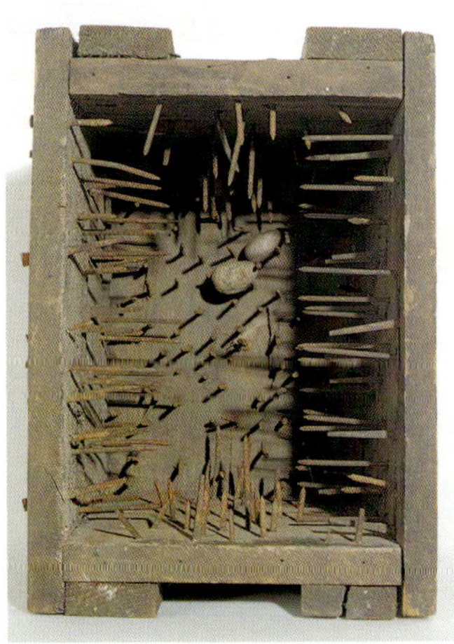

9.08 Joseph Cornell, *Untitled* (*Rattle and Music Box*), c. 1955, box construction, 3 1/2 × 10 1/8 × 7 1/4 in., The Menil Collection, Houston. Bequest of Jermayne MacAgy **9.09** Robert Rauschenberg, *Music Box* (*Elemental Sculpture*), c. 1955, wood crate with traces of metallic paint, nails, stones, feather, 11 × 7 3/4 × 9 1/4 in., Collection of Jasper Johns

Sounds, Silences

Cornell examines this duality between sound and silence. The work *Museum* (1949, private collection), is composed of several small vertical boxes, each containing an object. When the boxes are shaken, the object striking the sides emits a sound.[48] Wishing to explore a new sensation and surprise us, Cornell leaves one of them empty. Emitting no sound, it invites us, like Cage's *4′33″*, to listen to the silence.

Tunes coming from wound-up music boxes or from a ball moving over the little xylophone inside *Untitled* (*Rattle and Music Box*) (1955–59, fig. 9.08), the gentle sound of sand flowing like crystals from the ball that strikes glasses or the metallic sound of thimbles against mirrors in *Beehive* (1943–48, private collection)—these works demand active participation by the spectator-actor who can put them in motion, turn them and even shake them. *Music Box* (*Elemental Sculpture*) (c. 1955, fig. 9.09) by Robert Rauschenberg (1925–2008)—an artist who discovered Cornell's art in the 1940s—is a wooden case pierced with nails and tacks and includes many small stones, suggesting the same kind of collaboration. These creations are musical in the hands of the artist or collectors. Once exhibited, frozen behind glass, they become silent. It is no longer possible to even be aware of the acoustical capabilities encased within. If the existence of a sound for the privileged owner or the complicit spectator is no longer a secret, the artist can cultivate the mystery of its origin.[49] For *With Hidden Noise* (see fig. 3.09), a ball of string placed between two brass plates, joined together by four long screws, Marcel Duchamp (1887–1968) explained: "Before I finished it, Arensberg put something inside the ball of twine, and never told me what it was, and I didn't want to know. It was a sort of secret, and it makes a noise, so we called this a Readymade with a secret noise. . . . I will never know whether it is a diamond or a coin."[50] As for Cornell, he keeps the secret of the objects inside the little sealed boxes of *Museum* forever.

His whole life long, Cornell would consign to his diary his musical experiences, sources of feelings that were propitious for creativity. Traces of these sources were saved by the artist with the meticulous obsession of a collector, as he hoarded notes, books, newspaper articles, lithographs, and musical scores. Letting himself be guided by the associations that surged into his fertile imagination, he made of this amazingly rich storehouse the very substance of his works. Cornell expresses his fascination for artists who serve music with his enigmatic boxes, collages, and pamphlets, as he drew from musical language a new plastic and acoustical vocabulary.

Romantic in his musical impulses, modern in his discoveries, Cornell is indubitably European. In taking a position in the debate on sound in the cinema and, like his contemporaries Duchamp, Rauschenberg, and Cage, in his approach to art where performance and sound are closely linked together, he is a New York artist of his time.

Notes

1 Guillaume Apollinaire, "Parade" (1917), in *Apollinaire on Art: Essays and Reviews 1902–1918*, ed. Leroy C. Breunig, trans. Susan Suleiman (New York: Thames and Hudson, 1972), 452.

2 We refer here to Sandra Leonard Starr in *Joseph Cornell and the Ballet* (New York: Castelli, Feigen, Corcoran, 1983).

3 As his biographer Deborah Solomon explains, Cornell was in the habit of not unwrapping his records, taking pleasure in the simple idea of owning them. See Solomon 1997, 209.

4 Author's interview with Howard Hussey in Philadelphia on April 11, 2013.

5 "From steady work in cellar came up & walked out in a cool misty night. Full moon lighting up familiar objects of backyard; quinces still on tree, wooden bench, etc. Outlines of trees & branches, leaves. Tuned in this lyrical mood to Bizet's Symphony in C Major," Joseph Cornell, diary entry, October 3, 1949, cited in Caws 1993, 159.

6 See *The Business Biography of John Wanamaker, Founder and Builder, America's Merchant Pioneer from 1861 to 1922, with Glimpses of Rodman and Thomas B. Wanamaker* (New York: MacMillan, 1930).

7 Joseph Cornell Study Center, Smithsonian American Art Museum (hereafter SAAM), box 6.

8 See development below.

9 He cites Helen L. Kaufmann's *History's 100 Greatest Composers* in a non-dated diary entry, cited by Caws, 1993, 81.

10 Gérard Jean-Aubry, *La Musique française d'aujourd'hui*, 2nd ed. (Paris: Perrin, 1916): "yesterday awoke to desire to dip into the Aubry book on French music & renew acquaintance with passages that formerly meant so much of progress, enlightenment, even warmth & friendship—especially apropos of preoccupations with Satie, de Severac, and Chabrier," Joseph Cornell, diary entry, August 13 and 14, 1953, Joseph Cornell Study Center, SAAM, box 6.

11 For example, Robert Schauffler, *Beethoven: The Man Who Freed Music* (New York: Tudor Publishing, 1944); James Turner, *Mozart: The Man and His Works* (New York: Tudor Publishing, 1938).

12 Aaron Copland, *Music and Imagination* (Cambridge: Harvard University Press, 1952). Cornell could not but share the composer's point of view: "an imaginative mind is essential to the creation of art in any medium," 7.

13 Cited in Caws 1993, 449.

14 Ibid., 228.

15 Ibid., 11.

16 Cornell devoted a work to the twelve-tone scale of Webern and its ties to mathematics and images, *Webern's Room: Mathematics and Music* (1964–67, collage, private collection). See Howard Hussey, "Music in the World of Joseph Cornell," *Keynote: A Magazine for the Arts* 111, no. 3 (May 1979), 12.

17 On this subject, see Paul Griffiths, Paul Griffiths, *Modern Music: A Concise History from Debussy to Boulez* (New York: Thames and Hudson, 1978), 113–16.

18 Lou Harrison, "Music 'Recent Records and Concerts' by Lou Harrison," in *View*, series 5, no. 5 (Dec. 1945), 21.

19 Rollo Myers, *Erik Satie* (Paris: Gallimard, 1957), 46.

20 [Gentleman de velours]. Joseph Cornell Study Center, SAAM, box 6.

21 This is according to the statement by Howard Hussy, noted in Philadelphia on April 11, 2013. Eugène-Octave Debussy, born in 1873, died of meningitis at the age of three.

22 Vladimir Jankélévitch, *Ravel* (Paris: Seuil, 1956); reprint (Cambridge: Cambridge University Press, 1982), 73.

23 Ibid., 75.

24 "only 2 nights or so ago dream of Debussy playing the piano as in a store seen through spacious window," Cornell wrote in a diary entry of January 19, 1966. Cited in Caws 1993, 239.

25 Joseph Cornell Study Center, SAAM, *Mozart*, box 16.

26 Joseph Cornell Study Center, SAAM, *Rossiniana*, box 17.

27 Ibid.

28 The second quotation is from the original English, ibid.

29 Among the files with musical subjects one can also cite those that contain opera librettos, others that have scores for Italian melodies, and likewise a file, *Famagouste*, inspired by the dramatic poem *La Pisanella* of the Italian composer Ildebrando Pizzetti (1880–1968).

30 "[S]he is not beautiful, she is not ugly. She has something which has nothing to do with these two words born of Adam; she is the one we want and imagine, and everyone sees her in a different way. Her face is delightfully elongated: a nose short of knobbishness, an immense mouth for pleasure, two big, black, restless eyes a nail could not pin down." Vincenzo Bellini as copied by Cornell in the *Malibran* file, July 2, 1955. JCP, box 11.

31 Joseph Cornell and Elise Polko, *Maria*, reprinted in Ashton 1974, 135–42.

32 *The Parterre of Fiction, Poetry, History, and General Literature*, no. 140, Saturday, February 25, 1837, 89–91.

33 Cornell and Nathaniel Parker Willis, *Bel Canto Pet*, reprinted in Ashton 1974, 142–47.

34 Joseph Cornell Study Center, SAAM, February 1, 1954, box 6.

35 Stendhal, *The Life of Rossini* (London: John Calder, 1956), 369.

36 "What terms could I use to speak of the inspirations that Madame Pasta reveals by her song, and the aspects of sublime or singular passions which she knows how to let us perceive!," translated from Stendhal, *Vie de Rossini* (Paris: Michel Lévy Frères, 1854), 285.

37 See Caws 1993, 155; and Jennifer Mundy, "An 'overflowing, a richness & poetry': Joseph Cornell's Planet Set and Giuditta Pasta," *Tate Papers*, Spring 2004, http://www.tate.org.uk/download/file/fid/7230.

38 "to stories of the scintillating crown worn by Pasta," Joseph Cornell, diary entry cited in Caws 1993, 215.

39 "associated the Gris boxes with the nineteenth-century diva Maria Malibran. . . . the white cockatoos . . . are literally stand-ins for Malibran a 'bird of song'," cited by Solomon, 1997, 264.

40 "thinking of a 'parrot for Scarlatti'," Joseph Cornell, diary entry, December 18, 1954, cited in Caws 1993, 186–87.

41 Sonata for Harpsichord *L'Oiseau-Lyre,* Sonata in G Major, K. 391.

42 See Sandra Leonard Starr, *Joseph Cornell and the Ballet* (New York: Castelli, Feigen, Corcoran, 1983), 53.

43 "('caliph of Bagdad') music heard before town (memorable occasion)," Joseph Cornell, diary entry, May 5, 1954, cited in Caws 1993, 180.

44 Joseph Cornell Study Center, SAAM, *Caliph of Bagdad*, box 13.

45 See Solomon 1997, 42.

46 Cornell 1933, 77, reprint (New York: Arno Press, 1968).

47 Ibid., 81, 83, 87.

48 The author gives warm thanks to Jorge Helft for the demonstration.

49 See Kosinski 2005, 17–19.

50 Interview of Duchamp by James Johnson Sweeney in 1955, cited in Arturo Schwarz, *The Complete Works of Marcel Duchamp* (New York: Delano Greenidge, 1997), 644.

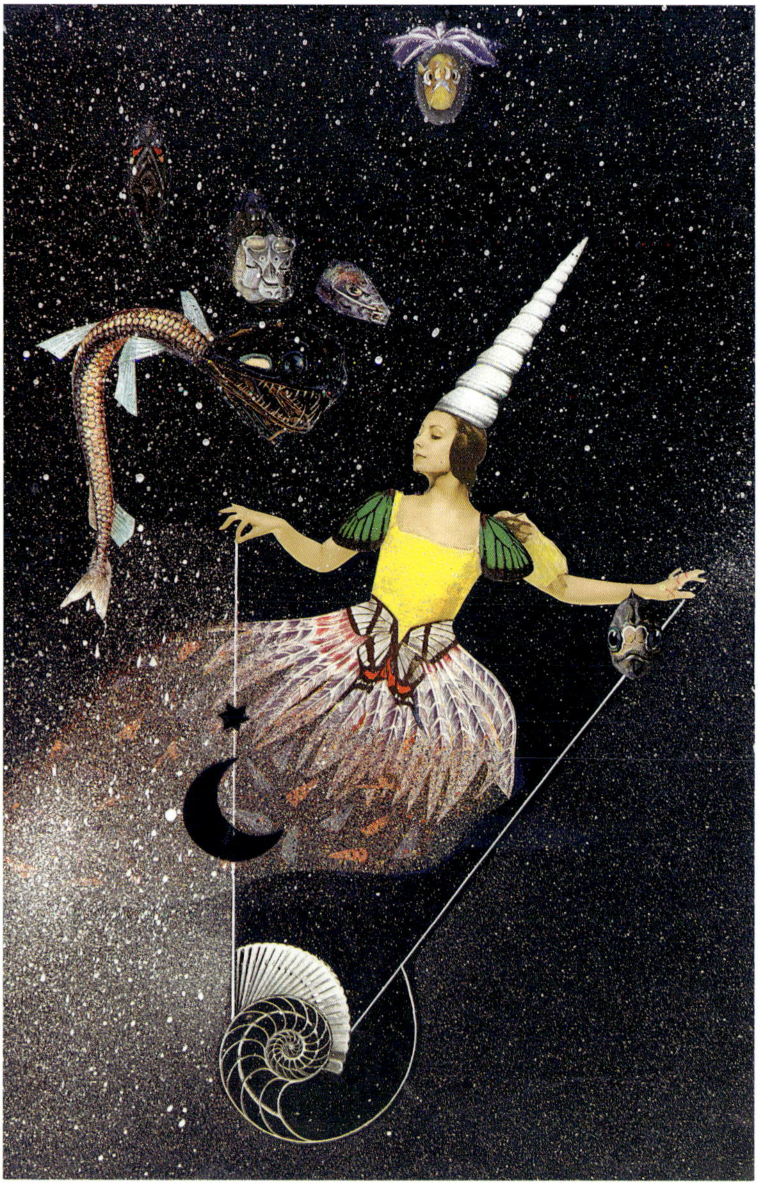

10.01 Joseph Cornell, *Untitled* (*Toumanova*), n.d., collage, 9 × 7 in., Smithsonian American Art Museum, Washington, DC. Gift of The Joseph and Robert Cornell, Memorial Foundation

The Circus Performer and the Dancer

Notes on Cornell and the Neo-Romantics

Patrick Mauriès

Arrival on the Scene

On a gloomy late afternoon in November 1931, a young man, as colorless and gray as his overcoat, pushed open the door of a Madison Avenue gallery that had only recently opened. This was not his first visit and the owner was beginning to wonder about the motives of this somewhat disquieting visitor. But after all, he thought, the presence of a human being is always better than plain dust. The young man, who was looking curiously over toward the photograph of a nineteenth-century dancer, wound up proposing an exchange between the grim and highly sought-after photographs of the Civil War and Nadar's portrait of George Sand—a proposal that perked up the interest of the gallery owner. The conversation went on and then, with closing time approaching, the young man furtively pulled out of his pocket a sheaf of collages for which he would like to have an expert's opinion. He added, under his breath, that despite appearances, his pictures had nothing to do with those of Max Ernst, hanging on the walls of the gallery, and that this difference mattered a great deal to him.

It was thus that Joseph Cornell made his entry incidentally into the history of art, if one is to believe his art dealer, Julien Levy, and the story he tells about it in his memoirs, almost a half century later.

The Russians

Five years earlier, across the Atlantic, all of artistic and sophisticated Paris—Noailles and Faucigny Lucinge, Cocteau and Kochno, Crevel and Miss Stein, accompanied by her dueña—were pressing at the doors of the Galerie Druet on the Rue Royale for the opening of an exhibit by a group that promised—so people said—to stir up a great to-do. There was nothing here that was very coherent, however; it was, rather, the result of a conjunction of circumstances. The young painter Pierre Charbonnier had invited some of his friends to share with him the walls of one of the most prestigious galleries in Paris, to which he had access through the auspices of his father-in-law. Many of these young artists already shared the redoubtable

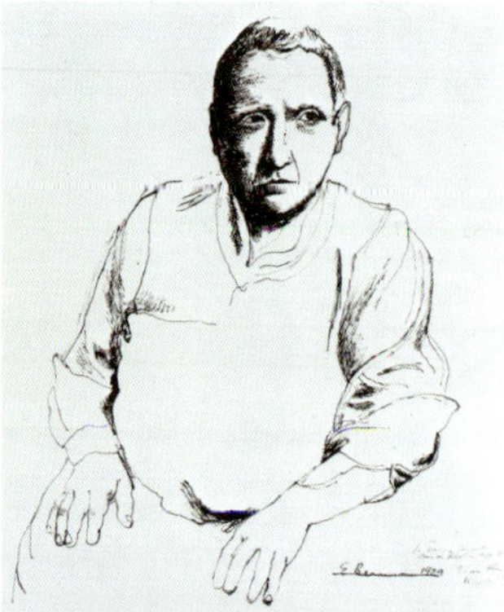

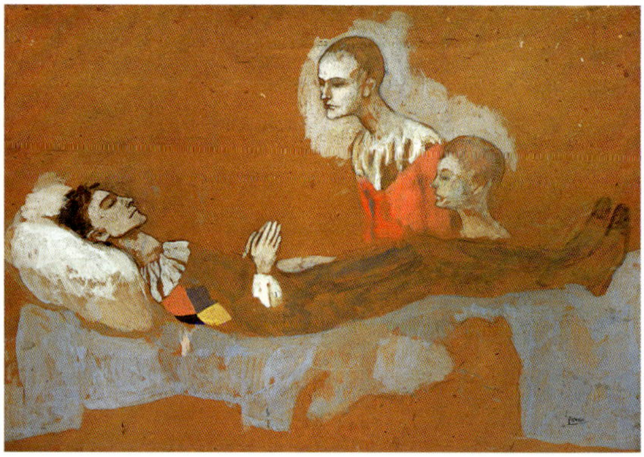

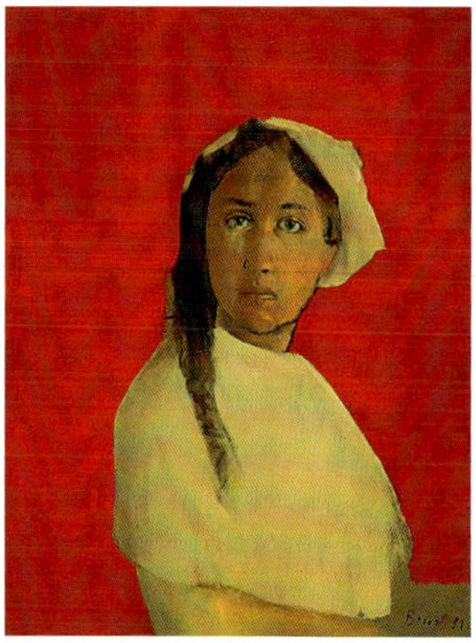

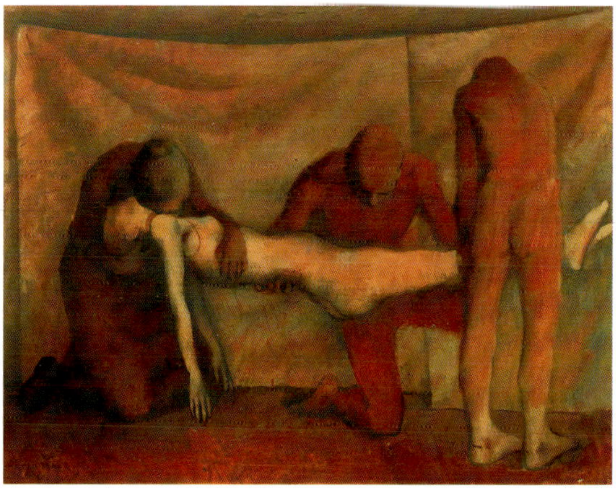

Left to right, top to bottom: **10.02** Eugene Berman, *Gertrude Stein*, 1929, pen and ink, Collection of Georges Hugnet **10.03** Pablo Picasso, *The Death of Harlequin* [*recto*], 1905, gouache over charcoal on cardboard, $26\frac{15}{16} \times 37\frac{11}{16}$ in., National Gallery of Art, Washington, DC. Collection of Mr. and Mrs. Paul Mellon **10.04** Christian Bérard, *Portrait of Tamara Toumanova*, 1931, oil on canvas, $32 \times 23\frac{3}{4}$ in., The Menil Collection, Houston **10.05** Pavel Tchelitchew, *Burial of the Acrobat*, 1930, oil on canvas, $25\frac{9}{16} \times 32\frac{1}{16}$ in., Williams College Museum of Art, Williamstown. Gift of James Thrall Soby, Class of 1928

privilege of having been honored by a look from the sententious Miss Stein (fig. 10.02), who called them the "Russian group." Three of them had indeed actually arrived from St. Petersburg a few years earlier via Berlin, but two of the others—the only woman in the group, Thérèse Debains, and the heir of a funeral home, Christian Bérard—were French, and, finally, Kristians Tonny, a sort of child prodigy, was Dutch. With the exception of the Dutchman, they were all around twenty-six years old, and the Russian group would be the subject of some dubious pages in chapter seven of *The Autobiography of Alice B. Toklas* before filling up a few paragraphs in histories of modern art under the name Neo-romantics, proposed by the critic Waldemar George.

Transatlantic

There is no prior evidence of a connection between these two episodes, with the exception of Levy, an outstanding art lover and dealer, who, over his lifetime, would promote the work of both the former and latter. But the connections between the actors in these two scenes are in fact deeper and the parallelisms more significant than at first sight. We might even be permitted to postulate, if not a community of spirit, then at least a set of elective affinities binding the solitary man from Utopia Parkway to this handful of artists who have been very quickly set aside at the outer edges of twentieth-century art.

Levy was not the only one to have already been interested in Cornell's beginnings at the same time as in the Neo-romantics. He was part of a small group of art lovers, living between New York and Boston, cosmopolitan and inquisitive—and, according to some, under the hold of the Junoesque hostess of *la rue de Fleurus*—who were immediately sensitive to the paradoxical aesthetic of the Neo-romantics and to the response they tried to bring to the exhaustion of conformism in early modernism. They include a financier and art historian (Edward Warburg), a balletomane (Lincoln Kirstein), a musician (Virgil Thompson), collectors and curators (James Thrall Soby and Chick Austin), and they would become the discreet agents, in all senses of the word, of the passage of artistic forms from Europe to the United States during those years, at the same time playing an essential role in the development of a truly American artistic landscape.

If Waldemar George—who would lose himself a bit later in the meanders of a return to the "tradition of French art"—tried to discern immediately the latent sense of the inaugural exhibit at the Galerie Druet (1926), it would be up to Soby, with *After Picasso* (1935), to write the only comprehensive book, still to this day, on the painters of the movement. A collector and friend of these young artists, he sketched out their biographies, the origins of the movement, extricated the differences among them, while connecting them to the great works of the beginning of the twentieth century, trying—with his nose, so to speak, pressed against events—to sketch out their future prospects.

Taking Up the Heritage

"A misnomer": that is how Levy retrospectively noted this first attempt to give it a name (and that which does not have a name, as we know, must struggle to come into existence). "Neo-romantic was perhaps a misnomer. Berman and his group, his brother Leonid, Tchelitchew, Bérard, and Tonny were Neo-Renaissance more precisely: romantic only in the trappings of melancholy and ruin, poverty and nostalgia, that were an integral part of their lives at this time." It was a label that, in trying to pin down a truth, nonetheless forced the activities of very different artists on the periphery of Surrealism (as, incidentally, was Cornell), fundamentally inassimilable to a group or a movement. Berman would in his turn come back to this theme in his belated *Appunti per un'autobiografia* (Notes for an Autobiography), a preface to an exhibition catalogue for Iolas in 1971: "An exhibit at the Galerie Druet earned us the label Neo-romantics by the critic Waldemar George. Actually we always refused to let ourselves be described as an organized group because each of us followed his own path without being concerned with the construction of a collective movement."

At most—but this is hardly unimportant—they were related by the proximity of their birthdates, between 1896 and 1906, a time when Picasso was developing his rose and blue periods, those very periods that would play a central role in their projects, if not their strategy, faced as they were with the formulas of late Cubism and with what "seemed destined to form the central core of art in the first half of the twentieth century." They were also confronted with the pure negativity of Dada and—even though they did not underestimate its importance—the cerebral approach of Duchamp. "In 1924," Soby notes ten years later, "the moment that had belonged to Dada faded away before a new era full of hope. The chaos of the post-war world was now succeeded by an ever stronger confidence and hope. A form of Romanticism up to then stifled by the war was beginning again to blossom without hindrance."

André Chastel would not be wrong later in speaking about a "Neo-romanticism," since for this generation—just as for those of artists of the second half of the sixteenth century confronted with Leonardo and Michelangelo—it was a matter of *taking up* the heritage from crushing masters, in this case Picasso (and de Chirico).

After Picasso—the title explains itself, wrote Soby, because these artists came after their elder in time ("and it was they, not he, who represented the most recent developments of modern art"), but also because they "originally derived from his work," from an essentially *nostalgic* part of his work.

Specters

A return to emotion, a search for poetic intensity, for an "unashamed poignancy," a form of art accessible to the greatest number of people, the reappropriation of figuration, and above all of the human figure, a stenography of the moment, in particular in Bérard's case, culminating in an atmosphere of intense melancholy, common to all these artists—such is the initial outcome of a "movement" that would mark, in tandem with Surrealism, the "renaissance of literary, narrative painting," if we are willing to strip these terms of any negative connotation (Waldemar George, for his part, would load everything with an ideological density, proposing "Neo-humanist" as another term for the group).

We cannot, however, reduce Neo-romanticism to a pure and simple movement of "reaction," inasmuch as it takes place naturally, in the eyes of Soby, in the succession of dialectical oppositions that structures the course of modern art. Cubism is opposed to the "monotonous libido" of expressionism, while the latter for its part found an alternative to impressionistic naturalism, with all of them positioning themselves against "the photographic realism of the nineteenth century." To sharpen the focus here, once again: Braque and Picasso had rejected the jolting dynamics of Fauvism in favor of Cubist balance, and a concern for construction going back, beyond Cézanne, to Seurat, Ingres, and Poussin. It became the task of the Neo-romantics to break free of the "idea of painting as architecture," so excellently represented by the approach of the two founders of Cubism, along with Gris, but which had wound up degenerating into a simple watchword.

Picasso, followed in this by the art world, was in the process of rejecting his production of the years 1903–5. Ignoring this rejection, the new generation sought on the contrary to reconnect with the stylistics of those years "as though it were a matter of dealing with the work of a dead and forgotten painter" (there is always something fundamentally spectral in Neo-romantic painting). In so doing, they were also reconnecting with what had inspired Picasso's blue and rose period: a figurative tradition deeply rooted in the nineteenth century and in popular culture, independent of any concern with a discontinuity and the dictates of any intellectual coterie.

The Circus Performer and the Dancer

The theme of the circus performer, so persistent in 1905 (which Picasso would return to in 1918 and constitutes something of a continuous baseline throughout his work), offers one of the most evident motifs of these ties with a visual culture of the previous century, where it represents a little space for dreaming as opposed to the somber reality of a rising capitalism and a devastating industrialization (fig. 10.03). As Jean Starobinski has shown in a famous study, it was already spreading widely with its related characters—tightrope walkers, Pierrot, Harlequin—in Nodier, Gautier, Baudelaire, Jules Janin, or Champfleury, and on through the exaltation, in particular, of the figure of Deburau, before finding a late, popular, and pathos-laden incarnation in Willette's Pierrot.

It is, further, the most visible transitional motif between Picasso and the Neo-romantics, but also among the different players in the movement, and among these and Cornell. The theme was tirelessly treated by Bérard, from *Cotillon* in 1932 to a set of wash drawings entitled *Les As du tapis* (Aces on the carpet); Tchelitchew (*Clown bleu* [Blue clown, 1929], *Clown à la nature mort* [Clown with still life, 1930], and *Burial of the Acrobat*, 1930, fig. 10.05); or Berman (*The Silent Dance* [1941], *Danses concertantes* [1944], *Armida* [1946], etc.). It blends into Cornell's main obsession with the figure of the dancing girl (often from the nineteenth century) and for that of the tightrope walker or the acrobat.

If this theme offers Picasso one of the multiple alibis that allow him to play with the figure of the artist, and his own image, for Cornell and the Neo-romantics it represents rather the highest expression of the human condition, from this ultimate point where it fulfills itself, breaking away from the laws of attraction, at the risk of vanishing—the emblem of a corporeal fragility.

Whereas the solitary man of Utopia Parkway did not cease dreaming about and fetishizing the body of the star dancer—so aptly named—in his mnemonic theater, from one end of his work to the other, Bérard, Berman, and Tchelitchew did not stop at using and varying these figures of artifice; they affirmed themselves immediately as painters of costume and theater. Berman sketched his first projects for the Hartford festival in 1936, then designed the sets and costumes for Serge Lifar's *Icarus* (1938), Frederick Ashton's *Devil's Holiday* (1939), and Balanchine's *Concerto Barocco* (1941). His career would thereafter be regularly paced by stage designs for the theater and ballets until his death in Rome in 1972.

A pioneer in this approach, Tchelitchew, marked like the Berman brothers by the adventure of the Ballets Russes, enjoyed some success from 1923 on in Berlin, with sets and costumes inspired by Constructivism. Those that he created five years later for *Ode*, at Diaghilev's request, break away from that influence, preluding his work for *Four Saints in Three Acts* in Hartford, for Balanchine's *Errante* and for the 1933 Ballets Russes, which had a determining influence on the evolution of contemporary ballet in the United States.

As for Bérard, he lost no time in becoming the chief theatrical, cinematic, and ballet stage designer of France from 1930 to his premature death in 1949, to the point of losing his way, according to some critics, as a painter. His first personal exhibit during his lifetime was presented at the Bignou Gallery in 1934; he was thinking about returning to painting the same year he died. His creations for dance and theater, perhaps even more so than those of his friends, left an indelible mark on the stage designing of his time—Cocteau's *La voix humaine* (The human voice) and Kocho and Sauguet's *La nuit* (The night) in 1930, *Cotillon* and *Mozartiana* for Balanchine in 1932 and 1934, Henri Sauguet's *Les Forains* (The fairground entertainers) in 1945.

Taglioni and Toumanova

The commonality of interest in this theme between Cornell and the Neo-romantics is not merely anecdotal; it had a direct impact on his career and his work. And it depended, once again, on the mediation—both unconscious and necessary—of Levy.

Having acquired an important portion of the collections of Serge Lifar—the dancer had accumulated them during the time he worked with the Ballets Russes and had now been invited to New York by the Metropolitan Opera—Levy made them the centerpiece of an exhibit in 1935, entitled *25 Years of Russian Ballet,* in which figured Bérard's Harlequins as well as works by de Chirico, Picasso, Bakst, or Cocteau, and an important set of costumes and sets by Tchelitchew. We can be permitted to consider this exhibit as an essential catalyst in Cornell's work insofar as the role of dance and the myth of the ballerina, in particular, are concerned. The exhibit neatly coincides, as Sandra Leonard Starr has noted, with the emergence of this theme in his work—Lifar, incidentally, being the only male figure admitted into his pantheon (*A Serge Lifar, en hommage*, 1933).

It was also on that occasion that Cornell met Tchelitchew. They established a deep friendship, further strengthened by the fact that the Russian painter soon introduced him to his compatriot, the weightless Tamara Toumanova (fig. 10.04), the main contemporary dancer—between Marie Taglioni and Fanny Elssler—to be the subject of collages (see fig. 10.01) and boxes (*Earring for Tamara Toumanova* and *Homage to Tamara Toumanova*, 1940; *Toumanova Snow Ball*, 1941; *A Swan Lake for Tamara Toumanova*, 1946, etc.).

A fascinating icon and an overwhelming idol (she has recounted how, overpowered by emotion, he took five steps back when they first met), Toumanova offers a prism through which to consider an essential aspect of Cornell's vision that, once again, draws him close to the Neo-romantics. A modern heir to the virtuosos of the golden century of ballet, she was their triumphant echo, their spectral prolongation into the middle of the twentieth century—the living proof of how the present cannot be separated from the past, of how they are bound in a game of perpetual exchanges, disruptions, and transformations. With Cornell, as opposed to the Neo-romantics, we find no desire to break with history and tradition that the first decades of the century had so radically sought to erase (this is one of the meanings of his refusal to see his collages assimilated to those of Max Ernst, of his opposing his "white magic" to the black magic of the Surrealists)

Ondine

An interpreter of the classical repertory as well as that of Balanchine, Toumanova fascinated Cornell, Starr writes, for "her ability to pass, like a chameleon, from a Romantic work set to Chopin's music—*Les Sylphides* (The sylphs)—to the complex modernity of a ballet orchestrated by Georges Auric (*La Concurrence* [The competition], 1931)." It was through Tchelitchew that she enters into Cornell's work and life in 1940, when the Russian painter "was obsessed with the idea of flooding Toumanova with light while dressing her with precious stones." This was a fantasy to which he gave life in Balanchine's *Balustrade*, on January 22, 1941, by dressing the dancing star in a black costume entirely covered with diamonds and rubies. The box entitled *Earring for Tamara Toumanova* (1940) is composed of diamonds and sequins that Cornell had surreptitiously recouped from the costume from which they had fallen during the rehearsals for *Balustrade*, a magical transfiguration of the trivial and the accidental by a new trick of "white magic."

At that same moment appears the other great dancing figure who dominates his work, a simple paper creature this time, born of his reading of stories about the ballet and albums of lithographs from the nineteenth century. Fanny Cerrito (1817–1909), alias Ma'am'zelle Cherry Toes, is inseparable in Cornell's imagination from the figure of Ondine, which she had interpreted in 1843. A legendary creature, emerging from the waves, Ondine is a figure who exists between two worlds, an immortal bursting into the finite world, a mistress of illusions who tries to pull the young fisherman Matteo down into the depths of the seas and who moves about the world using various faces, ungraspable and multifaceted, fascinating and dangerous, the emblem of desire and of its impossibility, of the fragility of the

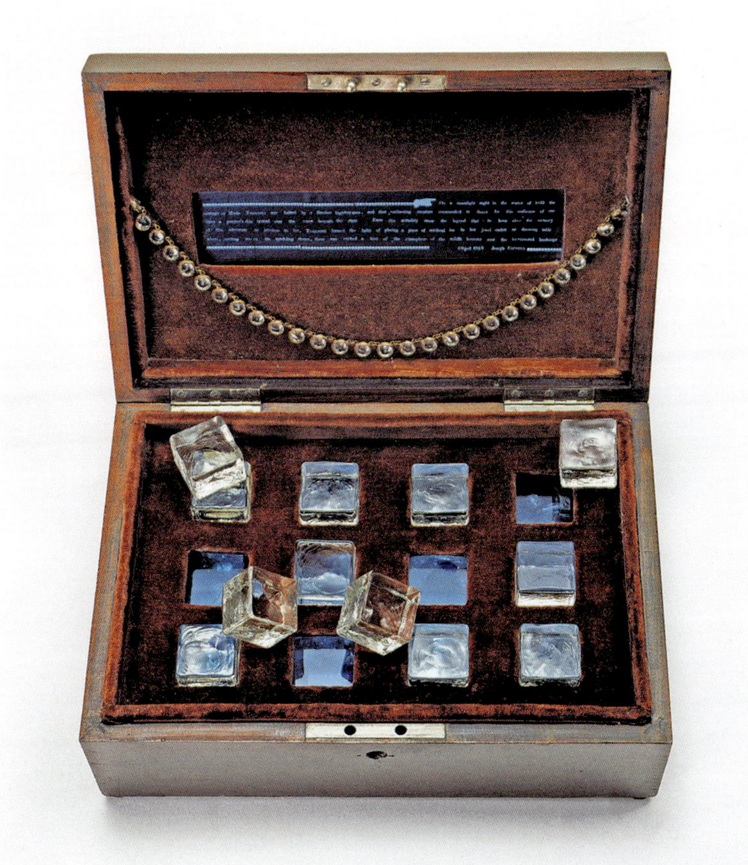

10.06 Joseph Cornell, *Taglioni's Jewel Casket*, 1940, box construction, 4¾ × 1⅞ × 8¼ in., The Museum of Modern Art, New York. Gift of James Thrall Soby

tie between body and mind. In an early box, around 1940, Cornell gathered the "traces of fugitive enchantments" she leaves behind before plunging into the sea: scraps of clothing, sequins, bits of fabric, and blue pearls scattered amid sand and seashells. According to Starr's inventory, Cornell would devote a second and then a third box to her in 1942 and 1943 (*Ondine Souvenir Case* and *Naples*), to which can be added *An Owl for Ondine* in 1954, with the whole series culminating in a small chest patiently elaborated between 1940 and 1960, entitled *Portrait of Ondine* (Smithsonian American Art Museum, Washington, DC), which he himself described as an "unauthorized biography of Cerrito."

Tchelitchew had preceded him on this path by designing the sets and costumes for Jouvet's production of Giraudoux's play *Ondine*, which "humanized the myth," at the Théâtre de l'Athénée, in 1939 (costume designs for *Ondine*, 1939, Bibliothèque National de France, Department of Theater Arts, Paris). Once again, there was nothing fortuitous in this coincidence; the theme of water, the representation of these spits of land eaten away by the sea, these shores where the elements are intermingled, melancholy hinterlands inhabited by hybrid creatures, the obsession with fluidity and metamorphoses—all these are present, and through their various effects and expressions they can be joined together with the works of Bérard, Tchelitchew, as well as the Berman brothers.

Mozartiana

A final myth common to these different works is highlighted in the list that Diane Waldman has drawn up of Cornell's recurrent motifs, in her interpretation of *The Crystal Cage (Portrait of Berenice)*, the famous collage published in *View* in 1943 (private collection). Here we find, side by side, Piero di Cosimo, Hans Christian Andersen, daguerreotypes, balloons, soap bubbles, Edgar Allan Poe, shooting stars, the Hôtel de l'Ange, solariums, snow, Gulliver, Carpaccio, the phases of the moon, Taglioni's ice cubes (fig. 10.06), landscapes in starlight, Queen Mab's palace, tropical bird feathers, Liszt, barometers, an owl, magic lanterns, bird cages, the Milky Way, Carlotta Grisi's aerial leaps—and Mozart.

As another figure of the sublime, a metaphor for the forces of art, Mozart represents the archetype of what Klossowski would have called the eternal adolescent; he is the most impressive of that "image of the child and the adolescent," who—as Edouard Jaeger noted, after Fernando Huici—"appears as an essential and constant element in [Cornell's] work." In the writings on the myth of the artist, he enters a world that echoes the portraits of young nobles and princesses by Bronzino and others, who are one of the leitmotifs of his boxes and collages. But Mozart obviously also represents much more. A paradoxical icon, he comes across, like the acrobat or the dancer, as the incarnation of absolute mastery, of transcendence through grace and harmony simultaneously with a vulnerable immaturity, of virtuosic innocence, of a life threatened with disappearance before being able to come fully into bloom. Like Mozart's music, he joins the most cheerful lightheartedness with the forces of tragedy, the pleasure taken in beauty with the feeling of finitude. Such is the fascinating contradiction in terms that inspires the vision that Bérard also offers us, with an equal intensity. When he sets out to be the set designer for Balanchine's *Mozartiana* in 1933 (fig. 10.07), he always only

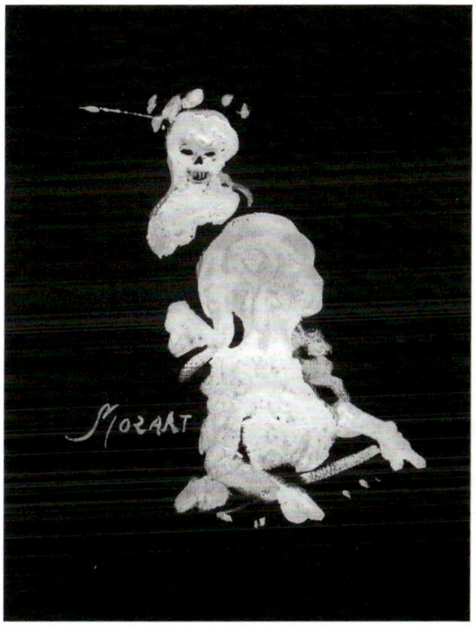

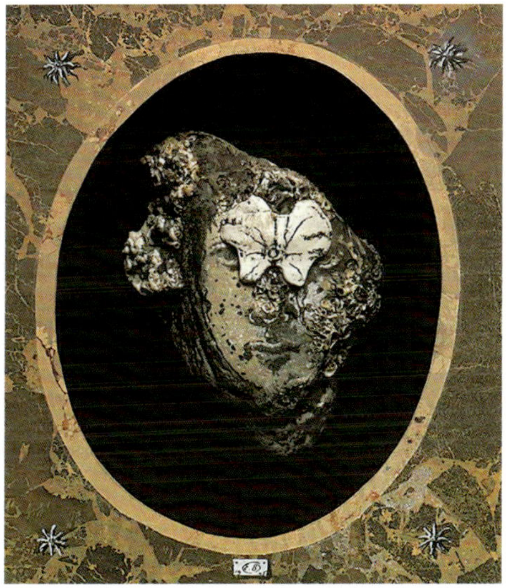

10.07 Christian Bérard, *Project for "Mozartiana,"* 1933, gouache on paper, Collection of Patrick Mauriès **10.08** Eugene Berman, *Untitled* (*Face on Stone*), 1945, ink on stone, paper, and velvet, 14 1/4 × 12 1/4 × 2 3/4 in., Collection of The Tobin Theatre Arts Fund, San Antonio

represents the bewigged child prodigy against a backdrop of allusive staging, in a constant dialogue with the allegory of death, a skeleton crowned with flowers or dressed for the ball. Such is the tone, in the musical sense of the word, that Eugene Berman would in his turn take up in a series of lithographs accompanied by a text by Raffaele Carrieri published in Milan in 1956 which he, in his turn, would entitle *Mozartiana*.

Theater and Fleeting Flashes

Such a constellation of motifs is only one aspect of the much closer relation of their vision and aesthetic values: life as theater, the world as illusion, the game of appearances, the ambiguity of reality and of the shadow it casts. There is never anything in any of these works other than displaced images, with false bottoms, representations of representations (which is what, incidentally, the term "neo-humanism"—overused perhaps, both historically and sociologically—conveys, like water passing through the meshes of a net). From 1930 on, the poverty of subjects in Bérard cannot of course be read independently of reference to Picasso and de Chirico, but also reference to French painting of the seventeenth century, as brought to light by the show in 1934 of *Peintres de la réalité* (Painters of reality) at the Musée de l'Orangerie, decisive for so many artists, from Balthus to Derain.

Similarly, Soby immediately saw that the nocturnal scenes in Berman's first period were above all "props for a romantic theatre" and that his Italy—the empty squares of Padua, Venice, or Ischia—were "still only theater, in which realism plays no role." Factories and actors emerge straight out of engravings by della Bella and Castiglione, from Palladio, the Bibbienas, and Piranesi, serving as a guiding light throughout his work, until his final years in Rome, even in the total revampings of his chromatic scales. His art was scientific, or "literary," to pick up Soby's expression, based on these multiple stratifications of memory, playing with an artistic repertory, with displacements and allusions, before finally illustrating allegorically, as a "neo-humanist" reading would have it, the condition of a Europe subjected to the forces of destruction.

The very space of Neo-romantic painting, thus, is as though magnetically charged: "Perspective and movement," continues Soby, "did not represent questions of pure technique, as had been the case for most of the Cubists; they had an emotional value for Bérard and a metaphysical one for Tchelitchew." And even if Tchelitchew might represent the cold, intellectualized and cerebral pole of Neo-romantic dramaturgy, with Bérard and Berman as the opposite pole, emotional and warm, they all share this taste for a doubled reality, loaded with echoes and allusions, vibrating with artifice. The perspective of these desolate worlds is always that of a theater stage.

It would be pointless to emphasize the parallelism with the minuscule constructions and altered perspectives of Cornell, constrained by the context of a box, playing with optical effects and discreet illusions. The similarities can even become astonishing when Berman, not content to utilize the ordinary effects of trompe-l'oeil—ornamented dial faces, broken window glass (which Cornell may for his part have inherited from Harnett and Peto, exhibited by Levy and reevaluated by Chick Austin in Hartford)—created true painting-reliquaries (fig. 10.08). Brought together by Levy in his 1947 study entitled *Eugene Berman, Paintings, Drawings, and Decor*, with its musical connotations of *Divertissements*, they are collages in three dimensions where painting and drawing integrate foreign objects: seashells, cork, sand, mica, driftwood—the very same that Cornell uses and which seem to offer us the remainders of a nature in perpetual transformation, attacked by time, sublimated into scrap, final leftovers of a reality subjected to the untiring sapping by destruction and death.

"The world of circus performers," writes Jean Starobinski, "is symbolically set between heaven and earth, between life and death, closer to death than to life, where everything arranges itself around the secret of a passage." Suspended space, the space of a labile reality, reflected by the deadened flash of a mirror, refracted by the light of a crystal, filtered by glass sheets, punctuated by fleeting flashes or coated with an artificial snow—these belong both to the settings created by Cornell's white magic as much as to the factories and ruins that compose Eugene Berman's theaters of melancholia.

Sources

Eugene Berman, *The Graphic Work of Eugene Berman* (New York: C. N. Potter, 1971).

Eugene Berman, *Eugene Berman* (Milan: Alexandre Iolas, 1971).

André Chastel, "Résurrection du maniérisme," *Une semaine dans le monde* (November 2, 1946).

Eugene Gaddis, *Magician of the Modern: Chick Austin and the Transformation of the Arts* in America (New York: Knopf, 2000).

Waldemar George, "Le Néo-humanisme," *Formes* 4 (April 1934).

Paris 1989.

Pavel Tchelitchew Drawings, ed. Lincoln Kirstein (New York: H. Bittner and Co., 1946).

Lincoln Kirstein, *Quarry: A Collection in Lieu of Memoirs* (Pasadena: Twelvetrees Press, 1986).

Lincoln Kirstein, *Tchelitchew* (Santa Fe: Twelvetrees Press, 1994).

Boris Kochno, *Christian Bérard* (Paris: Herscher, 1987).

Levy 1977.

Julien Levy, ed., *Eugene Berman* (New York: American Studio Books, 1947).

Patrick Mauriès, ed., *Le Trompe-l'oeil* (Paris, Gallimard, 1996).

James Thrall Soby, *After Picasso* (New York: Dodd, Mead, 1935).

James Thrall Soby, *Tchelitchew* (New York: Museum of Modern Art, 1942).

Jean Starobinski, *Portrait de l'artiste en saltimbanque* (Paris: Gallimard, 2004).

New York 1983.

Gertrude Stein, *The Autobiography of Alice B. Toklas* (Harmondsworth: Penguin Books, 1966).

Waldman 1977.

New York 1978.

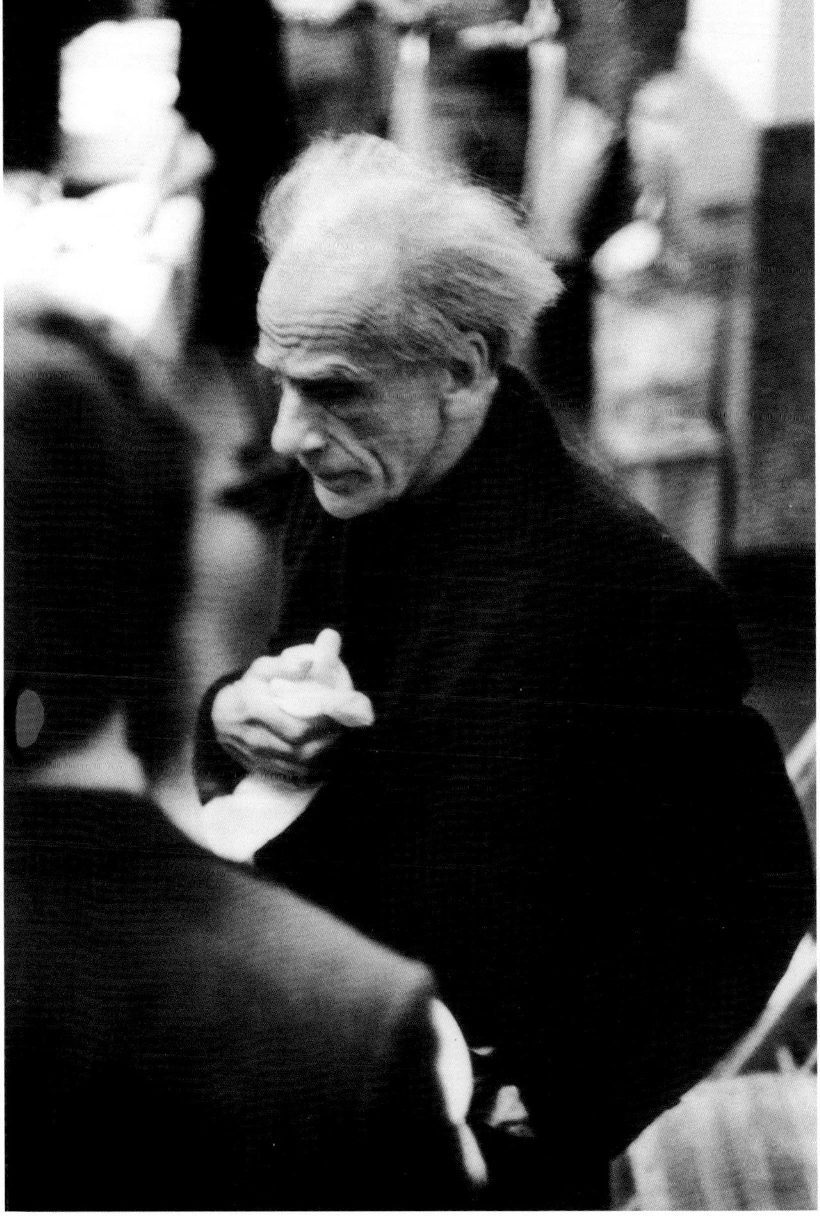

11.01 Fred McDarrah, *Portrait of Joseph Cornell*, c. 1970, Private collection

The Intuitive Space of Joseph Cornell

Howard Hussey

His work is filled with the white light of early morning—he and Herman Melville in this country have understood the concept of white the most richly.

—Robert Motherwell, 1953[1]

The very same white light of early morning was present in the Whitechapel Gallery when I arrived in London in late February 1981 to deliver a series of talks in association with Joseph Cornell's first major retrospective to travel outside the United States.

The central gallery of the Whitechapel, of too great a height for the intimate dimensions of Cornell's objects, caused their perfect scale to seem optically reduced. A false ceiling of white gauze devised by Nicholas Serota solved the problem. Lowered ingeniously, the transparent ceiling also permitted effective illumination from skylights higher up to pass through the gauze. Cornell's exposition was seen in a most enhancing blue-white radiance.

Earlier in his career, when he was perpetually troubled by exhibition lighting and deceptive gallery spaces, Cornell commented on one of many aspects of the problems he faced: "A new side of the work will come through when I least expect it. Even the lighting in a gallery will show me something I hadn't intended and very often this other something is what is seen and is in a very different light from the one it was taking shape in."

Cornell the task master, perfectionist, would have been pleased with the unexpected early morning radiance in the Whitechapel. He might have been hypnotized by it, over-sensitized as he was to the supernatural properties of the light he so loved in ice, in snow, candles, mirrors, crystals, clouds—such unearthly essences always arrested his attention, became light-traps, light prisons, to defy and challenge him, frustrate his self-taught skills to capture the fleeting symbols of his light-receptive visions, too many rare impressions and occurrences that were as quick as lightning continued to escape him.

In his workshop studio, where I saw him for the last time, I remember him at his most intense, lit by two naked light bulbs like two obsessions or two glaring unadorned hypotheses: One, the dream, the other reality, casting their twin radiance upon him, reminding me also of Cornell's correspondent personal ethic: To live to work, to work to live. Always the two were rediscovered anew, as if perpetually reborn again the moment the two light bulbs were turned on in the austere limbo of his workshop.

He once repeated a statement Duchamp made during the forties in New York City: "Painting had its back up against the wall for too long. I had to change all that. Joe, it was necessary that I should remove the wall." Cornell for a time offered Duchamp aid with the meticulous task of assembling the precision-made contents in several examples of Duchamp's *Boîte-en-valise*. A shy man and basically much too reticent for Duchamp (the ultra-sophisticated cosmopolite), Cornell habitually listened to M.D. with typical absent commentary. Joseph was well on with his own process of making walls dissolve or, at best, they must be an integrated part of his vision.

Cornell desired his objects and boxes to be able to go just about anywhere anyone wanted to take them to enjoy them. It did not matter very much where—a mountain peak, a roof top, a deserted beach, a cave in the cliffs—one could stop relating to walls and venture beyond into the interior life of the object occupying your own space with you.

While assisting Cornell for several paradoxical years, while serving him as gardener, secret agent, secretary, messenger, and the ghost of Franz Liszt, during these occupations I observed that he was also exploring a principle of uncertainty, or rather interrogating the principle because of another potential dimension hidden within. He was wanting the uncertainty of his experimental procedure to be part of the contemplative observer's conscious experience. In this it became clear to me how characteristic it was of Cornell to arrange the odds of a creative wager against himself. He was both in the center and on the periphery of his own creative clairvoyance.

"But my work may not last; it's too ephemeral." Even with all the uncertainties regarding the longevity of his objects, the endless labor delighted him like a series of surprise obstacle courses. He began to treat his experimental interests as obstacle-course games for the exercise and conditioning of the human spirit. Of his deeper motivations as experimenter-innovator, one was the intention to slow down his mind's variable perceptions, too much like the speed of light itself. The boxes and objects were conceived prodigiously nearer and nearer to his complex and wonderfully eccentric spatial intuitions.

From about 1940, Cornell was engaged in devising and revising his rediscovery of the philosophical toy into playful obstacle-course games. Science and metaphysics guided him in accordance with his interests. Inner space was treated as outer space; outer space became as familiar as inner space. The near and the far were synonymous, the drama of darkness and light became the intimacy and immensity of seeing and knowing. How utterly different what we see is from what we know.

Cornell wanted to sanction and preserve within his work the extra dimensional sense aspects of speed and light, with which events in the observable (phenomenal) world occurred, but he wished to represent symbolic equations of these events in a space and light that would define such ephemeral actualities, so they could easily be recognized and assimilated, even by a child.

Cornell needed his boxes, his obstacle courses, to aid him in his creative obsessions, intending to make of his daily life a continual series of monuments (intimate monuments) to all the moments of his earthly existence. The opening chapter of the book of Cornell's life should read like a sunrise.

I remember an occasion at 4:00 in the morning, while in the elation of a marathon of new ideas, he pondered how "The rising and setting of the sun is our newest and our oldest story, retold daily and each time with a unique variation (in detail) for the beholder!" As a visual motif in his middle and late collage work, sunrise and sunset offer the observer an immediate basic mood and a chronological identity. The effect is of coming home to a favorite room at a favorite hour.

Cornell accumulated files and dossiers filled to capacity with imagery and illustrations of every atmospheric effect in nature. The pursuit of such superterrestrial phenomena became an archive of formidable proportions. Such abundant reserves of imagery—never to be entirely absorbed in the collage series—exist now, in Washington, as a testimonial to Cornell's clairvoyant and visionary endowments as a humanist. Almost as far back as once upon a time, Cornell's extra-dimensional ambitions had become extra-dimensional life dedications. He was as determined to collect sunrises (and sunsets) as some of us collect wine labels or road maps, coins and postage stamps.

The concept of infinity kept him awake nights as a young student, a passionate insomniac completely surrounded by a space which no one could parcel up into cozy or comfortable boundaries, nor could such a continuous space be measured with provable or scientific accuracy.

In later years, a series of three-dimensional constructions bearing superterrestrial themes—*Winter Night Skies, Night Songs, Night Voyages*—began to evolve from Cornell's youthful memories and experiences as a student obsessed and frightened by astronomy. His archives held sufficient reserves of sunrise and sunset and he could re-address himself to an adolescent avocation: his fascination with the mysteries of the stars. An exploration with the constellations of both hemispheres was resumed; the material at hand contained enough of the past and the present and by implication of the future to occupy him for a total of fifty-odd years. Romantic navigations in the heavens was only one of seven major themes within the more expansive range of Cornell's kaleidescopic rediscovery of Natural Philosophy.

"Cornell has devised an experiment which completely overturns the conventional use of the object."

—Andre Breton[2]

The sage of Surrealism gave early recognition to the objects. Breton, however, was not praising Cornell's experiment as art per se, but endorsing the austerity and restraint Cornell brought to the overly indulgent field of visual perception. For Breton, the endeavor of higher learning and perception was inclusive of psychology, metaphysics, and ritual, but embraced art as well, all these categories involve space, time, and dreams as interrelated intuitive functions. Thus, Cornell considered Breton's support to be of and in direct accord with paths of interest that momentarily coincided.

The Surrealist cause never won Cornell completely. He did not wish for political exposure in public manifestations.

Like the quivering blue needle on a compass, Cornell's pure northern spirit sought for itself the most remote of all hyperborean retreats, Andromeda, Auriga, Cassiopeia. The sense of utter solitude in the vast expanses of the universe was what exalted the (symbolist) poet in him.

Cornell was nevertheless on the track of another marvelous potential: the one that preceded and then superseded Surrealism. The very one located within himself, a metaphysician who had no need to look for such potentials elsewhere.

The surreal aspect of a creative revelation in depth was brought home to him by the mystical presence of a seashell, a feather, a perfect cube of ice reappearing like a double exposure in the silent spectral harmony of his own interstellar solitude.

Cornell's personal ethic was rooted in the study of Natural Philosophy. His use of the word philosophy did not mean intellectual pursuits divorced from everyday life. This implies an attitude inherent to the real (actual) and metaphysical (universal) elements brought face to face in Cornell's naturally philosophical modes of exploration.

His work occasions a deeper learning (or teaching) as one of its more intriguing virtues—a way of life, a disposition toward nature and man, and an ethic for perceiving both.

The night themes also served as obstacle courses to detain for him the inexorable experience of life, his life, as a one-way trip into infinity. To a young friend he casually suggested: "Next time you happen to be on a beach, scoop up a thimbleful of sand and count the grains, see what happens."

Cornell cheerfully supplied our adventurer with the thimble. There followed a close examination of several of the sand boxes, sand fountains, and prisons, each example containing a fixed quantity of blue, yellow, white, or brown sand hermetically sealed in affecting patterns, abstractions, and forms which never yield to repeating any one configuration twice. If the concept of infinity inspired Cornell with the idea of sand fountains and prisons, it was because these objects were for him infinity machines in the generic sense of the hourglass, but more capable than an hourglass of inducing a creative trance or contemplative state of vision in the observer.

A fountain and a prison are light years away in contrast to each other. But Cornell saw them as spiritual forms and realities issuing from the same source. They would, therefore, yield astonishing intercommunication if one could hold the two together in a single-minded vision. Such unity of perception is contained in the principle of Cornell's philosophical toys—both the basic potential of being either fountain or prison, depending upon the observer's eye, mind, and emotional state when in contact with any such reversible precepts in art. Cornell's sand fountains and sand prisons will yield or withhold their secrets, depending upon the qualities informing our own best-known secrets, the shareable and the unshareable.

The philosophical toy is not a new or revolutionary conception. Cornell simply realized with a clear vision how to restore to the ancient idea and belief in games and play an appetite for mystery and contemplation.

What is the imagination? Is it an encyclopedic source of energy and information for the psyche, an intelligence navigating in time/space, like a satellite, transmitting an endless series of reports and discoveries to a correspondent receptor that wants to know more than it knows?

Should we not familiarize ourselves with the idea of infinity or the speed of light, and just exactly what are light years? Through the concept of toys, of play, of games, such observation, revelation, and surprise constitute the spiritual principle and legacy inherent in Cornell's work. He dreamed of a theater of the marvelous that would replace all obsolete systems of mass-organized education. His dream was so palpable, of such intensity, his inspiration so incredibly vivid, he lived his dream simultaneously with his everyday life, All things had become sacred to him. It was as if this dream finally, in an overflowing of the dream dimension, multiplied itself in cosmic response to Cornell's visionary desire and passed over all the obstacles and barriers to reality.

Cornell, the white magician, had become an alchemist, that man who forgets to eat and sleep. The man who has an infinite appetite for interrelations of things and causes. The foundation for Cornell's Theater of the Marvelous evolved gradually from his intimate relationship with ordinary, everyday objects, but they are not so ordinary from his point of view, all of them touched by or related in some way to the scale of a human hand and a knowledge of their metaphysical (universal) meanings.

The rediscovery of games and play as symbolic activities of a profound order suggested to Cornell a miraculous treasury of the real, part sanctuary, part museum, whose walls or boundaries can be seen through, a sacred zone, a special reserved place, small enough for a child to relate to, and then embrace and carry off. The would-be possessor is at the same time possessed by it.

Toys for adults is what he sometimes inferred, but such objects and inventions remain somehow theaters of infinity. They are meant for those who are intuitive to the wisdom contained in a philosophical toy: Play to Play. Is there something to win, perhaps only the formidable discovery of yet another universe hidden inside the one you were so sure you knew?

What we believe to be the facts may only be surface fictions of our own devising. Observe once again.

After several years, I had come to regard Cornell as the man without a country, who could never get lost because his home had become the entire planet.

To become a connoisseur of mysteries one must not be confused by that which is merely or momentarily mysterious and the significant mystery.

With his special friend, the poet Mina Loy, who sometimes behaved like his tutelary muse, Cornell shared many a secret because once, at a time when he needed it, she spoke one line of poetry that he understood as the great mystery, and thus he saw as a fountain or prison of Truth: "'Self' is the covered entrance to Infinity."

Notes

Previously unpublished in English, this essay was written in response to the presentation of the exhibition Joseph Cornell (organized by the Museum of Modern Art in New York) at the Whitechapel Gallery in London (March 2–April 12, 1981).

1 Robert Motherwell, "Preface to a Joseph Cornell Exhibition" (1953), in *The Writings of Robert Motherwell*, ed. Dore Ashton with Joan Banach (Berkeley: University of California Press, 2007), 169.

2 Breton 1941, 26.

3 Mina Loy, "Psycho-Democracy: A Movement to Focus Human Reason on the Conscious Direction of Evolution," *The Little Review* 8, no. 1 (Autumn 1921): 18.

Bibliography

Writings by Joseph Cornell

Caws 1993
Mary Ann Caws, ed., *Joseph Cornell's Theater of the Mind: Selected Diaries, Letters, and Files*, New York: Thames & Hudson, 1993.

Cornell 1936
Joseph Cornell, "Monsieur Phot" (1933), in Julien Levy, *Surrealism*, New York: The Black Sun Press, 1936, 77–88; reprint, New York: The Arno Press, 1968; reprint Adams Sitney, ed., *The Avant-Garde Film: A Reader of Theory and Criticism*, New York: New York University Press, 1978, 51–59.

Cornell 1942
Joseph Cornell, "'Enchanted Wanderer': Excerpt from a Journey Album for Hedy Lamarr," *View* 1st series, nos. 9–10 (Dec. 1942–Jan. 1943): 3; reprint Nendeln, Liechtenstein: Kraus, 1969.

Cornell 1943
Joseph Cornell, "The Crystal Cage (Portrait of Berenice)," *View* 2nd series, no. 4 (Jan. 1943): 10–16; reprint Liechtenstein: Kraus, 1969.

Cornell 1944
Joseph Cornell, "Taglioni, Charlotte Grisi, Cerrrito and Fanny Elsler," special issue of *Dance Index* 3, nos. 7–8 (July–Aug. 1944), with a cover designed by the artist; reprint New York: Arno Press, 1970.

Cornell 1945
Joseph Cornell, "Comment" and "Theater of Hans Christian Andersen," *Dance Index* 4, no. 9 (Sept. 1945): 139 and 155–59, with a cover designed by the artist; reprint New York: Arno Press, 1970.

Cornell 1946
Joseph Cornell, "Clowns, Elephants and Ballerinas," special issue of *Dance Index* 5, no. 6 (June 1946), with a cover designed by the artist; reprint New York: Arno Press, 1970.

Cornell 1954
Joseph Cornell, *Maria*, New York: Salamander Editions, 1954; reprinted in Dore Ashton, *A Joseph Cornell Album*, New York: Viking Press, 1974, 135–41.

Cornell 1955
The Bel Canto Pet: First Day of Locust Song, Spring 1955; reprinted in Dore Ashton, *A Joseph Cornell Album*, New York: Viking Press, 1974, 142–49.

Cornell n.d.
"Nebula, the Powdered Sugar Princess," n.d., *October*; 15 (Winter 1980): 40–48.

Selected Publications on Joseph Cornell

One-Artist Exhibitions

Cologne 1992
Bernd Growe, Ellen H. Johnson, and Robert Motherwell, *Joseph Cornell, 1903–1972*, Cologne, Galerie Karsten Greve, 1992.

Kamakura 1992
Sandra Leonard Starr, *Joseph Cornell*, Kamakura, Japan: The Museum of Modern Art, 1992.

Lyon 2013
Matthew Affron and Sylvie Ramond, *Joseph Cornell et les surréalistes à New York*. Paris: Editions Hazan, 2013.

Madrid 1984
Fernando Huici, *Joseph Cornell*, Madrid, Fundación Juan March, 1984.

New York 1967
Diane Waldman, *Joseph Cornell*, New York: The Solomon R. Guggenheim Museum, 1967.

New York 1976
Sandra Leonard Starr, *Joseph Cornell Portfolio*, preface by Robert Motherwell (1953), New York: American Dovecote and Shooting Gallery Co., 1976.

New York 1978
Richard L. Feigen, Howard Hussey and Donald Windham, *Joseph Cornell: Collages 1931–1972*, New York: Castelli, Feigen, Corcoran, 1978.

New York 1980
Kynaston McShine, ed., *Joseph Cornell*, New York: The Museum of Modern Art, 1980.

New York 1982
Sandra Leonard Starr, *Joseph Cornell: Art and Metaphysics*, New York: Castelli, Feigen, Corcoran, 1982.

New York 1983
Sandra Leonard Starr, *Joseph Cornell and the Ballet*, New York: Castelli, Feigen, Corcoran, 1983.

New York 1995
Donald Windham, *Joseph Cornell: Box Constructions and Collages*, New York: C&M Arts, 1995.

Paris 1980
Marie-Claude Beaud and Jean Le Gac, *Joseph Cornell*, with French trans. of a preface by Robert Motherwell (1953), Paris: Galerie Baudoin Lebon, 1980.

Paris 1989
Édouard Jaguer, *Joseph Cornell*, Paris: Galerie 1900–2000, 1989.

Pasadena 1966

Fairfield Porter, *An Exhibition of Works by Joseph Cornell*, Pasadena, CA: Pasadena Art Museum, 1966.

Philadelphia 1998 (traveled to Houston 1999)

Ecke Bonk et al., *Joseph Cornell / Marcel Duchamp . . . In Resonance*, Ostfildern-Ruit: Cantz Verlag, 1998.

Tokyo 1987

Sandra Leonard Starr, *Joseph Cornell: Box Constructions and Collages* and *Joseph Cornell: The Crystal Cage (Portrait of Berenice)* Tokyo, Gatoda Gallery, 1987.

Washington 2006 (traveled to Salem 2007 and San Francisco 2007)

Lynda Roscoe Hartigan, *Joseph Cornell: Navigating the Imagination*, New Haven: Yale University Press, 2007.

Selected Literature

Ades 1997

Dawn Ades, "Joseph Cornell," in *Surrealist Art: The Lindy and Edwin Bergman Collection at the Art Institute of Chicago*, London: Thames & Hudson, 1997, 28–99.

Ades 1980

Dawn Ades, 'The Transcendental Surrealism of Joseph Cornell', in New York 1980, pp. 15–42.

Andersen 2006

Wayne Andersen, "Joseph Cornell's 'Healthier Possibilities,'" *Common Knowledge* 12, no. 3 (2006): 420–42.

Ashton 1974

Dore Ashton, *A Joseph Cornell Album*, New York: Viking Press, 1974.

Blair 1998

Lindsay Blair, *Joseph Cornell's Vision of Spiritual Order*, London: Reaktion Books, 1998.

Bullot 1990

Erik Bullot, "Le Voyageur dans les glaces," in *Sortir du cinéma: Histoire virtuelle des relations de l'art et du cinéma*, Geneva: MAMCO, 2013, 141–63.

Caws 1989

Mary Ann Caws, "Collecting and Containing: Joseph Cornell and Mallarmé," in *The Art of Interference*, New York: Polity Press, 1989, 201–15.

Caws 1990

Mary Ann Caws, "Joseph Cornell: l'invention de la boîte surréaliste," *Études françaises* 26, no. 3 (1990): 79–86.

Caws 1997

Mary Ann Caws, "Constructing: Joseph Cornell's Metaphysics of Memory," in *The Surrealist Look*, Cambridge: MIT Press, 1997, 197–219.

Corman 2007

Catherine Corman, ed., *Joseph Cornell's Dreams*, Cambridge: Exact Change, 2007.

Edwards and Taylor 2007

Jason Edwards and Stephanie L. Taylor, eds., *Joseph Cornell: Opening the Box*, Oxford: Peter Lang, 2007.

d'Harnoncourt 1978

Anne d'Harnoncourt, "The Cubist Cockatoo: A Preliminary Exploration of Joseph Cornell's Homages to Juan Gris," *Philadelphia Museum of Art Bulletin*, 74, no. 321 (June 1978): 2–17.

Hartigan 1983

Lynda Roscoe Hartigan, *Joseph Cornell: An Exploration of Sources*, Washington, National Museum of American Art, Smithsonian Institution, 1983.

Hartigan, Vine, Lehrman 2003

Lynda Roscoe Hartigan, Richard Vine, and Robert Lehrman, *Joseph Cornell: Shadowplay Eterniday*, New York: Thames & Hudson, 2003.

Hartounian 1981

Helen H. Hartounian, "Joseph Cornell in 'View,'" *Arts Magazine* 55, no. 7 (March 1981): 102–8.

Hauptman 1999

Jodi Hauptman, *Joseph Cornell: Stargazing in the Cinema*, New Haven: Yale University Press, 1999.

Hennessey 1983

Christine Hennessey, "Joseph Cornell: A Balletomane," *Archives of American Art Journal* 23, no. 3 (1983): 6–12.

Hoving 2006

Kristen Hoving, "The Surreal Science of Soap: Joseph Cornell's First Soap Bubble Set," *American Art* 20, no. 1 (2006): 15–35.

Hoving 2009

Kristen Hoving, *Joseph Cornell and Astronomy: A Case for the Stars*, Princeton: Princeton University Press, 2009.

Hubert 1983

Renée Riese Hubert, "Patch and Paradox in Joseph Cornell's Art," in *Collage*, ed. Jeanine Parisier Plottel, New York: New York Literary Forum, 1983, 167–79.

Hussey 1979

Howard Hussey, "Music in the World of Joseph Cornell," *Keynote*, 3 no. 3 (May 1979): 6–12.

Jouffroy 1970

Alain Jouffroy, "Les Hôtels de Joseph Cornell," *Opus International*, 19–20, (Oct. 1970): 52–56.

Keller 1986

Marjorie Keller, *The Untutored Eye: Childhood in the Films of Cocteau, Cornell, and Brakhage*, Rutherford, NJ: Fairleigh Dickinson University Press, 1986.

Kelley 2003

Mike Kelley, "Hollywood Filmic Language, Stuttered: Caltiki the Immortal Monster and Rose Hobart," in *Foul Perfection*, Cambridge: MIT Press, 2003, 40–49.

Kosinski 2005
Dorothy Kosinski, *Dialogues: Duchamp, Cornell, Johns, Rauschenberg*, New Haven: Yale University Press, 2005.

Lawson 1980
Thomas Lawson, "Silently, by Means of a Flashing Light," *October* 15 (Winter 1980): 49–60.

Leppanen-Guerra 2011
Analisa Leppanen-Guerra, *Children's Stories and "Child-Time" in the Works of Joseph Cornell and the Transatlantic Avant-Garde*, Burlington, VT: Ashgate, 2011.

Leppanen-Guerra and Tashjian 2012
Analisa Leppanen-Guerra and Dickran Tashjian, eds., *Joseph Cornell's Manual of Marvels: How Joseph Cornell Reinvented a French Agricultural Manual to Create an American Masterpiece*, New York: Thames & Hudson, 2012.

Martin 1986
Richard Martin, "Some Lobsters, Some Elephants: Surrealist Reflections on Joseph Cornell's A Pantry Ballet (for Jacques Offenbach)," *Arts Magazine* 60, no. 6 (Feb. 1986): 30–32.

Michelson 1973
Annette Michelson, "Rose Hobart and Monsieur Phot," *Artforum* 11, no. 10 (June 1973): 47–57.

Mileaf 2003
Janine Mileaf, "Boxes, Books, and the Boîte-en-valise," in *A Transatlantic Avant-Garde: American Artists in Paris 1918–1939*, ed. Sophie Lévy, Berkeley, University of California Press, 2003, 163–72.

Moon 1998
Michael Moon, "Oralia: Joseph Cornell, Hunger, Sweetness, and Women's Performances," in *A Small Boy and Others*, Durham, NC: Duke University Press, 1998, 133–54.

Mundy 2004
Jennifer Mundy, "An "Overflowing, a Richness & Poetry": Joseph Cornell's Planet Set and Giuditta Pasta" (2004); www.tate.org.uk/research/tateresearch/tatepapers/04spring/cornell_paper.htm

O'Doherty 1982
Brian O'Doherty, "Joseph Cornell: Outsider on the Left," in *American Masters*, New York: Dutton, 1982, 317–56.

Pigott 2014
Michael Pigott, *Joseph Cornell versus Cinema* (London: Bloomsbury, 2014).

Porter 1966
Fairfield Porter, "Joseph Cornell," *Art and Literature*, 8 (April 1966): 120–30.

Schaffner 1999
Ingrid Schaffner, "Joseph Cornell," in *Deep Storage: Collecting, Storing, and Archiving in Art*, ed. Ingrid Schaffner and Matthias Winzen, Munich: Prestel, 1999, 102–5.

Schmied 1972
Wieland Schmied, *Joseph Cornell*, Hanover: Kestner-Gesellschaft, 1972.

Solomon 1997
Deborah Solomon, *Utopia Parkway: The Life and Work of Joseph Cornell*, New York: Farrar, Strauss and Giroux, 1997.

Staiger 2005
Janet Staiger, "Cabinets of Transgression: Collecting and Arranging Hollywood Images," *Participations* 1, no. 3 (Feb. 2005): www.participations.org/volume%201/issue%203/1_03_staiger_article.htm

Suárez 2007
Juan A. Suárez, "Joseph Cornell and the Secret Life of Things," in *Pop Modernism: Noise and the Reinvention of the Everyday*, Urbana: University of Illinois Press, 2007, 141–75.

Tashjian 1992
Dickran Tashjian, *Joseph Cornell: Gifts of Desire*, Miami Beach, FL: Grassfield Press, 1992.

Tashjian 1998
Dickran Tashjian, "'Vous pour moi?' Marcel Duchamp and Transgender Coupling," in *Mirror Images: Women, Surrealism, and Self-Representation*, ed. Whitney Chadwick, Cambridge: MIT Press, 1998, 36–65.

Tashjian 2005
Dickran Tashjian, "'Home Poor Heart': The Architecture of Cornell's Desire," in *Surrealism and Architecture*, ed. Thomas Mical, New York: Routledge, 2005, 41–52.

Waldman 1977
Diane Waldman, *Joseph Cornell*, New York: George Braziller, 1977.

Waldman 2002
Diane Waldman, *Joseph Cornell: Master of Dreams*, New York: Harry N. Abrams, 2002.

Publications on Surrealism

Selected Exhibitions

Boca Raton 1997
Michael Rosenfeld, *Surrealism and American Art, 1929–1949*, Boca Raton, FL: Boca Raton Museum of Art, 1997.

Hartford 2003
Eric Zafran, ed., *Surrealism and Modernism from the Collection of the Wadsworth Atheneum Museum of Art*, Hartford, CT: Wadsworth Atheneum, 2003.

London 1978

Dawn Ades, *Dada and Surrealism Reviewed,* London, Arts Council of Great Britain, 1978.

London 2001

Jennifer Mundy, ed., *Surrealism: Desire Unbound,* London: Tate Publishing, 2001.

Marseille 1986

Bernard Noël et al., *La Planète affolée: surréalisme, dispersion et influences, 1938–1947*, Marseille: Centre de la Vielle Charité, Paris: Flammarion, 1986.

New Brunswick, NJ 1977

Jeffrey Wechsler, *Surrealism and American Art, 1931–1947*, New Brunswick, NJ: Rutgers University Art Gallery, 1977.

New York 1936

Alfred H., Jr. Barr, *Fantastic Art, Dada, Surrealism,* New York: The Museum of Modern Art, 1936.

New York 1998

Ingrid Schaffner and Lisa Jacobs, eds., *Julien Levy: Portrait of an Art Gallery*, New York: Equitable Gallery, Cambridge: MIT Press, 1998.

New York 1999

Jacques Baron, et al., *Surrealism: Two Private Eyes. The Nesuhi Ertegun and Daniel Filipacchi Collections*, New York: Harry N. Abrams, 1999.

New York 2004

Susan Davidson and Philip Rylands, eds., *Peggy Guggenheim and Frederick Kiesler, The Story of Art of This Century*, New York: Solomon R. Guggenheim Foundation, 2004.

New York 2005

Isabelle Dervaux, *Surrealism USA*, New York: National Academy Museum, Ostfildern-Ruit: Hatje Cantz, 2005.

Philadelphia 2006

Katherine Ware and Peter Barberie, *Dreaming in Black and White: Photography at the Julien Levy Gallery*, Philadelphia: Philadelphia Museum of Art, New Haven: Yale University Press, 2006.

St. Petersburg 2000

William Jeffett, *Masterpieces of Surrealism*, St. Petersburg, FL: Salvador Dalí Museum, 2000.

Strasbourg 2000

Maria Lluïsa Borrás et al., *Les Surréalistes en exil et les débuts de l'école de New York:* Strasbourg, Musée d'Art Moderne et Contemporain, 2000.

San Antonio 2004

Michael Duncan, *High Drama: Eugene Berman and the Legacy of the Melancholic Sublime*, San Antonio, TX: McNay Art Museum, 2004.

University Park 2004

Ingrid Schaffner and Colin Westerbeck, *Accommodations of Desire: Surrealist Works on Paper Collected by Julien Levy*, University Park, PA: Palmer Museum of Art, Penn State University, Pasadena, CA: Curatorial Assistance, Inc. 2004.

Selected Literature

Breton 1941

André Breton, "Genesis and Perspective of Surrealism" (1941), trans. Laurence Vail, in *Art of This Century*, ed. Peggy Guggenheim (New York: Art of This Century, 1942).

Breton 1945

André Breton, *Le Surréalisme et la peinture*, New York: Brentano's, 1945; reprint: Étienne-Alain Hubert, in collaboration with Philippe Bernier and Marie-Clarie Dumas, ed., André Breton, *Œuvres complètes* (vol. 4), Paris: Gallimard, 2008.

Breton 1978

André Breton, *What is Surrealism? Selected Writings*, ed. Franklin Rosemont (New York: Monad Press, 1978).

Breton 1937

André Breton, *Mad Love*, trans. Mary Ann Caws (Lincoln: University of Nebraska Press, 1987).

Ford 1991

Charles Henri Ford, ed., *View: Parade of the Avant-Garde*, New York: Thunder's Mouth Press, 1991.

Levy 1936

Julien Levy, *Surrealism,* New York: Black Sun Press, 1936.

Levy 1977

Julien Levy, *Memoir of an Art Gallery*, New York: G. P Putnam's Sons, 1977; reprint with an introduction by Ingrid Schaffner, Boston: MFA Publications, 2003.

Miller 2007

Angela Miller, "'With Eyes Wide Open': The American Reception of Surrealism," in *Caught by Politics: Hitler Exiles and American Visual Culture*, ed. Sabine Eckmann and Lutz Koepnick, New York: Palgrave, 2007, 61–94.

Sawin 1995

Martica Sawin, *Surrealism in Exile and the Beginning of the New York School*, Cambridge: MIT Press, 1995.

Zafran 2000

Eric M. Zafran, "'I am Not a Madman': Salvador Dalí in Hartford," in *Dalí's Optical Illusions*, ed. Dawn Ades, New Haven: Yale University Press, 2000, 38–61.

Zlotsky 1986

Deborah Zlotsky, "'Pleasant Madness' in Hartford: The First Surrealist Exhibition in America," *Arts Magazine* 60, no. 6 (Feb. 1986): 55–61.

Illustration Credits

Every effort has been made to identify and contact the copyright holders of the images published in this book. Should you discover an error, please contact the publisher. The following have granted permission to reproduce illustrations in this book.

© 2015 Artists Rights Society (ARS), New York / ADAGP, Paris. Courtesy Philadelphia Museum of Art: 3.09

© 2015 Artists Rights Society (ARS), New York / ADAGP, Paris. Courtesy The Menil Collection, Houston. Photo: Robert Mates: 10.04

© 2015 Estate of Pablo Picasso / Artists Rights Society (ARS), New York: 10.03

© Artists Rights Society (ARS), New York / ADAGP, Paris. Courtesy Collection of Patrick Mauriès, Paris: 10.07

© Bibliothèque nationale de France: 3.01, 3.02, 3.03

© bpk, Berlin / Hamburger Kunsthalle / Elke Walford / Art Resource, NY: 1.06

© CNAC/MNAM/Dist. RMN-Grand Palais / Art Resource, NY: 2.02

© Edward Owen / Art Resource, NY: 6.08

© Getty Images, St. Louis, MO. Courtesy Private Collection: 11.01

© Man Ray Trust / Artists Rights Society (ARS), NY / ADAGP, Paris 2015, 3.04

© Man Ray Trust / Artists Rights Society (ARS), NY / ADAGP, Paris 2015 / CNAC/MNAM/Dist. RMN-Grand Palais: 3.06

© Taryn Simon. Courtesy Gagosian Gallery: 6.06

© The Joseph and Robert Cornell Memorial Foundation / Licensed by VAGA, New York, NY: 1.01, 1.07, 8.06

© The Joseph and Robert Cornell Memorial Foundation / Licensed by VAGA, New York, NY & SPDA, Tokyo: 9.07

© The Joseph and Robert Cornell Memorial Foundation / Licensed by VAGA, New York, NY. Courtesy Bibliothèque Nationale de France: 3.05

© The Joseph and Robert Cornell Memorial Foundation / Licensed by VAGA, New York, NY. Courtesy Collection of Carol and Douglas Cohen: 9.06

© The Joseph and Robert Cornell Memorial Foundation / Licensed by VAGA, New York, NY. Courtesy Joseph Cornell Study Center, Smithsonian American Art Museum, Washington, DC: 5.01

© The Joseph and Robert Cornell Memorial Foundation / Licensed by VAGA, New York, NY. Courtesy National Gallery of Art, Washington, DC: 2.04

© The Joseph and Robert Cornell Memorial Foundation / Licensed by VAGA, New York, NY. Courtesy of Anthology Film Archives, New York: 6.09

© The Joseph and Robert Cornell Memorial Foundation / Licensed by VAGA, New York, NY. Courtesy of the Collection of Marguerite and Robert Hoffman: 2.07, 9.05

© The Joseph and Robert Cornell Memorial Foundation / Licensed by VAGA, New York, NY. Courtesy of The Fralin Museum of Art at the University of Virginia: pages 13–17

© The Joseph and Robert Cornell Memorial Foundation / Licensed by VAGA, New York, NY. Courtesy of The Museum of Modern Art, New York: 8.07

© The Joseph and Robert Cornell Memorial Foundation / Licensed by VAGA, New York, NY. Courtesy of The Philadelphia Museum of Art: 7.01

© The Joseph and Robert Cornell Memorial Foundation / Licensed by VAGA, New York, NY. Courtesy Peabody Essex Museum, Salem, MA: 5.05

© The Joseph and Robert Cornell Memorial Foundation / Licensed by VAGA, New York, NY. Courtesy Private Collection. Photo by Matt Suib: 9.04

© The Joseph and Robert Cornell Memorial Foundation / Licensed by VAGA, New York, NY. Courtesy Private Collection. Photo by Michael Tropea: 1.02, 1.03, 1.05

© The Joseph and Robert Cornell Memorial Foundation / Licensed by VAGA, New York, NY. Courtesy Private Collection. Photo by Tom Powell: 9.02

© The Joseph and Robert Cornell Memorial Foundation / Licensed by VAGA, New York, NY. Courtesy Richard L. Feigen: 7.05

© The Joseph and Robert Cornell Memorial Foundation / Licensed by VAGA, New York, NY. Courtesy San Francisco Museum of Modern Art: 3.08

© The Joseph and Robert Cornell Memorial Foundation / Licensed by VAGA, New York, NY. Courtesy Satoshi Yokota: 7.02

© The Joseph and Robert Cornell Memorial Foundation / Licensed by VAGA, New York, NY. Courtesy Smithsonian American Art Museum: 10.01

© The Joseph and Robert Cornell Memorial Foundation / Licensed by VAGA, New York, NY. Courtesy The Art Institute of Chicago: 9.03

© The Joseph and Robert Cornell Memorial Foundation / Licensed by VAGA, New York, NY. Courtesy The Menil Collection, Houston, Bequest of Jermayne MacAgy. Photo: Hickey-Robertson, Houston: 9.08

© The Joseph and Robert Cornell Memorial Foundation / Licensed by VAGA, New York, NY. Photo courtesy of Allan Stone Projects, New York: 4.02

© The Joseph and Robert Cornell Memorial Foundation / Licensed by VAGA, New York, NY. The Robert Lehrman Art Trust, courtesy of Aimee and Robert Lehrman: 1.10, 2.05, 4.01, 4.04

© The Joseph and Robert Cornell Memorial Foundation/Licensed by VAGA, New York, NY. Courtesy Mark Kelman: front and back covers

© The Museum of Modern Art, New York: 8.01–8.04

© Victoria and Albert Museum, London: 1.04

Art © Robert Rauschenberg Foundation/Licensed by VAGA, New York, NY: 9.09

Courtesy Art and Picture Collection, The New York Public Library: 2.03

Courtesy Center for Creative Photography, University of Arizona © 1991 Hans Namuth Estate: 9.01

Courtesy Collection of The Tobin Theatre Arts Fund: 10.08

Courtesy INSTITUT Gustave Courbet—Association des Amis de Gustave Courbet et du Musée, Ornans: 4.09

Courtesy Joseph Cornell Study Center, Smithsonian American Art Museum, Washington, DC: 5.02–5.04, 6.01–6.05, 6.07, 7.04

Courtesy Matthew Affron: 7.03

Courtesy Musée de l'Impression sur Etoffes, Mulhouse: 4.08

Courtesy of Anthology Film Archives, New York: 8.05

Courtesy of The Dean and Chapter of Canterbury: 1.08

Courtesy of The Museum of the City of New York: 2.01

Courtesy of Williams College Museum of Art, Williamstown: 10.05

Courtesy Ségolène Le Men: 4.03, 4.05, 4.06, 4.07, 4.10

Courtesy the Collection of Georges Hugnet: 10.02

Joseph Cornell Papers, 1804–1986, Bulk 1939–1972, Archives of American Art, Smithsonian Institution: 1.09, 7.06; 7.07 a,b

The Museum of Modern Art, New York. Gift of James Thrall Soby. Digital image © The Museum of Modern Art/Licensed by SCALA/Art Resource: 10.06

The Museum of Modern Art, New York. Gift of Mrs. Gerald Murphy Fund. Digital image © The Museum of Modern Art/Licensed by SCALA/Art Resource: 2.06a, 2.06b

Unless otherwise noted, all works by Joseph Cornell are © The Joseph and Robert Cornell Memorial Foundation/Licensed by VAGA, New York, NY

Index

About the Contributors

Matthew Affron is The Muriel and Philip Berman Curator of Modern Art at the Philadelphia Museum of Art. He has written extensively and curated exhibitions on Cubism, abstract art, and modern art and politics. He co-organized the exhibition *Joseph Cornell et les surréalistes à New York / Joseph Cornell and Surrealism* (Musée des Beaux-Arts de Lyon and The Fralin Museum of Art, University of Virginia, 2013–14).

Stephen Bann is emeritus professor of History of Art at the University of Bristol. His books involving the history of "curiosity" are *Under the Sign: John Bargrave as Collector, Traveler, and Witness* (1994) and *Ways around Modernism* (2007).

Émmanuel Guigon is director and chief curator of the Musée des Beaux-Arts et d'Archaéologie de Besançon. His publications on the found object include *L'Objet surréaliste* (2005) and *Le surréalisme et l'objet* (2013).

Lynda Roscoe Hartigan is The James B. and Mary Lou Hawkes Chief Curator, Peabody Essex Museum, Salem, Massachusetts. A Cornell scholar of long standing, she organized the retrospective exhibition *Joseph Cornell: Navigating the Imagination* (2006–2008).

Jodi Hauptman is senior curator in the Department of Drawings and Prints at The Museum of Modern Art, where she has organized numerous exhibitions of modern and contemporary art, most recently *Henri Matisse: The Cutouts* (2014–15). She is the author of *Joseph Cornell: Stargazing in the Cinema* (1999).

Howard Hussey is an artist. He served as Joseph Cornell's studio assistant from 1966 to 1972 and has published a number of essays on Cornell and his work.

Ségolène Le Men is professor in the Department of History of Art and Archaeology, Université de Paris Ouest Nanterre La Défense, and senior member of the Institut de France. Her publications include *Courbet* (2007) and *Livres d'enfants, livres d'images* (1989).

Camille Lévêque-Claudet is curator of Old Master and Modern Art at the Musée Cantonal des Beaux-Arts, Lausanne, where he organized the exhibition *Giacometti, Marini, Richier: la figure tourmentée* (2014). He assisted in the organization of the exhibition *Joseph Cornell et les surréalistes à New York / Joseph Cornell and Surrealism* (Musée des Beaux-Arts de Lyon and The Fralin Museum of Art, University of Virginia, 2013–14).

François-René Martin is professor at the École Nationale Supérieure des Beaux-Arts de Paris and at the École du Louvre. His publications include *Grünewald* (2012) and the forthcoming *Grünewald et ses critiques*.

Patrick Mauriès is a journalist, writer, and independent scholar. He is author of *Fragments d'une forêt* (2013) and *Cabinets of Curiosities* (2002).

Anne Morra is associate curator in the Department of Film at The Museum of Modern Art, where she is involved in an ongoing research project on Joseph Cornell's films.

Sylvie Ramond is director and chief curator of the Musée des Beaux-Arts de Lyon. She has organized numerous exhibitions, most recently *Joseph Cornell et les surréalistes à New York / Joseph Cornell and Surrealism* (Musée des Beaux-Arts de Lyon and The Fralin Museum of Art, University of Virginia, 2013–14), *Soulages XXIe siècle* (2012), and *1945–1949: Repartir à zero* (2008). She is one of the authors of *Grünewald* (2012).